OPERATION JOB SEARCH

A Guide for Military Veterans Transitioning to Civilian Careers

OPERATION JOB SEARCH

A Guide for Military Veterans Transitioning to Civilian Careers

JOHN HENRY WEISS

Skyhorse Publishing

Skyhorse Publishing books may be purchased in bulk at special discounts for sales promotion, corporate gifts, fund-raising, or educational purposes. Special editions can also be created to specifications. For details, contact the Special Sales Department, Skyhorse Publishing, 307 West 36th Street, 11th Floor, New York, NY 10018 or info@skyhorsepublishing.com.

Skyhorse® and Skyhorse Publishing® are registered trademarks of Skyhorse Publishing, Inc.®, a Delaware corporation.

Visit our website at www.skyhorsepublishing.com.

10 9 8 7 6 5 4 3 2 1

Library of Congress Cataloging-in-Publication Data is available on file.

Cover design by Rain Saukas

Print ISBN: 978-1-63450-563-5
Ebook ISBN: 978-1-5107-0156-4

Printed in the United States of America

CONTENTS

DEDICATION

OPERATION JOB SEARCH is dedicated to the memory of Sergeant Chris Kyle . . . veteran, Navy Seal, Silver Star medal recipient, husband, father, son, patriot, and American sniper.

Sergeant Kyle struggled with his transition from military to civilian life after 1,050 days of active duty in Iraq and Afghanistan, where his role as a sniper saved countless lives of fellow American combatants. His transition to the civilian world after discharge included volunteering his services to help other veterans making the same journey. In the process, Sergeant Kyle lost his own life.

We urge all veterans and non-veterans to view the story of his life in the movie *American Sniper* and to read his book *American Sniper: The Autobiography of the Most Lethal Sniper in US Military History*.

Thank you for your service to America, Sergeant Kyle. Rest in peace.

FOREWORD

Transitioning to the civilian world of work is a daunting task for military veterans, one that requires preparation and just plain hard work. I can best illustrate what all military veterans experience by telling you my own transition story.

I am a graduate of the United States Military Academy at West Point, and due to injury, I was forced to retire in 2010. This was one of the scariest times of my life. Even with all the support that the Military offers separating Service Members, I was reentering a world I did not truly understand, the civilian world of work. After spending ten years learning and applying my skills within the military, how was my time as a Field Artillery Officer supposed to translate to the civilian sector?

The last time I had checked potential employers like IBM and Coca-Cola, they were not calling for employees to fire, or set up fire direction centers, or to jump out of perfectly good airplanes, things that we routinely did in the military. I took survey after survey to determine how my military skills could help me transition to a post-military civilian career, but unfortunately the results of those surveys led me to accept a corporate position that brought me absolutely zero job satisfaction.

I accepted a corporate position but yearned for the military job that I had serving my colleagues and country, and I refused to believe I would never have it again. Searching to find what would bring me the most civilian job satisfaction, I left the corporate world knowing one thing: I wanted to help people and I wanted hands-on interaction.

During my search I spent hours on the computer and in local bookstores, scouring all material that would point me in the right direction. Frustrated that most of the material I found did not apply to me or my military experience, I thought I was going to be stuck just going to work day in and day out . . . unhappy. Is this what all of the long hours, long days, and long years added up to? Fortunately, the answer to that question was a resounding "no."

I knew there was a better way and began by assessing my personal strengths and aspirations. I remembered how much I loved physical training with my Soldiers, and the importance of being prepared to fight. With this in mind, I concluded that I could translate this into a civilian career focusing on helping people stay physically fit. This realization led my wife and me to begin our strength & conditioning facility, Kings of Fitness, in 2012. After three years in business, I realized that I had found the job satisfaction I wanted!

Now, I share this information because through hard work and research I was able to figure things out for myself. It took me two years to learn what I wanted to focus on post-separation, and it was worth the effort. Time is our most valuable commodity in the transition process. You cannot retrieve wasted time so you need to use every resource at hand to make a successful transition.

OPERATION JOB SEARCH is the resource I was looking for back in 2010, and I am happy to tell you that this book is available to you now. All military veterans face the inevitable challenge of rejoining the civilian workforce. Take advantage of the information and experience that the author, John Henry Weiss, shares on every page, and let this book be the vehicle that makes your transition to the civilian world easier. ***Always remember, if I could do it, you can too! Best of luck, veterans!***

                                           Kiel King, CPT, U.S. ARMY RET.

PREFACE

It was back-to-school time across America, and this particular September day was proceeding in an orderly and traditional manner for most students, teachers, and parents. However, this was no ordinary school day at Emma E. Booker Elementary School in Sarasota, Florida. The school principal, Gwen Rigell, had been preparing for this day for the past six weeks, ever since she received word from the Secret Service that a dignitary from Washington, DC, would be visiting the school and talking with the second grade students and their teacher, Sandra Kay Daniels.

Students and their parents could not help but notice changes at Booker. Hall and classroom bulletin boards were informative and attractive. Floors glistened, no doubt in response to the frequent applications of cleaning agents and polishes by the maintenance staff. The front office and entrance sported a new coat of paint. Community volunteers had spruced up the landscaping at the outside entrance to the school, and the grass was an eye-catching shade of dark green. Most notable of all was the new and larger American flag that greeted visitors at the entrance to Booker Elementary School. Booker was nothing less than spit-shine perfect.

The special day arrived and administrators, teachers, and children began entering the school at 8:00 a.m. It was a beautiful, cloudless day across the country, one of those late summer days where you are happy to be alive and living in America. At 8:15, Principal Rigell went on the intercom and announced,

Children, this is a special day. President George W. Bush will be visiting our school to tell us about an exciting new education program called

The No Child Left Behind Act. It is the most significant piece of education legislation in the history of our country. President Bush and Senator Edward "Ted" Kennedy wrote this bill. It is a good example of what can happen in America when both Republicans and Democrats put the welfare of the people before partisan politics. Please be on your best behavior. Be courteous to President Bush and his staff. He will be visiting every classroom to say hello and will spend extra time with the second graders. Some of you will have a chance to participate in a reading lesson with the President. Show him how smart you are and all of us will be proud of you. Today, September 11, 2001, is a special day in the life of Booker Elementary School!

At 8:30, President Bush and his entourage arrived. After a warm welcome by the principal, he toured the school commenting on its orderly appearance and lavishing compliments on Gwen Rigell and her staff. Then, he entered the second grade classroom to a round of applause and settled into one of those diminutive elementary school desks, as the teacher, Sandra Daniels, led the class through a reading lesson. This was excitement never before witnessed in an elementary school classroom in America. Who could have imagined the President of the United States actually participating in a classroom lesson? Everyone could see that President Bush was enjoying the event, even though his knees were bent like a pretzel to fit under the small desk. Then something unexpected happened. A presidential aide, Andy Card, entered the classroom, hurriedly approached the President, and whispered in his ear, "Mr. President, a plane hit the second World Trade Tower. America is under attack." With those words, life in America and the rest of the world changed forever.

The President was outraged but sat quietly to digest the significance of the event and plan the next step while the reading lesson continued. He was not paralyzed by fear, as critics would later say attempting to disparage the President's behavior. Several minutes later, he left the classroom quietly, careful not to upset those innocent second graders, and conferred in private with his aides. Then he communicated with Vice President Cheney, who was in Washington. Immediately thereafter, the President ordered Combat Air Patrols to the skies across America. It was his first official act in the War on Terror. Then he departed on Air Force One to Houston and eventually Washington, DC, surrounded by F-16's from the Ellington Air Force Base. A new kind of war had begun, one where the enemy wore no uniform and flew no flag. No one knew what lay ahead.

9/11 was also the beginning of a new era for the women and men serving in our Armed Forces. Until this time, military life for most of them involved domestic strategic planning, training, staffing, and maintaining the various Operations Centers—behind-the-scenes activities that go unnoticed when a country is not at war. Now the mission had changed to wage a war unlike all others, one that would see millions of US troops deploying from America to Iraq and Afghanistan. Most would return to America alive and unharmed, but others would return physically or mentally wounded. And, unfortunately, some would return to Dover Air Force Base in Delaware in a flag-draped coffin.

9/11 was the seminal event that created our present day population of veterans. After multiple deployments, millions have been discharged from active duty and face challenges that often go unnoticed: rehabilitation from physical or emotional wounds, problems reuniting with family and friends, and adjustment to a new America.

Above all else, veterans face the challenge of navigating the civilian world where having a job is the difference between living as a self-sufficient human being and going on welfare, leaving spouses, partners, and children at the mercy of the safety-net system. Veterans are not satisfied with this kind of future. They return to the homeland confident that in a country where the active workforce numbers 155,000,000, they will find a decent job... quickly. However, many veterans find that breaking into the civilian workforce is beyond their level of experience, and job hunting continues for twelve months or more. Veterans need the support of all Americans, which is why I wrote **OPERATION JOB SEARCH**, a guide to help veterans accomplish their new mission—transitioning to the civilian workplace.

John Henry Weiss

INTRODUCTION

OPERATION JOB SEARCH (OJS) is a book for US military veterans, female and male, seeking civilian employment after discharge. It provides information for navigating the world of civilian employment and rubrics for civilian job searching. For most veterans, understanding the civilian workplace and transitioning to a civilian job is a challenging operation.

A job search is comparable to a military operation, which states the objective and then follows through with strategies to accomplish the mission. It all sounds so simple. *Plan your work. Work your plan. Success will follow.* But does it really happen that way? The reality is what all veterans experience: job hunting is a complicated challenge, one they did not anticipate. Some veterans conjecture that civilian job hunting can be summed up by the phrase "Welcome to the Real World."

I wrote this book to help military veterans through the challenges associated with transitioning to the civilian workforce.

The five main premises of **OPERATION JOB SEARCH** are:

1. **Serving in the military was a true work experience.** Most civilian hiring authorities have little or no military experience, which makes it difficult for them to understand that veterans applying for a position bring as much or more to the table as those who did not serve. It is the responsibility of the job-hunting veteran to educate company hiring managers who are making personnel decisions.

2. **Company hiring authorities and human resources directors do not hire military resumes, Tweets, YouTube videos, or social media stories.** Companies hire military veterans who

have the intelligence and energy to find them and build a personal relationship. Smart veterans do that by leaving the house to seek military friendly employers at venues such as job fairs, trade shows, conferences, business parks, and even more pedestrian places like coffee shops and restaurants. Starbucks and Chipotle come to mind.

3. **Work in the civilian world is a means to becoming self-sufficient, which is providing your own food, shelter, clothing, transportation, insurance, and other necessities required to function independently.** This is different from the military, where the *big three*—food, shelter, and clothing—came free of charge or at a greatly reduced price compared to costs for identical items in civilian life.

4. **Job-hunting is a multi-step process.** It requires making a viable business plan, establishing an operations center (a home office in civilian-speak), honing written and verbal communication skills, translating the MOS (Military Occupation Specialty) into civilian language, creating a career profile, and more. It goes beyond preparing a resume and braving an interview.

5. **Veterans must leave the house to attend trade shows and job fairs.** At these events, veterans will meet hiring managers from hundreds of potential employers in the flesh and under one roof.

One of the key features of **OJS** is the identification of companies that are honest and ethical places to work based on our research and personal experience.

The writing style of **OPERATION JOB SEARCH** is informal, conversational, inspiring, entertaining, and instructional. Chapter length is brief, reflecting the style of communication in the digital world. **OJS** does not talk down to veterans as so many sources do both in print and online. You will not find *any* patronizing talk in this book. We believe that veterans have the intelligence, energy, and passion to become self-sufficient and self-actualized human beings and as such deserve discourse on an adult level.

Real life stories of both military and non-military personnel from my experience in the retained search business highlight the critical importance of key topics such as flawless spelling and grammar in written documents. For example, we illustrate the importance of error-free written communication by relating the experience of Patti from St. Louis, who lost a director-level position paying $200,000 because of a spelling error on her resume.

Understanding the civilian workplace is part of the job-hunting process. An important chapter on terminology and business numbers provides a review of civilian workplace terminology and current business-speak. For example, here is a list of the characteristics of the veteran population entering the civilian workforce. The data was provided by the Bureau of Labor Statistics, the Census Bureau, the Pew Research Center, the Veterans Administration, and other sources.

- There are approximately 20 million veterans living in the United States, 1.5 million of whom are women.
- The unemployment rate for all returning military personnel entering the civilian workforce is 2.5 percent above the national average at any given time. Double that number for female veterans.
- For newly minted veterans, the unemployment rate has averaged approximately 20 percent over the past five years, truly a national crisis.
- The unemployment rate for post-9/11 veterans is higher than the national averages.
- Among post-9/11 Iraq and Afghanistan veterans, 33 percent have been unemployed for longer than one year; 17 percent have been unemployed for more than two years.
- Approximately 29 percent of veterans 25 and older have a bachelor's degree or higher.
- 3.6 million veterans have a service-related physical disability or PTSD.

- Approximately 160,000 military personnel are discharged from service each year.
- At the end of 2015, there were 722,000 unemployed veterans.
- Over 6.1 million veterans served the country between 1990 and 2013.

As you will learn in **OPERATION JOB SEARCH**, the civilian workplace is all about the numbers.

OJS provides numerous links to corporate websites and other information sources. Links are active in the digital version, requiring only a click on an iPad, tablet, or smartphone to reach an important information source. Those reading the print version need only enter the URLs on their iPads or smartphones to gain immediate access to important information, such as the locations and dates of job-hunting events.

The principles in **OJS** apply equally to female and male veterans, but women face additional problems, which is why I have included separate chapters identifying their challenges and offering solutions.

Each chapter in **OJS** concludes with these items:

1. **Chapter Takeaways**—rubrics critical to the job-hunting process that we presented in the chapter.
2. **The Veteran's Library**—suggested readings that elaborate on the chapter content.

OPERATION JOB SEARCH is the market's only *complete* guide to job hunting and career education written specifically for transitioning military personnel. The Internet and several books contain bits and pieces of advice and information on the process generally, but **OJS** brings it all together between two covers.

You may read **OJS** sequentially from first chapter to last, or you may go directly to those chapters with immediate appeal. Take a moment now to review the Table of Contents to see the scope and sequence of **OJS**. You will not be disappointed.

Finally, **OJS** reflects my everyday experiences as an executive recruiter working in the civilian world of work, not that of an academic theorizing about the workplace. *All of OJS is the real deal.* Welcome to the real world of civilian employment, Veterans. Welcome to **OPERATION JOB SEARCH.**

PART I

The Process of Transitioning to the Civilian Workplace

If American business does not earn sufficient revenue to earn a fair profit, this Government cannot earn sufficient revenues to cover its outlays. If American business does not prosper and expand, this Government cannot make good its pledges of economic growth. Our foreign policies call for an increase in the sale of American goods abroad, but it is business, not Government, who must actually produce and sell these goods. Our domestic programs call for substantial increases in employment, but it is business, not Government, who must actually perform these jobs.

*—John F. Kennedy, US Navy Veteran
and 35th President of the United States*

Chapter 1

Self-Assessment.
Aptitude. Fulfillment.
Mission. Purpose

The job-search lexicon is replete with words and terms that we *think* we understand, but when put to the test, many veterans often misunderstand the civilian definitions. Self-assessment, aptitude, mission, fulfillment, purpose, interests, vocation, resume, interview, cover letter, follow-up letter, workplace etiquette, career profile, social media profile, job fairs, job descriptions, job offers, etc. Had enough?

If we were to rank the words and terms that veterans need to explore, the following would be at the top of the list: self-assessment, aptitude, purpose, mission, fulfillment, and interests. All deal with learning who we really are and what we want to do with the rest of our lives. All veterans have had career counseling before and after discharge and one would think the transition to the civilian workplace would not be a problem. Think again, because learning who we really are is a continuing and imperfect process.

The sequence of events for finding a job frequently is thought to be something like this. Counseling. Discharge. Preparing a resume. Looking at online job boards. Submitting resumes. Finally, an employer makes you a job offer that provides compensation to become a self-sufficient human, in addition to providing life purpose, fulfillment, and happiness! Slam-dunk. Mission complete! Unfortunately, that is not the real world of civilian job searching for veterans. It is more than firing off resumes to every job posting on the boards. It is a process that begins with two distinct objectives.

CIVILIAN JOB-SEARCH OBJECTIVES

There are two parts to a civilian career search:

1. Finding work that pays enough to buy food, shelter, clothing, insurance, transportation, healthcare, education, recreation, and other necessities.
2. Finding work that is interesting, fulfilling, and purposeful.

How do we reach both objectives? Can an eight-hour workday really be the one and only vehicle to fulfill all of our human needs and desires? What do we do with the remaining sixteen hours? Do we compartmentalize our lives into one meaningful segment called "work" and the other into a part called "off-time"? The answer is obvious. We need to make our work time and off-work time come together to be complete human beings.

SELF-ASSESSMENT

Where do we begin this practical search for the basics, and how do we define those transformational activities that bring life satisfaction? It all begins with learning who we really are and what it is that makes life meaningful and worth living.

It all sounds so simple. Do what you love, and you will never work a day in your life! How many times have you heard that old canard? However, who are you? And what do you really like to do? Military service left little time for self-assessment, which is why many veterans spend an inordinate and unnecessary amount of time on self-assessment as they make the transition to civilian life. Some seek career coaching, others seek online help, and others seek advice from the clergy. **OJS** believes there is a better way. Let's simplify the trip. Learning who you really are involves two basic steps:

1. Finding what your greatest *interests* are.
2. Finding what it is that you do well, your *aptitude*.

For example, if you place art, numbers, and skyscrapers at the top of your interest list, and mathematics has always come easy to you (your aptitude), your career path might include work as an architect, a general building contractor, a structural steel worker, or a carpenter. All of these careers pay substantial wages, enough to enable you to pay for the basics and have money left over to contribute to charitable causes. In addition, you get satisfaction from seeing the beautiful buildings you created provide a place for other people to live and work.

The best resource for uncovering your interests and aptitudes is to study the *Occupational Outlook Handbook* published by the US Department of Labor. It is available online from the publisher, JIST Publishing (www.jist.com), from Amazon, and from Barnes and Noble. This book lists every imaginable job in the marketplace along with a job description, salary range, projected need, and more. Read this book, and you will find interests you never thought you had. This book is one of the most valuable resources on the market for every veteran job hunter.

THE SELF-ASSESSMENT TEMPLATE

A practical way to go about your self-assessment project is to create a print or digital template titled "Self-Assessment."

Title the first column "My Main Interests" and list ten things, in order of priority, that arouse your interest. The first item might be "Information Technology."

Title the second column "My Aptitudes and Abilities" and list what you are good at doing. One item at the top of your list might be "Verbal Communication."

Title the third column "My Experience." "Teaching and Giving Directions" might be at the top of your list.

In the fourth column of your template, write "Possible Jobs and Employers."

Now combine the first three items in columns 1, 2, 3: *technology, verbal communication, and teaching.* Now go to the fourth column, write down the kinds of jobs that require these three interests and abilities. Here are some possible choices:

- Selling software applications
- Selling technology hardware such as computers, tablets, and smart phones
- Customer service work with a technology company like Comcast, Google, or Verizon
- Consultant work with a consumer technology provider like AT&T
- Teaching customers how to use applications at an Apple consumer store
- Teaching at the K-12 or college level if you have the credentials

The next logical step in the process is to find companies that provide those job opportunities. Go to the Internet and enter each of the six job categories listed above. I did just with "software applications." I found hundreds of leads, including "10 Enterprise Software Companies to Watch."

LIFE PURPOSE

Go to Google and enter "life purpose." You will get millions of hits. Why? Because everyone asks, "Why am I here on Earth? What can I do with my time that is important?" For most people, answering these questions circles back to work, and they ask, "What kind of work can I do that is meaningful?" Most of us begin thinking about those questions only after graduation from college or high school, or after discharge from military service. What is it you can do to make sense out of work? What kind of work can you do to give purpose to your life? Truth be known, most of us slug through our careers asking those questions from our first job to our last job. It seems that we never find all the answers, but that is a good thing because constant seeking for truth keeps your mind working and growing.

When Have You Arrived?

Most job seekers believe that finding an answer to the life-purpose question lies in finding the right job, one that gives fulfillment, happiness, joy, and peace. "If I can just find the right job, I can put those warm and fuzzy questions behind me and get on with life." Some people do just that. They find a job that they like and believe they have arrived. The life-purpose questions cease. The company is great. The boss is a gem. The job title impresses. All is good but what happens when the job disappears, if you are laid off because your company was sold and the new owners bring in a replacement for your job? You reported happy for work at 8 a.m., and at 5 p.m. you and the job are history. All of a sudden, you have *unarrived,* and it is back to the life purpose questions. The moral of the story is this: when you believe you have arrived, you stop asking questions. And when you stop asking questions and seeking answers, you stop growing.

Now there are more questions. "What is work about? Is it a means to bring purpose and fulfillment to my life? What happens if I get another job that I love and the same thing happens?"

The confusion stems from a misguided understanding of the meaning and purpose of work and our place in the workplace. Life purpose transcends the workplace. Work is just one part of it. But what does that activity called "work" really mean?

THE MEANING AND PURPOSE OF WORK

Let's cut through the hype from the millions of Internet hits, thousands of books, the dozens of TV programs, and countless sermons from the pulpit. All seem to be shouting, "I have the answers! Listen to me!"

For a moment, let's put aside the philosophy and words of traditional wisdom and try to get a handle on the meaning of work from history. Back in the Neolithic era, about 12,000 years ago, people were hunters and gatherers. There was no such thing as "work." The main concern was to stay alive. Survival was the operative word. There were no Targets to buy clothing. There were no Walmarts to buy food. There were no Home Depots to buy lumber to build shelters. People found their own necessities for survival. They depended upon nobody else. Anthropologists call all of these survival activities "the hunt."

Fast forward, and we see people trading their time for survival items. They performed some kind of service for a neighbor and in return, they received food, or an article of clothing (maybe a bearskin shawl), or maybe some reeds to build a rudimentary shelter. At some point in time, people began to call this arrangement W-O-R-K. The model has become more sophisticated throughout the millennia, but the constant is this: work, whether in the late Neolithic era or today in the twenty-first century, is primarily about survival. The meaning and purpose of work is to make money to become self-sufficient, to provide our own food, shelter, and clothing, plus modern-day needs like insurance, transportation, education, technology devices, and recreation. What? The purpose of work is to make money? "How crass!" the academics might cry.

Our meaning of work will not make friends among university sociologists and philosophers. They do not like words like "money," "profits," "selling," and "marketing." I have had this discussion many times, and when I suggest to critics that they should sign over their entire paycheck to a favorite cause, maybe a nonprofit organization focusing on saving the snail darter in Northern California, I get a blank stare in return. Working for self-fulfillment alone makes no sense.

MONEY AND THE WORKPLACE

Successful workers who have made a lot of money from their jobs have been targets for criticism. All of us have heard the chatter. "Business people are greedy! Increase taxes on those wealthy bastards! Level the playing field. There's no social justice in America. Close the gap between the haves and have-nots. Narrow the economic divide."

Now examine the flip side of making a lot of money. When you make money from your job, you become self-sufficient. You do not need to tap the wealth of family and friends to survive. You do not need government handouts. Instead, you take the excess money from your job and donate it to your own worthy cause. It is called charitable giving, philanthropy, or giving back.

As an example of what a wealthy American can do with BIG money, take Mark Zuckerberg, the CEO of Facebook. In 2015, he donated *$73 million* to the San Francisco General Hospital to build a new trauma center. Of course, not all Americans make Zuckerberg's kind of money, but the point is this: all workers can make charitable giving a part of their monthly expenses. Give back in proportion to what you make.

Does work mean anything else besides making money? Do we spend eight to twelve hours per day on the job just to make money, even if we might *hate* what we are doing? Of course not. There is more to it than that . . . after we make enough to become self-sufficient and provide for our needs and those of our dependent family members. (We cannot forget the kids. With the average cost of a college education standing at about $30,000 per year, we need to make money.)

The role of money in our culture generally, and the workplace specifically, is critically important. In fact, I wrote an entire chapter on the subject. See Chapter 39, "Charitable Giving, Philanthropy, and Community Outreach."

ALL JOBS HAVE MEANING, PURPOSE, AND VALUE

All jobs have meaning. All jobs have purpose. All jobs have value. Even jobs that are not highly regarded have meaning and purpose. For example, think about the job of the trash collector, euphemistically called "sanitation engineer." There is nothing overly complex about this job, but it provides a vital service to the community. Imagine what your life would be without these workers. Is this job less valuable than that of an accountant or physician? These jobs, too, provide a necessary service to the community, but like so many other jobs, they can be downright boring. But what job is not boring at times? Jobs do not exist to give you a high 24/7.

Many job candidates, veterans and non-veterans alike, have a misguided interpretation of the meaning of work. They believe what is on TV and listen to the media hype. How many times have we seen ads for Microsoft or Google showing workers having a jolly old time on the job floor? It is not ping-pong all day for tech workers. They have work goals to meet, and many spend more than twelve hours a day accomplishing them. And how about those ads for National Car Rental, showing the corporate executive beaming with pleasure as she runs down the aisle to her upscale rental car? Truth be known, working as a corporate exec and traveling 50 percent of your time is not happy task. It's a stressful job, and it is boring much of the time. There is nothing exciting about spending your time on airplanes, in rental cars, and in hotel rooms.

All jobs exist to provide a product or service for other human beings, whether it is the job of a priest or minister who provides counseling and comfort, the job of a teacher who assists students with the learning process, or that of an active duty soldier carrying an M16 and working in a combat zone. If we look at the end product of our work, we can always find meaning and purpose, but what about fulfillment?

FULFILLMENT AND MISSION

Too often, we believe that work should answer all of our prayers. It should provide substantial wages. It should provide peace, joy, and happiness. It should provide fulfillment. And it should provide a sense of mission. Job coaches and happiness gurus have filled millions of digital and print pages telling workers what fulfillment on the job *should* mean, what kind of mission all workers *should* have.

Seeking fulfillment and mission is a personal endeavor. Others can only offer suggestions to help you through the process. The definition I like best is that *job fulfillment and mission means helping others in meaningful ways.* Helping others could mean performing surgery on a victim of pancreatic cancer or selling long-term disability insurance to a worker with a spouse and three kids. If you look into the silent corners of any job, you can find fulfillment, because every job deals with a product or service designed for another human being.

Consider the insurance industry, believed by many to be one of the most boring industries on Earth. Can it provide fulfillment? Well, yes it can. For example, recently my insurance agent drove me to distraction urging me to buy a long-term disability insurance policy. Finally, I caved in and bought the policy. Three days after the policy took effect, I was involved in a serious bicycle accident that totally disabled me for six months. Without that policy I would have been unable to pay the mortgage and car loan, unable to pay for food and other necessities. Who said that selling insurance is a meaningless job?

There is no one definition of job fulfillment or mission. It means different things to different people. To Mother Teresa it meant one thing, and to Bill Gates it means something else. What should it mean to you? Nobody can provide the answer for you. You must discover that on your own using some of the suggestions in **OJS** and other sources. Your curiosity and search for answers means that you are seeking meaning and growing.

Research the fulfillment issue at your leisure, and be sure to view a digital posting on the subject by *Forbes*, www.forbes.com. This ever-popular business site weighed in on the fulfillment issue, and we urge you to read the August 1, 2013, piece "The Foolproof Guide to Finding True Career Fulfillment."

MOVING FORWARD

A job alone will not provide purpose, fulfillment, and mission. All of these are life issues that go beyond the workplace. Your search for life meaning encompasses all that you do at work, after work, and on weekends.

Do not spend months dealing with these philosophical topics. It will sap your energy like nothing else and take time from your job search. Use the tools in **OPERATION JOB SEARCH** and you will find the Promised Land of employment with meaning. We guarantee it.

CHAPTER TAKEAWAYS

- Uncover your areas of interest by reviewing the *Occupational Outlook Handbook.*
- You can find life purpose in your time off from work.
- Every job has meaning. Every job has purpose. Every job has value.
- Job fulfillment and mission are personal.
- When you believe you have "arrived," you stop growing.
- The basic purpose of work is to become self-sufficient.
- There is nothing wrong with making money, lots of it, provided you use it wisely and give back to others in proportion to your wealth.
- BECOME SOMEBODY.

THE VETERAN'S LIBRARY

United States Department of Labor. ***Occupational Outlook Handbook.*** JIST Publishing Co, 2015.

Chapter 2

Working for a Corporation or a Small Business

Many veterans lacking professional experience in specialized areas like medicine, law, or education will most likely exercise the default choice: working for a large corporation, like Microsoft or Boeing, or a small business. One is not better than the other. Large corporations have much to offer, including generous benefits like a contributory IRA, while small businesses require less work experience and formal education and provide a relaxed work environment. Pursuing one or the other is a matter of personal preference.

Contrary to street wisdom, the majority of civilian workers are employed by small businesses, not large corporations like General Electric (305,000 employees) or Walmart (2.2 million employees). However, all companies fall into one of the major industries that keep our workforce employed. Let's have a look at some of these industries, broadly defined.

MAJOR US INDUSTRIES
All corporations and small businesses fall within major industries. Some of the most obvious are:

- The Clothing Industry
- The Education Industry

- The Energy Industry
- The Financial Industry
- The Food Industry
- The Healthcare Industry
- The Insurance Industry
- The Petroleum Industry
- The Shelter Industry
- The Technology Industry
- The Transportation Industry

In addition, there are other fast growing industries that veterans might explore, like the "Green Industry," which is concerned with making our local environment and Planet Earth a more healthful and desirable place to live.

Note that we excluded "Government" from the list. This is a special employment category with distinct characteristics that will be covered in Chapter 5.

OJS INDUSTRY FAVES

The workplace is vast, and it takes considerable time to determine where to begin looking for a civilian job. Here are some of our favorites based on personal experience, research, work experience, and anecdotal information from a variety of sources. We call them **OPERATION JOB SEARCH FAVES** (**OJS FAVES**). These are industries that employ millions of workers and provide an opportunity to take home more than a paycheck (i.e. work satisfaction). Some of our faves are:

- Education
- Energy
- Healthcare
- Insurance
- Security
- Technology
- Transportation

All are growth industries that offer endless job opportunities for both men and women veterans. Here is a brief review of each industry to get you moving in the right direction.

THE EDUCATION INDUSTRY

The broadly defined Education Industry consists of for-profit companies like Phoenix Online University, DeVry Institute, McGraw-Hill Education, Scholastic, and Highlights for Children. There are nonprofits, too, like Educational Testing Service (ETS), and The College Board.

These companies are scattered throughout the USA and offer jobs spanning the entire range of specialties like sales, marketing, finance, editorial, product development, information technology, and human resources. Workers in the Education Industry find much job satisfaction, because the products are instructional materials and services for K-12, higher education, and adult education, which benefit individuals and the country as a whole. Here is an example of the influence a worker in this industry can have.

Margaret of New Jersey

Margaret was an editor with a large K-12 publishing company and specialized in producing social studies texts and materials. Some of the products she completed included American History texts, World Cultures texts, and US Government texts. Thousands, perhaps millions, of students using these core products acquired the concepts and skills necessary for an understanding of United States history and government because of Margaret's work. If you are seeking work satisfaction, it does not get better than working in the Education Industry.

Companies in the Education Industry. OJS Faves

I compiled this list based on my personal experience with each company as an executive recruiter, as well as research. There are many other good companies in the Education Industry, particularly educational technology companies, many of which are entrepreneurial. Jobs in this industry may require a background in teaching or education administration.

Educational Testing Service, www.ets.org. ETS produces testing and assessment products for K-12 and higher education and is noted for producing the SAT exam. It is based in Princeton, New Jersey, and employs thousands of workers at its home office and satellite offices throughout the country. ETS is a good example of a *nonprofit* company, one that does not have shareholders. This status permits ETS to plow back its profits into product research and development. Annual revenues exceed $1 billion. Not bad for a "nonprofit" company! Check the website for current job listings.

Highlights for Children, www.highlights.com. This Columbus, Ohio, education company produces print and technology instructional materials for the K-12 market. The company has been in business for generations and is noted for its elementary school magazine *Highlights for Children*. Sound familiar? You probably read this magazine when you were in elementary school. Explore the website for job opportunities across the nation, as Highlights has four subsidiary companies, which are active in all fifty states.

Measured Progress, www.measuredprogress.org. This New Hampshire company has been in business for close to thirty years producing both formative and summative testing and assessment products for K-12 school districts and state departments of education. The company produces its products in both traditional pen-and-pencil format and in digital format. Check the website for job opportunities.

MIND Research Institute, www.mindresearch.org. Based in Irvine, California, MIND publishes K-12 technology products for mathematics instruction. Many of its products grew out of research at the University of California. One of its most successful elementary school math programs incorporates music in its various lessons. Why? Because music is a mathematical discipline and has broad appeal to every student group. Jobs at MIND span domestic and international sales, marketing, information technology, product development, and human resources. Check the website for job opportunities. MIND employs workers across all fifty states, as well as internationally.

Scholastic, www.scholastic.com. Without a doubt, this NYC-based company is a true icon in the Education Industry, because it publishes high-quality print and digital products covering a wide range of topics. In addition to curriculum-related products, Scholastic publishes trade books for school-age children, such as the immensely popular *Harry Potter* and *The Hunger Games* series. This company is the world's largest publisher of children's book titles and employs close to ten thousand workers. Check out the website for job opportunities in editorial, sales, marketing, information technology, and finance. The company employs workers in every state, and has regional sales offices throughout the country.

I recently checked the Careers page on the Scholastic website and found over one hundred postings spanning occupations ranging from truck drivers to editors. The company prefers to hire workers who have an education background for jobs in editorial, human resources, marketing, and sales. For other jobs, like those in transportation or warehousing, an education background is not required.

THE ENERGY INDUSTRY

The energy industry is one of the largest in the world and includes petroleum companies, natural gas companies, LPG companies, nuclear energy companies, solar energy companies, and many others. This industry employs millions of workers in jobs that require very specific STEM (science, technology, engineering, and mathematics) skills, as well as jobs that require sales, marketing, and finance skills. This industry is noted for paying above-average wages and offering attractive

benefits. Here are two examples to get you started exploring this treasure trove of job opportunities.

Clean Energy, www.cleanenergyfuels.com. The company, headquartered in Newport Beach, California, is a leader in the movement to
use clean burning natural gas to power trucks, buses, and automobiles.
It has established hundreds of natural gas service stations throughout
the west and southwestern states. Its mission statement reads: "Clean
Energy is changing the way North America fuels its vehicles. Energy
independence is an undisputed goal for our nation, and we at Clean
Energy know just how realistic and attainable that goal is with natural
gas fuel. Moving forward in our thinking as well as in our vehicles
means a safer, healthier planet for all of us."

Exxon Mobile Corp, www.exxon.com. The world's largest petroleum company is the Texas-based gas and oil producer Exxon Mobile
Corp. Exxon's 2014 revenues exceeded $450 billion, and the company
employs 77,000 workers. In the Houston area, Exxon, in partnership
with a number of community colleges, is spending millions of dollars to train future veterans for jobs in the petroleum segment of the
energy industry. The company has an excellent record for diversifying
its workforce. OPEC (Organization of Petroleum Exporting Countries) no longer dominates the Energy Industry. The United States is
now the world's leading producer of natural gas and will soon become
the number one producer of oil as well. All of this bodes well for jobs in
the Energy Industry, one that traditionally has a soft spot for veterans.

A Note to Female Veterans about the Petroleum Industry

Some stereotypes of the typical oil and gas worker are: big burley macho
guy; beard; heavy drinking; cursing; dirty clothes; manipulative. Think
again. According to a recent Bureau of Labor (BLS) report, 46 percent
of the new jobs in the petroleum business went to women. No, that is

not a mistake. Check this out at www.BLS.gov. Once again, the numbers tell it all. Regardless of your gender, religion, race, and ethnicity, go for any job in an industry that interests you. Work stereotypes are falling fast, and the playing field is quite level.

THE HEALTHCARE INDUSTRY

Included in this industry are pharmaceutical companies that produce prescription drugs and over-the-counter medications, medical device manufacturers, hospitals, and physical therapy treatment centers, just to name a few. It is a robust industry, one that will see exponential growth as millions of baby boomers reach their senior years and require more frequent health services.

Companies in the Health Industry. OJS Faves

Cleveland Clinic, www.my.clevelandclinic.org. Located in Cleveland, Ohio, this medical treatment center encourages returning military personnel to contact human resources for employment opportunities. They have a special category on their website for military, so check it out. This is one of the finest medical treatment hospitals in the country. Reliable sources rank Cleveland near the top of all US hospitals for cardiac care. It is also noted for its philanthropic ventures and community outreach initiatives.

Johnson & Johnson Pharmaceutical Co., www.jnj.com. J&J produces not only lifesaving medicines, but also everyday health and grooming products. Almost everyone reading this book will have J&J products in their medicine cabinets. This is a giant international company that dates back to 1886. It generated $71 billion in sales in 2013 and employs 128,000 workers. J&J is military friendly. The CEO, Alex Gorsky, graduated in 1982 with a Bachelor of Science from the US Military Academy at West Point, New York. He spent six years in the United States Army, finishing his career with the rank of captain and earning the Ranger tab and Airborne wings.

J&J works with a number of organizations helping veterans transition to civilian employment. For more information about Johnson & Johnson's initiatives for veterans, go to www.jnj.com/heroes. Watch the "Honoring Veterans" video.

Medtronic, www.medtronic.com. This is the world's largest medical technology company. It is based in Minneapolis, Minnesota. Medtronic produces life saving devices like defibrillators and heart stents. It was founded in 1949, employs 50,000 workers, is active in 140 countries, and had revenues exceeding $17 billion in FY 2015. Medtronic is noted for its community outreach programs and philanthropic ventures, particularly in the Twin Cities area. Medtronic is military friendly.

Pfizer Pharmaceutical Company, www.pfizer.com. Pfizer is an icon in the pharmaceutical business and employs thousands of workers in a diverse array of jobs. It is one of the best in the business and is a military friendly employer.

This list of companies could go on for several pages, which attests to the vigor of this industry. In fact, when in March 2015 *Fortune* magazine listed the top 100 companies to work for, nineteen of them, almost 20 percent, were healthcare companies.

Healthcare Companies for Women

Fortune, in the same issue, also listed the top ten companies for women. Seven of these were healthcare companies. They are:

- Atlantic Health System
- Baptist Health South Florida
- Children's Healthcare of Atlanta
- Meridian Health
- Novo Nordisk
- Scripps Health
- Wellstar Health System

Work in the Healthcare Industry consists not only of medical professional jobs, such as doctor, nurse, midwife, or physical therapist. The industry employs many workers in non-clinical jobs as well, such as information technology, sales, marketing, finance, and human resources. One does not need experience in clinical healthcare to work in this booming industry. Transitioning women veterans could not find a better list of companies to explore for potential job opportunities.

THE INSURANCE INDUSTRY

Some consider this industry boring and concerned only with making money at the expense of policyholders. Who wants to do something as unexciting as selling policies for life insurance, auto insurance, homeowners insurance, short- and long-term disability insurance, flood insurance, and retirement instruments like annuities? Insurance is just an invention by greedy corporate executives to make money, right?

Well, think again. Interestingly, the insurance industry in the United States was founded by none other than Benjamin Franklin, who recognized insurance as an instrument to minimize risk and deal with unforeseen occurrences, like a fire that might consume your home and all of its contents. In so doing, Ben gave birth to an industry where it is almost impossible to fail. It is an industry that employs some of the most brilliant mathematical minds on earth. These mathematical geniuses are the actuaries. They deal with massive amounts of data to determine risk levels and price their products—insurance policies—accordingly.

In addition, insurance products are necessary for living as a responsible self-sufficient human being. Insurance policies provide monetary benefits to policyholders who suffer misfortunes, whether it is an illness that costs thousands of dollars to treat or an accident that causes temporary or permanent disability resulting in loss of wages. Here is an example of what workers in the insurance industry can do to minimize risk for you and me.

Chicken Man

It was a beautiful early autumn morning, and I was riding my bike through a rural area in suburban Philadelphia, Pennsylvania. The area was dotted with small farms, some of which raised chickens. While I was riding past a farmhouse with chicken coops nearly reaching the road, a bantam chicken darted from weeds growing along the shoulder and ran into the front wheel of my bike. I had no time to outmaneuver this fast-moving beast, so down I went. I suffered a fractured pelvis, a torn rotator cuff, a concussion (despite wearing a helmet), and multiple lacerations, contusions, and abrasions. I was partially disabled for eight months after fourteen days in the hospital, surgery, and intensive physical therapy. During that time, I had no income or disability payments from my employer. The expenses, however, continued as usual. I was responsible for home mortgage payments, car payments, insurance payments, food, clothing, medicine, and so on. You get the picture.

Here is how the insurance industry rescued Chicken Man, as a TV reporter who put my story on the 11 p.m. Philadelphia news called me. I would have defaulted on the mortgage and car loan but for a long-term disability insurance policy that I had purchased from Northwestern Mutual Insurance Co. and that had become effective only three days before the accident. That policy covered almost 100 percent of my expenses during my disability. Without it, I could not have survived financially. Here's the rest of the story.

Joanne Rescues Chicken Man

Joanne, the insurance agent who sold me life insurance and homeowners insurance, had been after me for months to buy a long-term disability insurance policy because my employer did not provide that in my benefits package. Smart guy that I thought I was, I told Joanne that I was in good health and my chance of ever needing long-term disability insurance was minimal. "Wrong," she said. "On any given day, you could be hit by a truck and become incapacitated for the rest of your life. Long-term disability is more important than life insurance for individuals with family responsibilities. Chances of incurring long-term disability for a middle-aged person are much greater than those of dying." I refused to listen to Joanne, but she kept after me until in a moment of frustration I said, "Okay, Joanne. Get off my case! Write up the damn policy and don't bug me anymore." She did just that. Three days later, I was hit, not by the proverbial truck, but by the chicken. To this day, I thank Joanne for taking the time to educate me about the unknown risks that we face every time we get out of bed in the morning.

What did Joanne get out of this? First, she received commission on the policy, and she received great satisfaction from performing a good deed for another person in the course of her work. Thanks, Joanne. Without you, I would have ended up on welfare.

Who said insurance is a boring industry suitable only for aggressive insurance agents with no interest in anything but bringing home the bacon? This is a good industry, one that can provide not only a handsome income, but also much job satisfaction. Some say that insurance is boring. **OJS** says that boring is good when you are talking about an industry that offers long-term employment opportunities, good income, and a chance to provide helpful services for other human beings. It does not get much better than that.

Companies in the Insurance Industry. OJS Faves

Mass Mutual Insurance Co., www.massmutual.com. You cannot argue with over one hundred years of continuous profitable operations. Does long-term employment, good wages, and job satisfaction sound interesting? Try Mass Mutual.

Northwestern Mutual, www.northwesternmutual.com. This outstanding life insurance company, with home offices in Milwaukee, Wisconsin, and regional offices throughout the country, has been in business since 1907. Yes, this company has been in business for over 100 years, which means they are doing something right for their customers and their employees. Northwestern employs close to 6,000 workers in a wide variety of positions covering sales, marketing, finance, underwriting, and human resources. Total company assets are $120 billion. However, the Northwestern story does not end here.

Northwestern also funds a childhood cancer foundation to help find a cure for this terrible disease affecting millions of children each year. It's called the Northwestern Mutual Foundation.

Northwestern is a good example of how workers and companies can use the large amounts of money they make to do something good for the community. Northwestern is a company you should explore for job opportunities. The last time I checked, there were openings for sales representatives in Boston and other locations.

State Farm Insurance Company, www.statefarm.com. This is the world's largest automobile insurance company, and many say it is the best on the street. Many of its agents have made State Farm a family business, and frequently there are several generations of State Farm agents in one location.

USAA, www.usaa.com. United Services Automobile Association is a multiline insurer offering a variety of insurance products. Insurance is a booming business, and this nationwide insurer has reserved jobs in all departments of the company for returning veterans. In addition, there are special programs for veterans and their spouses, such as those sponsored by the Junior Military Officer (JMO) program. The JMO program helps transition JMOs into the company and provides the opportunity to acquire the knowledge, skills, and awareness needed for a potential USAA leadership career. You will find sixteen program opportunities on their website, each relating to a specific functional area within USAA.

THE SECURITY INDUSTRY

The security industry has been growing exponentially because of cyber-crime against both government agencies and companies. It includes a wide variety of initiatives: preventing cheating on exams; securing private property; protecting financial information; protecting confidential data, both private and governmental; and reducing the threat of terror attacks. There are many companies in the security industry and each limits its activities to one or two specialties. Here are two examples.

Caveon, www.caveon.com. This company specializes in preventing cheating on academic exams, like the SAT, and on various certification exams. Their list of clients includes the College Board, IBM, Microsoft, Atlanta Public Schools, American Board of Internal Medicine, Hewlett Packard, and the Association of Government Accounts. Caveon is an interesting place to work that is expanding its staff across all departments nationwide.

Raytheon, www.raytheon.com. This company is a defense contractor and builds weapons systems used for our national protection. However, Raytheon also builds cyber security systems to get rid of hackers, worms, trojan horses, and other forms of cyber warfare. Check out their website and review the career pages for exciting job opportunities.

THE TECHNOLOGY INDUSTRY

Technology is an industry that requires special attention, so we have devoted three chapters to the topic. See Part III.

THE TRANSPORTATION INDUSTRY

Many interesting companies fit into this category and many of them are household words. One thing is certain in this world, in addition to death and taxes: there will always be a need to move people and goods from one place to another. This industry includes companies involved with automobiles, airplanes, boats, trains, railroads, trucks, bicycles, and all companies that offer support items like tires, batteries, rails, seats, and windows.

Companies in the Transportation Industry. OJS Faves

Boeing, www.boeing.com. Rick Stephens, a Boeing senior vice president and Marine Corps veteran, said that Boeing has hired 3,000 veterans in the past two years. Boeing will need thousands of additional workers as orders for the new 757 Dreamliner keep pouring in. By the way, tune out the media noise on the lithium ion battery problems. Boeing solved this problem, and the Dreamliners are flying safely. When you get to the Boeing website, access the Boeing "Military Skills Translator," a very useful device to tell you how your military skills translate to a civilian job.

Boeing is the world's largest aerospace company and employs 170,000 workers across sixty-five countries. It is headquartered in Chicago. Add to this Boeing's special program to hire and support transitioning military personnel, and you have a company that should be on your list of potential employers. To learn more, go to the website and click on the "Careers" page. Then click on "Military." Land a job with this company and you will be a happy veteran.

FedEx, www.fedex.com. FedEx has become a household word. It is the world's largest delivery service. A veteran of the Vietnam War, Marine Captain Fred Smith, who is the present day CEO, founded it in 1971. His service awards include the Silver Star, Bronze Star, and Purple Heart (two). Is it any wonder that FedEx is the most military friendly of all transportation companies?

Hertz, www.Hertz.com. Hertz has made a concerted effort to find jobs for veterans and has created a special website to provide information. The website even names the person in charge of their military program. She is Leigh Anne Baker, Senior Vice President and Chief Human Resources Officer. We like Hertz for its transparency.

Lockheed Martin, www.lockheedmartin.com. When you open this website, one of the first things you will see is a close-up of the new F-35 Lightning II jet fighter. It is worth the trip to Lockheed's website just to see this new fighting machine. Click on "Careers" and the first heading is "Separating Military Personnel." Next, click on "Military" for an exciting ride to what may be your next job.

Southwest Airlines, www.southwest.com. If you like profitability in a company profile, then Southwest Airlines is for you. The company was founded in 1967 and is headquartered in Dallas, Texas. Southwest has been profitable every quarter for the past twenty years and has provided thousands of jobs for workers across the country. While other airlines have been going broke, Southwest has been making money. Under the leadership of their affable CEO Gary Kelly, they are doing something right. People like to work at Southwest.

Toyota, www.toyota.com. Toyota is headquartered in Japan but manufactures all of its automobiles sold in America right here in the USA. The Toyota Camry is the most popular car in America, which speaks well for Toyota's quality and customer service. Visit their website for a long list of jobs available throughout the US. Toyota recognizes the efforts of veterans by giving all who served a $500 discount on all Toyota cars and trucks in addition to any other price promotions. One thing you should understand about auto companies is that many of their jobs are located at retail locations like Fred Beans Toyota in Flemington, New Jersey. In Chapter 18, "Where to Find Employers. Who Is Hiring?" I will tell you about an interesting job I saw advertised while having my Toyota Avalon serviced.

Union Pacific Railroad, www.up.com. Union Pacific is the largest US railroad and operates primarily in states west of the Mississippi River. The original company was founded by an act of Congress in 1862 and is headquartered in Omaha, Nebraska. The company employs 43,000 workers, and its annual revenues exceed $20 billion.

Most of us think of railroad employees as train conductors, ticket sellers, and locomotive engineers. However, the visible workforce accounts for only a small percentage of employees. Behind the scenes are hundreds of thousands of workers involved in sales, marketing, finance, technology, and engineering. Moreover, as the US petroleum industry continues to grow exponentially, the railroads are growing in tandem because oil and gas need to be transported from wellhead to refiners throughout the country.

Veterans seeking jobs often overlook this booming industry. According to the Association of American Railroads (AAR), some 500 companies and organizations in the railroad industry are seeking to hire about 5,000 veterans. These companies include freight carriers, inter-city passenger and commuter railroads, and rail supply companies. As a growing number of current railroad employees look toward retirement, the number of job openings will begin to rise in future years. Ed Hamberger, president of the AAR, said, "Today, roughly 23 percent of the railroad workforce is eligible to retire by 2015."

Ray LaHood, former US Department of Transportation secretary, indicated that 25 percent of the industry's current employees are veterans. "Our veterans have the skills and real-life experiences that we need to help rebuild America," he said in a CNN interview.

Veterans, do not overlook this booming industry. It offers jobs in every state of the country, and these are good jobs with security, attractive wages, and excellent benefits.

OJS LARGE COMPANY FAVES: CHEMICALS ENTERTAINMENT. FINANCE. FOOD. RENTAL. TECHNOLOGY

The usual route that many veterans follow is to look on the job boards and scour the social media for leads to job opportunities with *any* company that may be hiring. The next step they take is to send a resume to a position number or job number (i.e. Position 1276). That is foolish, as we already know, because finding a job involves making a personal connection with a hiring manager. There is a better way to find good potential employers in large companies.

Search for companies that have been in business for many years and that have been profitable. Target companies whose products and services are in constant demand throughout the business cycle and which have a good reputation for fair play with their workers. Why spend your time throwing darts at the entire board of American goods and services producers?

To get you headed in the right direction, here is a list of **OJS** large company favorites. It is not by any means a complete list, but it will give you an idea of what we consider important and the criteria we used in assessing these employers. Note that our list includes both goods and services producers and spans a number of industries.

The Blackstone Group, www.blackstone.com. This company is one of the world's leading investment and financial advisory firms and is headquartered in New York City. It has eight regional offices spread throughout the country and offices abroad as well. Blackstone services include the management of corporate private equity funds, real estate opportunity funds, hedge funds, mezzanine funds, senior debt vehicles, proprietary hedge funds, and closed-end mutual funds. Blackstone recently announced its intention to focus on the Aerospace and Defense industries and has already appointed a senior executive, Jim Albaugh, to manage this operation. He had been CEO and president of Boeing Commercial Airplanes.

Blackstone CEO Steve Schwarzman recently announced that the company plans to hire 50,000 military veterans during the next five years. It has established a management training program that is already up and running and has partnered with President Obama, First Lady Michelle Obama, and Vice President Biden to implement a nationwide initiative called "Joining Forces" to encourage private companies to hire and train military personnel. The New York City phone number is 212–583–5000. Call and ask for instructions about how to contact the hiring managers for their various departments.

This may take some time, but stick with it until you find the right person.

Coca-Cola, www.coke.com. This 100-year-old company has provided jobs for millions of people not only in the USA, but also throughout the world. It treats its workers well and is in reorganization mode. Many of Coca-Cola's workers are nearing retirement age, and younger workers are taking over. They have new ideas, use technology effectively, and are positioning the company to reach new levels of performance and revenue.

Costco, www.costco.com. The company makes money two ways: by selling its products to customers and from membership fees. Its products include anything from fresh foods to tires. Annual revenues are approximately $24 billion, as a lot of money is spent on groceries and household goods. Costco has nowhere to go but up, and that means job opportunities for workers across America. Moreover, Costco, one of the largest companies in the world, has made a commitment to hiring returning military veterans. Costco employs 174,000 workers, most working behind the scenes in real estate, finance, marketing, technology, supply chain management, purchasing, construction, and human resources. Among big box retailers, Costco ranks number one in wages paid to store employees: $21 per hour.

By the way, Costco sells more wine, imported and domestic, than any other company in the world. And that's not all. In 2015, Costco sold 140 million rotisserie chickens and 140 million hot dogs. Hungry for a good job, a hot dog, a rotisserie chicken, and a nice bottle of wine from the Loir Valley in France? Work with Costco.

Disney, www.disney.com. Go to the website, click on the "Careers" button and then on "Working Here." Then click on "Heroes Work Here," and you will find a wealth of information about initiatives Disney has to help transitioning military personnel get started on a meaningful career. You will see quotes from veterans about their work experience at Disney in a variety of positions involving finance, sales, security, and technology.

Dow Chemical, www.dow.com. Dow is the world's second largest chemical company after BASF and has home offices in Midland, Michigan. Dow produces products used in almost every facet of our lives. Under the leadership of its CEO, Andrew Liveris, the company has grown exponentially worldwide and has won many "best employer" awards in countries around the world. Many consider Dow one of America's best employers, as it has a reputation for creating a diverse workforce where everyone is welcome. Dow employs over 55,000 workers and has sales revenues of approximately $60 billion. Dow was founded in 1897 and is military friendly.

FedEx, www.fedex.com. See the **OJS Faves** list for the Transportation Industry above.

General Electric, www.generalelectric.com. GE has its fingers in many manufacturing pots and is a very profitable company. It was founded in 1892 and employs approximately 310,000 workers. Annual revenues top $145 billion. GE, headquartered in Fairfield, Connecticut, is a multinational conglomerate, which means that it manufactures and produces a multitude of diverse products that are sold in many countries. Many GE products, such as power plants and engines, are used by the US military. The company has an excellent record for philanthropy and community outreach, in addition to being military friendly.

General Mills, www.generalmills.com. "Wheaties. Breakfast of Champions." General Mills has been serving up this breakfast cereal in its iconic orange box for the past eighty years. General Mills is doing a lot right, like producing foods that customers enjoy and find nutritious. General Mills employs 41,000 workers and generates $18 billion in annual sales. This is one of the leading food companies in the world. It is based in Minneapolis, Minnesota. Go to the General Mills website for details about their veterans initiatives and for job listings. Companies stay in business this long only if they produce products that customers find valuable and a work environment and culture that employees find gratifying.

When it comes to community outreach, General Mills is at the top of the pack. Over the past thirteen years, its Box Tops for Education program has raised over $300 million for schools across the USA. In addition, its various foundations have awarded over $535 million to charitable organizations. Individual employees have bought into the General Mills culture, too. Eighty percent of General Mills' workers donate time to work with nonprofit organizations like Habitat for Humanity and Meals on Wheels.

General Mills has also been designated a Yellow Ribbon Company by the Governor of Minnesota for its commitment to recruiting, hiring, training, and supporting veterans.

Home Depot, www.homedepot.com. Where else can you find houseplants, light bulbs, home appliances like dishwashers, and sheets of plywood for home construction under the same roof? This is a very profitable company with locations across the USA and abroad. The company employs 365,000 workers and its annual revenues are approximately $80 billion. Home Depot was recently ranked 30th in the *Forbes* list "The Top 100 Military Friendly Employers."

IHG, www.IHG.com. The Intercontinental Hotels Group includes famous names like Holiday Inn, Holiday Inn Express, Intercontinental Hotels, Crown Plaza, and others. When you find the "IHG Careers" page, click on "Apply," and then click on "Create a Profile." Next, click on "View Veterans Jobs." Here you will find more than 1,000 jobs organized by job title and location, both domestic and international.

Johnson Controls, www.johnsoncontrols.com. Johnson Controls is the world's leading provider of controls mechanisms for the building and automotive industries. Annual revenues exceed $42 billion. JC has a very active program for veterans, and we urge you to review the website. Click on "Careers" and then on "Transitioning US Veterans" to access an interesting description of their military program. Be sure to view the videos made by former servicemen and women employees describing the company culture. The names of these men and women are on the screen. Who knows, you might know one of them.

Lowe's, www.lowes.com. A WWII veteran, Carl Buchan, founded this major home supply company. Over the years, the company has taken good care of military personnel. Click on "Careers" and then on "Military" for more information and a listing of job opportunities. Lowe's is ranked 38th in the *G.I. Jobs* listing of the Top 100 Military Friendly Employers. Lowe's boasts of having hired more than 14,000 veterans recently. In addition, Lowe's participates in the Military Spouse Employment Partnership, an initiative devoted to finding job opportunities for spouses of military personnel employed at Lowe's. Read more about it on their website.

McDonald's, www.mcdonalds.com. This company is expanding its fast food menu constantly and is located in countries all over the world. It has been in business for over sixty years and employs approximately 2 million workers in 100 countries. Its annual revenues are approximately $30 billion. Over the years, it has been a leader in community outreach. McDonald's corporate headquarters are located in Oak Brook, Illinois, a suburb of Chicago.

Qualcomm, www.qualcomm.com. This company is a global semiconductor designer and a manufacturer and marketer of digital wireless telecommunications products. It is one of the best in the business and has been around since 1985, which is a long time in the digital technology business. Qualcomm is based in San Diego and employs 30,000 workers. Qualcomm has collaborated with Manpower San Diego to provide a number of information technology scholarships *exclusively for returning military personnel who served in Iraq and Afghanistan.* Check with Manpower San Diego and Qualcomm human resources for more information about this and other programs for veterans.

Salesforce.com, www.salesforce.com. This is the preeminent cloud computing company headed by a highly respected CEO, Mark Benioff. Recently the company created a new division dedicated to the institutional school market because colleges and universities are moving to the cloud. The stock price has been moving up steadily over the past three years because company revenues have been increasing, and because investors consider Salesforce.com to be the best of breed. The company has an excellent track record of service to the community and contributes to worthy causes.

Starbucks, www.starbucks.com. A few years ago, people asked, "What can a coffee house do for America? What's all the fuss about another coffee joint?" Well, for starters, a good cup of joe in the morning is the traditional way that most Americans begin their day. It is part of our culture. However, there is more to this story than drinking coffee.

Starbucks has provided both part-time and full-time jobs for millions of Americans from coast to coast, and it treats them fairly. Many workers who started as baristas (don't you love the job title?) moved up to management positions and executive level positions. In addition, the CEO, Howard Schultz, has made a concerted effort to bring jobs back to America by using only American manufacturers to provide essential items such as paper coffee cups, which are manufactured in Ohio. In 2015, Starbucks initiated an online college scholarship program for all employees.

Starbucks is not only America's coffeehouse. With the recent acquisition of Teavana Holdings, it is America's teahouse as well. Starbucks has a bright future and we recommend that you check out the website for job opportunities. You will see jobs in supply chain operations, finance, global development, information technology, retail sales, coffee roasting house operations, and many others.

For the seventh year in a row, the Ethisphere Institute has included Starbucks in its list of the world's most ethical companies. *Fortune* magazine has listed Starbucks among the 100 best American companies for employment. The company has been in existence since 1971, and we predict it will still be here when you are looking for an encore career. Did you look at the Career Center section of the website?

Texas Instruments, www.TI.com. TI is eighty years old. It is not a Johnny-come-lately to the technology world, and it produces more than calculators. TI produces technology products like RFID barcodes and sophisticated semiconductors, those little beasts that make your digital toys run. TI has a presence in thirty-five countries and employs 35,000 workers. Annual revenues top $14 billion. The company is based in Dallas, Texas, and has offices scattered throughout the USA and abroad.

TI has a reputation for treating its workers like family despite its size, which explains why people work there for many years. TI has one of the best mentoring programs in the business, and one of its most attractive benefits is a profit-sharing program that has made many workers very wealthy.

Please note that TI is very deliberate when it comes to hiring workers at any level for any position, which is probably one of the reasons why this is such a successful company. The hiring process could span several months, but it is worth the time and effort.

Tiffany & Company, www.Tiffany.com. This American icon of upscale jewelry and fine home furnishings has been in business since 1837. Do you want to work in a pleasant environment surrounded by beautiful objects of art for the home and personal adornment? Do you get high looking into a flawless two-carat diamond? If you answer "yes" or even "maybe," the next step is to check out their website. By the way, if you are bilingual (French/English), check out Tiffany job opportunities in Paris, France.

United Rentals, www.unitedrentals.com. This is one of the largest tool and equipment rental companies in the world, and it offers many interesting opportunities for returning veterans. Under the "Careers" menu, click on "Military Recruiting." This company has great respect for the values and skills you learned in the military and is one of the best 100 military friendly employers. One of the testimonials is from Marc Elig, U.S. Army, CW-5, who advises veterans not to discount the skills learned in the military, because companies like United Rentals will translate those skills into positions within the company.

Verizon, www.verizon.net. The country's largest wireless carrier offers employment opportunities in all states and is at the forefront of all forms of digital communication. The array of jobs with this communication giant is impressive. If your interests include communications and technology and you have military work experience in either field, Verizon may be the right place for you.

Walmart, www.walmart.com. This is America's largest employer and the world's largest retailer, because it offers the number one requirement for survival—food—at reasonable prices. This non-union employer has incurred the wrath of organized union bosses who want to break the successful Walmart model. Do not fall for their negative attacks against Walmart. This is a great company with many job opportunities for entry-level and experienced veterans. Worldwide it employs 2.2 million workers and annual revenues exceed $45 billion. The company has a policy of promoting from within, and in the past year it promoted 170,000 workers to positions of greater responsibility and higher pay.

Walmart is one of the most military friendly companies and has made a commitment to hire 100,000 veterans over the next five years. In fact, Walmart hired 40,000 veterans between Memorial Day 2013 and Memorial Day 2014, a confirmation that it is serious when it comes to hiring veterans. William Simon, president and CEO, recently said, "Let's be clear. Hiring a veteran can be one of the best decisions any of us can make. These are leaders with discipline training and a passion for service."

Check out their special website for veterans, www.walmartcareerswithamission.com.

Whole Foods, www.wholefoods.com. This company deserves an A+ for leading America toward better eating habits by selling foods that are free from chemicals and pollutants harmful to our health. In addition, the CEO is committed to working with the community to provide assistance to those in need. Based in Austin, Texas, Whole Foods is one of the most socially responsible companies in the world. The company employs approximately 60,000 workers, and its annual revenues are more than $12 billion. *Fortune* magazine ranks Whole Foods in the top 100 best companies for workers. Whole Foods has an excellent benefits program for its employees and a career path for workers seeking long-term employment.

These are just a few of the large companies that hire hundreds of thousands of workers each year. Explore the career pages of these large companies and apply for a position that matches your profile, remembering to send your resumes and career profiles to the human resources director or department hiring manager by name. Smart veterans never send career information to "Employment Manager" or "Position #257." Successful job hunting means establishing a relationship with a named person in a position to hire job candidates such as you.

SMALL BUSINESSES ARE BIG EMPLOYERS

The Bureau of Labor Statistics (BLS) defines small businesses as those companies employing fewer than 500 workers. A small business can be anything from a corner deli employing three or four workers to a niche technology firm with several hundred workers. *Small businesses employ over 50 percent of all workers.*

Working for a small business, as opposed to the large companies listed above, offers both considerable advantages and considerable challenges. Many small businesses, particularly storefront entrepreneurial businesses like restaurants or florist shops, have greater sensitivity to disruptions in the economic climate. They are subject to going out of business at the first hiccup in the economy because they depend on day-to-day revenue to stay alive. Large companies usually have cash reserves to carry them through lean times, or they have readily available sources of borrowed cash.

Generally, working for a small business carries more risk for workers than working for a large corporation. Small business owners usually do not have the resources to provide salaries and benefits offered by large firms. Many small businesses do not offer retirement plans, such as a 401K, in their benefits packages, and many offer only legally required minimum medical and hospital insurance. Paid vacation, sick days, and holidays are not offered by some small businesses, and other employee amenities are sparse. Compensation is usually less in a small business than it is in a large corporation.

On the plus side of the equation, small businesses can be more flexible in providing personal time off (without pay, of course) and often have more relaxed work rules. Usually the culture is friendlier and employers are more flexible on job requirements. Previous work experience and formal education requirements are not as rigid as they are in a large company.

Owners of small businesses usually carry out the hiring process personally, while large companies hire recruiters to conduct candidate searches or post their openings on numerous job boards. The hiring process in a small business is frequently abbreviated. Frequently, a job candidate receives an offer immediately after the first personal interview. The process with a large company can be tedious and take thirty to sixty days, or more, beginning to end. However, once you are hired by a small business, promotions to a higher rank may come more quickly than they would in a large corporation.

Where should you cast your lot, small business or large company? It is not an easy answer and one that frequently comes down to personal preferences, needs, and circumstances. For example, assume that you are divorced with two children and many bills to pay and you need cash now. Your chances for quick employment are better with a small business than they would be with a large company where the process could stretch on for six months. It comes down to this: you take what you can get to pay the bills and be self-sufficient, even if the compensation is below what you would like.

SPECIAL HELP FOR WOUNDED VETERANS

The content of **OJS** is instructive for all veterans, even those living with physical disabilities or PTSD. The rules of the game apply to all, but those with disabilities face special challenges. They will find additional job-hunting resources at organizations such as the Wounded Warrior Project, www.woundedwarriorproject.org; Paralyzed Veterans of America, www.pva.org; Wounded Heroes Foundation, www.woundedheroesfund.net; the US Department of Veterans Affairs, www.VA.gov; and the Society for Human Resource Management, www.shrm.com.

MOVING FORWARD

Evaluating an employer, large or small, is an important task and it takes time. It is worth the effort, however, because you do not want to work for a company whose products and culture are not compatible with your interests, agenda, and values. For more help on evaluating a company, go to Chapter 33, "How to Evaluate a Company, Its Culture, and Executive Staff."

CHAPTER TAKEAWAYS

- All companies and small businesses are part of a larger entity called an industry.
- The hiring process in a large company is more detailed and lengthier than it is in a small company.
- In our economy, you take what you can get in order to pay the bills and become self-sufficient.

- A record of community outreach is one important factor in evaluating a company.
- Companies with a long and successful record of profitable business operations are usually good employers.
- Military friendly companies are sensitive to the needs of veterans. Place them at the top of your list of potential employers.
- The *Occupational Outlook Handbook* is a valuable job-hunting resource.

THE VETERAN'S LIBRARY

Jim Cramer and Cliff Mason. *Jim Cramer's Stay Mad for Life: Get Rich, Stay Rich (And Make Your Kids Even Richer)*. Simon & Schuster, 2007.

Jim Cramer. *Jim Cramer's Real Money*. Simon & Schuster, 2009.

Troy Adair, Ph.D. *Corporate Finances Demystified*. McGraw-Hill, 2011.

US Department of Labor. *The Occupational Outlook Handbook*. JIST Publishing Co., 2015.

Time Inc., *Fortune* magazine. *Fortune* is published monthly, print or digital, at a reasonable cost to subscribers.

Chapter 3

Military Friendly Companies

Companies that render preferential treatment to veterans are military friendly companies. A number of organizations specialize in rating these companies, and occasionally they revise the lists to reflect new data and information. Sometimes there are companies that go unnoticed. You can find them other ways, like at job fairs held exclusively for military veterans.

How can veterans use these listings? How can they help in your job search? First, realize that military friendly companies do not guarantee a job to every veteran who submits a resume. Veterans must use the rules of engagement listed in **OJS**, one of which is to meet with company hiring managers *in the flesh* to build a personal relationship. Merely submitting a resume will produce meager results. The reason is that companies do not hire resumes; they hire living, breathing veterans who have the smarts to find a way to meet them personally. It makes no difference whether you are seeking a job in transportation, such as driving an eighteen-wheeler for Walmart, or a job as an IT coordinator for Johnson & Johnson, or a job as human resources director for Nordstrom.

USING LISTS OF MILITARY FRIENDLY EMPLOYERS

Many job seekers make the basic mistake of scouring the job boards for listings and then submitting a resume to any company for any job that comes close to their interests and qualifications. That is not the way to begin. It is important to make a job search plan, one that clearly delineates what you will be doing day by day. When you are construct-ing the part of your plan targeting specific companies, always include military friendly companies posted by the ranking organizations. That is the most productive method to add focus to your job search.

WHAT DOES "MILITARY FRIENDLY" REALLY MEAN?

There is no universally accepted definitive meaning for this term, but in general it means that companies are interested in hiring veterans *and* have established processes to attract their candidacy. Some companies use the term "Military Friendly" to attract veterans because they truly believe veterans bring something extra to the table, such as focus, ded-ication, passion, reliability, discipline, leadership skills, diversity, punc-tuality, and work ethic.

Other companies use the term as a marketing tool. Labeling your-self as "Military Friendly" makes good press, but sometimes it stops there. The most serious military friendly companies have set aside a certain number of jobs that will go only to military veterans, both men and women. Target companies that make such a promise. Two that come to mind are Blackstone and Walmart, both of which we described in the previous chapter. Also, some military friendly companies have established employment programs for spouses of veterans, and these should be at the top of your contact list. Three such companies are First Data, Lowe's, and Walmart.

MILITARY FRIENDLY RANKING ORGANIZATIONS

My Internet search for ranking organizations led me both to well-known places and to others that are not highly visible. Usually the rankings focus only on the so-called Top 100, but **OJS** will take you beyond that point. Begin your search for military friendly companies using these resources:

Military Friendly, www.militaryfriendly.com. This website is one of your best resources for finding military friendly employers. This organization breaks down the list into ten sectors and updates the list annually. These sectors are:

- Defense
- Diversified Services
- Energy
- Finance
- Healthcare
- Manufacturing
- Retail
- Security and Corrections
- Technology and Telecommunications
- Transportation

Military Friendly uses reliable data for its evaluations and chooses only the best from among 5,000 companies. Energy, defense, and finance are industries that frequently rise to the top of their list. Some of the top companies on their latest list are:

- *Combined Insurance Company.* The company has committed to hiring 4,000 veterans over the next two years.
- *United Services Automobile Association (USAA).* Fourteen percent of this company's employees are veterans. Here's what USAA recently said to veterans seeking civilian employment: "'We know what it means to serve' is more than a slogan. We respect and honor what the men and women in our military risk for us, and what their families go through to support them. Not only have you proven yourself in service to our nation, but you also know our members better than anyone—and can share your unique experiences through service to our members."
- *Baker Hughes.* This company is a global oilfield services provider and has an excellent record of accomplishment hiring veterans for a variety of technical positions.

- *Union Pacific.* This is the largest railroad in the USA; it employs over 45,000 workers in a variety of positions. For a complete description of Union Pacific and an analysis of the railroad industry, see Chapter 2.
- *Allied Barton Security Services.* Allied employs 55,000 highly trained security workers targeting higher education, commercial real estate, healthcare, finance, government and other industries. The company dates back to 1957 and is based in Conshohocken, Pennsylvania, a Philadelphia suburb. Victory Media selected the company as a 2015 Military Friendly Spouse Employer. Learn more about the company's regard for veterans on its website, www.alliedbarton.com. When we reviewed the website, we found a phone number that veterans can call to learn more about Allied's programs for veterans and their spouses. The number to call is 866–825–5433.

Interestingly, nineteen financial services companies are in the top one hundred. Some of them are: Bank of America, KPMG, PriceWaterhouseCoppers, First Command Financial Services, and Deloitte.

The entire list includes a diverse group of companies, some of which are household names like McDonald's, Accenture, Aetna, First Data, JP Morgan Chase, General Electric, Lowe's, Verizon, Sprint, Walmart, Home Depot, and Hewlett Packard. All value the skills and training that military personnel acquired while in service. Many have special training programs for veterans, and some even provide preferential treatment for military spouses. In addition, new companies are added to the list based on new data points. For example, Google announced in December 2014 that it launched a special program to lure veterans to seek employment there. Review www.google.com/about/careers/veterans/index.html for more information.

While you are visiting this site, look for a listing of job fairs for veterans.

The Department of Veterans Affairs (VA), www.va.gov. The VA holds career fairs and expositions for veterans in almost every state around the calendar. Here you will find hundreds of military friendly companies seeking veterans for a variety of jobs. Go to the website for more information and a description of what takes place at these career expos.

One of the best VA events is held in Washington, DC, each year. It is called the Veterans Career Fair and Expo, and it brings together private sector employers and civil service employers (government agency employers) who are seeking veteran job candidates. This event is particularly well suited for veterans living the the Mid-Atlantic states who are within easy driving distance to Washington.

Joining Forces, www.whitehouse.gov/joiningforces. In 2011, the White House initiated a program to help veterans transition to civilian jobs. First Lady Michelle Obama and Dr. Jill Biden, wife of Vice President Joseph Biden, spearheaded the drive to assist veterans and their spouses transitioning to the civilian job market. Joining Forces is a consortium of government and civilian organizations that includes the US Department of Veterans Affairs, the US Department of Labor, the US Department of Defense, the US Chamber of Commerce, state and local government organizations, and a number of civilian companies like United Parcel Service (UPS) and Xerox. Since its founding, civilian employers in the Joining Forces consortium have hired over 550,000 veterans.

Department of Defense (DoD) Contractors, www.defense.gov. The DOD publishes a list of all companies under contract to do business with this major government department. All companies that do business with the Department of Defense are military friendly. The list includes:

- Lockheed Martin
- Boeing
- Raytheon
- General Dynamics Corporation
- Northrup Grumman Corporation

Go to the website to access this list and add the listed companies to your job search plan for review. You must apply directly to the companies to explore their job opportunities. DOD will not do this for you.

GI Jobs, www.gijobs.com. We recommend this site because it publishes an annual select list of twenty jobs offered by Military Friendly companies. Go to the site and click on "Top 20 Hot Jobs for Veterans." In addition, you will find valuable information to help you in your job search.

Recruit Military, www.recruitmilitary.com. Some of the best military friendly companies are not on published lists. They will be on the floor of job fairs held exclusively for veterans throughout the country. This site provides a valuable service for veterans by listing the location and dates for all veteran's job fairs each year. Job fairs and conventions are the best places for networking because hiring managers for each individual company are always working in the company exhibit booths. These are the people you need to know in order to get a job.

Bradley Morris, www.bradley-morris.com. This is the premier recruiting firm dedicated to searches for military veterans. The company seeks candidates who are former military officers, noncommissioned officers, and technicians for placement in a variety of jobs with thousands of employers throughout the country. Bradley Morris holds Conference Hire Events in many states around the calendar and visits bases, too. Many of the Bradley Morris staff members are former military personnel.

MILITARY FRIENDLY INDUSTRIES. OJS FAVES

After extensive research into industries especially friendly to veterans, I found two sectors that hold significant promise for veterans. They are manufacturing and railroads. Some sources consider both to be outdated sectors, but nothing could be further from the truth.

MANUFACTURERS

The National Association of Manufacturers is reaching out to help veterans as much as possible through a number of programs. The need for workers in the manufacturing sector is acute. According to the Institute for Veterans and Military Families (IVMF) at Syracuse University, there are an estimated 600,000 advanced manufacturing jobs unfilled in the United States. More than 82 percent of manufacturers report they cannot find people to fill their skilled production jobs. Furthermore, up to 2.5 million manufacturing jobs will open up within five years as older workers retire.

Companies such as Alcoa, Boeing, Lockheed Martin, and General Electric are making a concerted effort to recruit veterans, and I urge you to contact these companies. Manufacturing companies are dead serious about hiring veterans. Just these four companies alone have hired close to 65,000 veterans in the past ten years.

RAILROADS

Job seekers often overlook this booming industry. It is an excellent place to seek job opportunities. Many job seekers think of railroad jobs only in terms of what they see while riding a commuter train (e.g. engineers and conductors). However, for every visible railroad worker, there are thousands working behind the scenes in a variety of interesting and lucrative jobs. This industry seeks to hire veterans because of their skill sets and work ethic. For a more detailed description of this industry, see Chapter 2.

MOVING FORWARD

Is it really worth the time and effort to explore employment with the so-called military friendly companies? **OJS** responds to that question with an unqualified "yes." Most are large companies that have been in business for decades and are highly profitable. Explore their websites for information about their programs for veterans and the procedures for gaining employment there. Always explore the website's "Career" pages and zero in on one or several jobs that you find attractive and that are in harmony with your military work profile. Remember, never submit your resume to a job number or an entity without a name, like "employment manager." Even when you are dealing with military friendly companies, you must follow the rules for civilian job hunting in **OJS**, one of which is to submit your resume or career profile only to a named person with a title. Doing otherwise is like sending your credentials to another galaxy.

CHAPTER TAKEAWAYS

- Follow the general rules for civilian job hunting. Military friendly companies do not hire just any veteran who knocks on the door.
- Frequently review the websites of organizations ranking military friendly companies.
- Some companies use the term "military friendly" as a marketing tool. Distinguish companies serious about helping veterans from those who just give lip service.

THE VETERAN'S LIBRARY

Forbes **magazine**, www.forbes.com/forbes. Make a habit of visiting this site frequently for important business information.

Chapter 4

Starting Your Own Business or Buying a Franchise

Join the thousands who have started their own businesses instead of working for someone else. The fact that you have a wide array of skills learned in the military, a college degree, or both does not mean that you *must* work for a big corporation or a small business. Working for a company, particularly a large one where the ground rules can be oppressive, may not be your idea of a good time. Many of your colleagues feel the same way.

Veterans have an enviable record of success running their own businesses. According to Military.com and other corroborating sources, approximately 3.6 million veterans run their own show. That translates into 25 percent of the veteran workforce.

But how do you start your own business? What must you do before hanging out a sign with your name on it? Isn't it true that most business owners have money in the family and are mostly upper class? To clear up those misconceptions, here is the profile of people who start their own businesses according to an article that appeared in the *Wall Street Journal*: "Less than 1 percent come from extremely rich or extremely poor backgrounds. 71.5 percent come from a middle class background. 70 percent used their own savings as the source to fund their own businesses." So much for the stereotypes of business owners. I like numbers. They always set the record straight.

PORTRAITS OF SUCCESSFUL VETERAN BUSINESS OWNERS

Who are some of these successful entrepreneurs? Are there any good examples of veterans who decided to make it on their own instead of casting their lot with a company? The answer is a resounding "yes." Here are two inspirational stories of veterans who started their own businesses.

Captain Kiel King of New York (U.S. Army Ret.)

First, I am medically retired as a Captain. Upon returning to the United States from Germany, I spoke with the Lucas Group, an executive recruiting firm that specializes in placing military personnel. My Bachelor's Degree is in Chemistry & Life Sciences, but it did not come into play while taking my interview with the Coca-Cola Bottling Company. I was hired after the first interview. I started with Coca-Cola a month after leaving the military as a Production Manager, but, after one year, I was not truly working in a field that I enjoyed. I believe I was hired due to my leadership experience in the Army and my education at West Point. After a bit of soul searching I decided it was important to continue my education in an area that I truly loved and went back to school to complete a graduate degree in Physical Rehabilitation Sciences.

I have since started my own company called Kings of Fitness, where we operate under the mission to educate, motivate, and inspire individuals to live a healthy and physically active lifestyle. While I was in the Army, helping people was extremely important to me, and now that I am medically retired, helping people is still the most important thing that gives me true job satisfaction. I did not feel I had that with Coca-Cola as great as they were with bringing me in.

I also had the fortunate opportunity to work with the Wounded Warrior Project on maintaining an updated resume. They are absolutely an amazing organization that cares. I still hear from them once a month when they check in to see how I am doing.

All veterans can learn from Captain King's story. After his medical discharge, he immediately prepared to make the transition to the civilian workforce. He did not just hang out for six months thinking about it. Coca-Cola hired Captain King after the first interview, which indicates how impressed the company was with the communication and leadership skills he had learned in the Army. After a year, he did some soul searching and found that working for someone else was not what he really wanted to do. His inner core was taking him in another direction. He returned to school for an MA in a field he liked, physical rehabilitation, and then started his own business. It's an inspiring story, and here is what we can learn from Captain King:

- Education must continue after discharge.
- Take advantage of the many sources of help for veterans like the Wounded Warrior Project.
- Start a business that grabs your interest and provides meaning to your life.

Kevin Treiber, Medic 91A (Ret.), Yardley, PA

Kevin served as a medic in operations Desert Storm and Desert Shield. After discharge, he enrolled in a local community college for a year and then moved on to the University of North Carolina for his BSN in Nursing. Following several years in the nursing profession, Kevin founded his own business, TDY Medical Staffing, Inc., www.tdymedical.com, where he is President and CEO. His company is a provider of contract medical, administrative, clerical, allied health, nursing, and other professional services for assignments with federal and state governments and commercial organizations. TDY is a VA-verified Service Disabled, Veteran Owned Small Business. Established in 2008 to address the shortage in government healthcare personnel, TDY has since evolved to service every sector including medical and administrative personnel. TDY offers clients integrated staffing solutions that ensure coverage in every department or unit of a workplace. Clients select flexible assignment options ranging from per diem shifts to extended year contracts.

Like so many of his colleagues, Kevin faced significant challenges during his transition, but used his military training, his intelligence, energy, and passion to overcome them. His sage advice to all transitioning veterans is a simple but profound message: THERE IS NO CHALLENGE YOU CAN'T OVERCOME. NEVER STOP TRYING!

HOW TO GET STARTED

The rules of business entrepreneurship apply to everyone, not just veterans. There are not two sets of rules. Consider what Richard Branson, founder and CEO of Virgin Airlines, said in his first blog post for LinkedIn in 2012: "As LinkedIn is a business that started in a living room, much like Virgin, which began in a basement, I thought my first blog on the site should be about how to simply start a successful business." Here are Branson's five top tips:

1. Listen more than you talk.
2. Keep it simple.
3. Take pride in your work.
4. Have fun, success will follow.
5. Rip it up and start again.

These are the first steps that Richard Branson took when founding Virgin Airlines, one of the most successful airlines on the planet. Branson always has good ideas for entrepreneurs and has authored twelve books about starting and operating businesses. I've listed two of them in **THE VETERAN'S LIBRARY** at the end of this chapter.

By the way, Branson did not have a college degree when he founded Virgin Airlines. His age? Twenty-four. Go to LinkedIn periodically and read Branson's blogs. You will receive advice from one of the world's most successful business owners at a terrific price—free. You can learn much from him. He's been there, done that, without a college degree, without family money, while working from a basement office to plan his work and work his plan.

FAMOUS ENTREPRENEURS

If you explore how other entrepreneurs founded their businesses, the story will be similar to Branson's. Take Bill Gates, the founder of Microsoft. He dropped out of Harvard after his sophomore year and founded Microsoft. His age? Twenty-one. He had no family money and a middle-class background.

Here are two more examples of successful entrepreneurs. Steve Jobs and Steve Wozniak both dropped out of college after their first year and founded Apple Computer working out of a garage. Both were in their early twenties. Then we have Larry Ellison, founder and CEO of Oracle, who bypassed college altogether and founded one of the world's largest software companies.

In addition, let's not forget Mark Zuckerberg, the CEO of Facebook, another person with big dreams and little appetite for continuing his education at Harvard. He dropped out of college and founded Facebook. Mark is in his early thirties and his start-up, Facebook, is a publically held company. Mark's net worth exceeds $30 *billion*, much of which he donates to charitable causes.

OJS is not saying that only college dropouts launch successful businesses. Individuals start businesses with little or no college experience. And let's be realistic about the money. Not every entrepreneur will establish a billion-dollar business, but what's wrong with a cool million? That sounds like a big number, but after you establish a business with your name on it, a million will sound like chump change.

I WANT TO DO IT MY WAY

These behemoths in the technology world all began as someone's dream, which was refined into a viable business in someone's garage or basement. (I'm not sure why garages and basements are so attractive to entrepreneurs. That's just the way it is.) If Captain King, Bill Gates, and Mark Zuckerberg could do it, so can you. The business you start does not have to be another Microsoft in order to be successful. There are thousands of small businesses founded, owned, and operated successfully by someone who had the courage to say, "I want to do it my way." Here is a good example of a veteran who did it his way.

Colonel Harland Sanders

Harland Sanders was born in 1890 and spent the first forty years of his life working a variety of jobs. As a child, he learned to cook family-style meals from his mother while working on a farm. In 1902, he enlisted in the Army and was honorably discharged after serving for a limited amount of time. He had no clear career path and bounced from job to job, working primarily for railroads. At nights, he worked on a law degree by mail correspondence from La Salle Extension University, a forerunner of today's online universities. After practicing law for a brief time, he accepted an offer from the Shell Oil Co. to operate a gas station in Corbin, Kentucky. A true multitasker, Harland began cooking and selling meals from his own house adjacent to the gas station. One of his specialties was chicken, not fried or baked, but cooked in a new device called a pressure cooker. Word spread that his chicken was the best you can buy, and he gave up the gas station business and opened restaurants that featured his specialty. At about the same time, the Governor of Kentucky commissioned Harland as a Kentucky Colonel, an honorary title.

In 1940, Harland created and promoted his "secret recipe" for his now-famous chicken, attracting rave reviews from food critics who spread the word nationwide. In 1952, he franchised his first restaurant and named it Kentucky Fried Chicken, and the rest is history. Colonel Harland Sander's story proves that successful entrepreneurs do not have to be technology gurus like Gates or Zuckerberg. Any smart veteran using his intelligence, energy, and passion can do the same.

If the thought of founding a company that has your name on it really turns you on, go for it! There are many books and websites offering ideas about how to get started, and there are many support groups ready to help veterans accomplish their goal. First, let's explore the different types of business models you might pursue.

STARTING YOUR OWN BUSINESS AS A SOLE PROPRIETOR

Can you really start your own business, as did Sanders, Zuckerberg, and Gates? How long does it take before you can make serious money to become self-sufficient? There are many visible examples of small businesses that are successful. Take a walk down Main Street USA and talk with the owner of a storefront business and you will get the answer. Here are examples of small businesses started by people who had a dream and ambition.

Marlon from Brazil

A good example of a start-up business is a company named "Floors by Marlon Corp." This New Jersey-based company does one thing: install and refinish hardwood floors in homes and businesses. This is a story of a man who immigrated to the US in 2003 knowing very little English. His name is Marlon.

Marlon has been in the flooring business for the past ten years after immigrating to the US from Brazil to seek better job opportunities. After researching businesses that have a long life cycle, he decided to work in the construction business. This was a smart move, because this is a "shelter" related business and, as we learned earlier, it is one of the big three along with food and clothing. He began working for a flooring installation company and after only two years of experience felt that he knew enough to start a business of his own. He started his own entrepreneurial business, and the work came in mainly through referrals from customers who were satisfied with the quality of his work and his fair prices. Soon he needed help, so he hired workers on a part-time basis to meet his requirements.

Fast forward to 2016. Marlon has three people working for him and just spent $25,000 on a new truck and floor-sanding equipment. Marlon does not have a college degree, but he applied his intelligence, energy, and passion to make it on his own. You can, too.

You do not have to work for a large company to become a self-sufficient worker. If the entrepreneurial life is appealing, select something that you really like and pursue it. It does not have to be glamorous, but it does have to fulfill a need that people will always have for goods or services.

WHAT KIND OF BUSINESS CAN I START?

The list of business ventures is endless, but a good place to start is to envision a business in which you have an interest or a passion. Food. Shelter. Clothing. Transportation. Technology. Insurance. Education. Healthcare. These are necessities for all people regardless of age, gender, geography, race, and religion. Apply the same rules that you did for seeking work in the corporate environment. Learn your main field of interest, your aptitudes, and your work experiences in the military and then translate all into a business service.

Businesses on Main Street, USA

The next time you leave the house, look at the businesses on either side of Main Street. A majority of them will be selling food, shelter, clothing, and related products. The point is this: if you want to strike out on your own as an entrepreneur rather than work for someone else, just do it. Play to your passion. Do something that turns you on every day, as Branson said.

Ideas for Your Own Business

Here are five entry-level start-up ideas to get you thinking about your own business:

1. Produce and sell the number one life-sustaining product—food. Remember Colonel Harland Sanders and KFC.
2. Provide services for homes and businesses, as Marlon did.
3. Sell products of any kind as an independent sales representative.
4. Go to school to earn certification in a field of interest, as did Captain King and Medic Kevin Treiber.
5. Follow your passion, as Richard Branson did.

Let's talk for a minute about number three, which is the least expensive way to start working on your own. Independent sales reps carry products related to one specific industry. Take cutlery, for example. Sales reps working in this narrow market niche might carry products for three or more different manufacturers, both domestic and foreign, and sell them to restaurants, both large and small, or to wholesalers, companies that distribute and sell not only knives but also related products, such as metal cooking pots and pans. I know a sales rep who sells only knives in the Mid-Atlantic region, and he makes a small fortune. His slogan? "My products are a cut above the rest."

STARTING YOUR OWN BUSINESS IN A PARTNERSHIP

Another way to start your own business is with a partner who has similar interests and values. Selecting the right partner is an important first step and requires a complete examination of that person's skills, energy, intelligence, passion for self-employment, ethics, values, and interest in the ideas you have for starting a business. Researching your potential partner is critical. If you select just a good friend instead of a *good potential business friend* who is compatible with you in every way, your business could turn into a nightmare. Many entrepreneurs have failed because they selected the wrong partner.

Here is a good example of a successful partnership.

> ## Chris from Silver Spring, Maryland
>
> *Chris said good-bye to the corporate world and turned his interest in cinematography into a thriving video production company. This is not a business for the faint of heart. It requires exceptional written and verbal communication skills, bottom-line business skills, creativity, imagination, and technical expertise. While Chris possessed all of those qualities, the time requirements for operating a successful media business were significant. Chris found a partner with similar values and skills, and together they founded Rafferty-Weiss Media (www. raffertyweiss.com). Check out their website for a peek at a successful and creative partnership with a nationwide reputation for producing products of excellent quality.*

STARTING YOUR OWN BUSINESS WITH A FRANCHISE

A popular way to start your own business is to purchase a franchise, but how this type of business operates is frequently misunderstood. The franchise industry focuses primarily on products and services related to the big three: food, shelter, and clothing. Some popular franchise businesses involve restaurants, cleaning services, real estate, hotels, and a variety of retail stores.

How a Franchise Works

There are two entities involved in the franchise operation. First is the *franchisor*, which is the company that owns the brand name, like McDonald's. The other part is the *franchisee,* the person who buys the product name and sells the franchisor's products at an individual store. The franchisor, or parent company if you will, provides the location, training, marketing and sales support, advertising, and other requirements needed to operate a business. The company charges the individual store operator a franchise fee to begin the business, and takes a percentage of the business revenues.

Of course, the first franchise names that come to mind are McDonald's, Burger King, Dunkin Donuts, Starbucks, Dairy Queen, Chipotle, KFC, and ServPro Cleaning Services. Almost all of the individual stores in the fast food market are franchises. Purchasing one costs serious money. For example, McDonald's requires a minimum of $250,000 in cash to own the franchise. You cannot borrow this amount; it must be $250,000 that is unencumbered, and that is just the beginning. Before you are finished, it will cost anywhere from $600,000 to $1.5 million to purchase a McDonald's franchise.

However, other franchise opportunities are interesting and available for as little as $10,000. There are hundreds of websites that provide information, not only about cost, but also about the process. One that I like is "Top 100 Franchises"(www.top100franchises.net).

When I last checked this website, I found franchises in the $10,000 to $200,000 range. One that I like is ServPro, a house cleaning and restoration business that has an excellent nationwide reputation for good service. The franchise cost is $25,000. At the high end was a Checkers drive-in restaurant, where a franchise will cost approximately $200,000.

Franchise Resources for Veterans

There are a number of online sources to learn more about franchise operations and opportunities:

Entrepreneur, www.entrepreneur.com. This resource is available in magazine format, too. Recent issues have contained interesting articles about veterans who started their own businesses.

Vetfran, www.vetfran.com. This is a division of the International Franchise Association, which recently reported that veterans own one in seven franchises in the US, approximately 66,000 businesses.

GI Jobs, www.gijobs.com. Recently G.I.Jobs listed the following top franchises for veterans:

1. Pillar to Post Inspection Services
2. Jan Pro Franchising
3. Aire Serv
4. Mr. Appliance Corporation
5. WIN Home Inspection
6. Mr. Electric
7. Jani-King
8. Amerispec Home Inspection Services
9. Matco Tools
10. Anytime Fitness

There are many veteran friendly franchises available. Just google "veteran friendly franchises" and you will come up with two days of information to research.

RESOURCES FOR VETERAN ENTREPRENEURS

Recently *Forbes* ran an article titled "The Best Organizations for Entrepreneurs." You can access this article online for interesting and valuable sources of support to start your own business. Navigate this list for information about how to start a business and how to network with others doing the same thing.

US Small Business Administration, www.sba.gov. This is your best source for information about starting your own business. It has many free online education programs that will tell you step-by-step how you go about launching your own business. The SBA operates "Operation Boots to Business: From Service to Startup," a program specifically for veterans. The introduction from the website identifies their mission:

> Boots to Business is an entrepreneurial education initiative offered by the US Small Business Administration (SBA) as an elective track within the Department of Defense's revised Training Assistance Program called Transition Goals, Plans, Success (Transition GPS). The curriculum provides valuable assistance to transitioning service members exploring self-employment

opportunities by leading them through the key steps for evaluating business concepts and the foundation knowledge required for developing a business plan. Participants are also introduced to SBA resources available to help access startup capital and additional technical assistance.

Make this your primary resource for information and online courses for starting your own business. **OJS** recommends the SBA website over all other sources of information for veterans.

Veteran Women Igniting the Spirit of Entrepreneurship (VWISE), www.SBA.gov. This is a program for female veterans sponsored by the Small Business Administration and its partners, such as Syracuse University. It teaches entrepreneurial business skills and encourages women to start small businesses. VWISE is a three-part program offered online through Syracuse University. For details go to www.Whitman.syr.edu.

Entrepreneurship Bootcamp for Veterans with Disabilities (EBV), www.anderson.ucla.edu/entrepreneurship-bootcamp-for-veterans. This unique program offers hands-on experiential training. It was designed for disabled veterans of Operation Enduring Freedom and Operation Iraqi Freedom. The program is offered in partnership with several universities and is available at no cost to veterans. Go to the website for details and a look at inspiring stories of disabled veterans who have made the transition aided by the EBV programs.

US Department of Veterans Affairs (VA), www.va.gov. The VA is the first place most veterans go for help. It's a comprehensive site, so be prepared to spend a good amount of time accessing and reviewing many VA programs for transitioning veterans. When you access the website, enter "employment transition programs" for information about using the VA to your benefit.

Entrepreneurs Organization, www.eonetwork.org. This organization provides general information about starting businesses anywhere in the world. EO requires a hefty membership fee, so study the site carefully to learn if the benefits are right for you.

The Technology Council of Greater Kansas City, www.kcnext.com. Specializing in Kansas City area tech jobs, the organization offers support and advice for entrepreneurs. It focuses on technology applied to all industries including healthcare, telecommunications, digital media, and more. Their sponsored events are perfect for networking.

Built in Chicago, www.builtinchicago.org. BIC concentrates on technology opportunities in the Chicago area. This organization boasts 40,000 members who are business owners or employees of entrepreneurial businesses. An attractive feature of this site is a posting of Chicago area companies in hiring mode. Check this out if you live in the Chicago area or in a nearby state.

Corporate Alliance, www.corporatealliance.net. This organization has offices in California and Utah and provides support, training, and networking services for entrepreneurs across the country. Its mission is to provide introductions and networking opportunities for members regardless of their level of experience. Corporate Alliance hosts networking events at various locations in western states like California, Utah, and Nevada.

OKAY, WHERE'S THE MONEY?

All entrepreneurs ask, "Where do I get the money to start a business?" It is a valid question. Some businesses can begin with absolutely nothing in the bank account, others require substantial amounts of money. How much money you will need depends on what you intend to do. Let's get practical and explore how you can find the resources to start your business:

1. **Your own personal savings.** Some businesses do not cost much to begin operating. $1,000 could be enough to get you started.

2. **Family money.** Many entrepreneurs find start-up money from parents and other family members. Tapping into family money comes with serious risk. Trust is involved. If you are exercising this option, prepare a detailed business plan and present it to your parents or other family members just as you would to a loan officer at a bank. If parents or siblings say, "No!" move on to other family members, like a favorite aunt or uncle, or better yet, your grandparents. Grandparents love their grandchildren and will do most anything to make them happy and successful. There is one caveat about asking family members for money: vow to repay every cent of the loan. You are not a charity case, and your parents and other family members have their own lives to lead. Present a written statement for family members stating when you will begin repaying the loan and how much each payment will be.

3. **Banks.** Local banks make money by lending money to entrepreneurs like you. You must create a detailed business plan to get a banker's attention, and you can do that with a little help. There are online sources that give advice about preparing a credible business plan. Approach the most local of banks in your area, an independent bank, not a branch of Wells Fargo. The process is to learn the name of the bank loan officer and make an appointment for a personal interview to present your business plan, your resume, and career profile. This is a no-nonsense deal, so dress accordingly. Bankers are not impressed with sneakers, backpacks, t-shirts, waist-length hair, and visible tattoos. Your veteran status helps, but banks are interested primarily in the bottom line. They make every effort to minimize risk, even when dealing with veterans.

4. **Angel funding sources.** These are individuals or small organizations that provide seed money to entrepreneurs. Finding these sources takes time and research. You can find these sources online by networking through social media like LinkedIn or through loan officers at a local bank.

5. **Loans from Government Organizations.** The SBA, VFW, Wounded Warriors, and the Department of Veterans Affairs (VA) offer a variety of low-interest loans to veterans. Also, check your state government programs for veteran loan programs.

What can be more exciting in the civilian world of work than doing it your way? Chris from Silver Spring did it. So did Marlon from New Jersey. So did Bill Gates. So did Mark Zuckerberg. So did Colonel Harland Sanders. So did Captain Kiel King. So can you!

MOVING FORWARD

The business of starting your own business does not have to be complicated. The beginning of any entrepreneurial adventure is planning and research, so I'll repeat an **OJS** rule: *Plan your work. Work your plan.*

Owning a business requires your undivided attention and much time. However, if you like what you are doing, the time factor becomes insignificant. This oft-repeated advice rings true. *Do what you love, and you will never work a day in your life.*

CHAPTER TAKEAWAYS

- Plan your work. Work your plan.
- Follow your passion.
- Select a business that provides basic goods and services for consumers.
- You alone can make a difference by applying your intelligence and energy to an idea about which you are passionate.

THE VETERAN'S LIBRARY

Richard Branson. *Losing My Virginity*. Virgin Books, 2013.

Richard Branson. *Like a Virgin: Secrets They Won't Teach You at Business School*. Virgin Books, 2012.

Lewis Schiff. *Business Brilliant: Surprising Lessons from the Greatest Self-Made Business Icons*. Harper Collins, 2013.

Stephen Fishman. *Working For Yourself: Law & Taxes for Independent Contractors, Freelancers and Consultants*. NOLO, 2011.

Brian Tracy. *GOALS: How to Get Everything You Want, Faster Than You Thought Possible*. Barrett-Koehler, 2010.

Bill Aluet. *Disciplined Entrepreneurship: 24 Steps to a Successful Startup*. Wiley, 2013.

Chapter 5

Working for the Federal, State, or Local Government

The American workplace is divided into the public sector and the private sector. The public sector consists of all elected and appointed government jobs at the federal, state, and local levels. The public sector employs more than twenty million workers in jobs as diverse as President of the United States, Chairman of the Joint Chiefs of Staff, Senator, Secretary of State, Ambassador to China, State Representative, Mayor, and Administrative Assistant for the Building Inspector of a small town in Wisconsin.

In addition, there are thousands of workers employed by the political parties. Both the Republican National Committee (RNC) and the Democratic National Committee (DNC) have national headquarters in Washington, DC, and regional offices in every state. Start exploring this sector by checking out these websites for job openings: www.RNC.org and www.DNC.org. You may be pleasantly surprised to find a number of interesting jobs with the party of your persuasion.

At the end of 2014, the total number of federal, state, and local government employees totaled approximately 22,000,000. Yes, you read that right: *twenty-two million*. Of that number, the federal government alone employs approximately 16,000,000 workers. These numbers are from the Bureau of Labor Statistics and the Census Bureau.

Veterans have always been favored for government jobs at every level. These jobs pay well and offer excellent comprehensive benefits and security.

LOCAL GOVERNMENT JOBS

Jobs in towns, cities, or counties are just around the corner and offer attractive opportunities for veterans. For those who are seeking a career in government or politics, this is a good place to start.

Here you will learn at the grassroots level how government works and the role you can play in it. Former Congressman from Massachusetts Tip O'Neill said, "All politics is local." All successful politicians must know how it works on their own turf, at the local level.

How do you get started? Easy. Begin by accessing your local government website. You will find a list of both full-time salaried jobs and part-time hourly-pay jobs. There are specific instructions for applying for all government jobs, one of which is to apply online. If you see something you like, complete the application, submit it, and go to the next step, which is making a personal visit. *Do not sit at home and wait for an answer.*

Put on your business attire and with your career profile or resume in hand make a personal visit to the government office. Tell the receptionist you are there to see the mayor, or the highest-ranking official for that government entity, about job opportunities. Should you really ask to see the highest-level official? The short answer is "Yes." Tell the gatekeeper (the receptionist or administrative assistant) that you might be her boss someday, so she should take care to steer you in the right direction. Injecting a sense of humor into your conversation with a gatekeeper is a good way to build a relationship, which will make reaching the right person much easier. These are key players in the employment process. If you cannot arrange a personal visit with the mayor or other high-level official, ask the receptionist to give your credentials to the mayor or the mayor's administrative assistant. Several days later, follow up by calling the mayor or the administrative assistant to make sure they received your resume. Remember to request a personal interview.

Many times, government jobs at any level are awarded to those who know a prominent government official or businessperson. If you have family members or friends who work in government or business, use that person's name as the referral agent. Networking is often a key factor in obtaining a government job.

STATE GOVERNMENT JOBS

Follow the same process to explore jobs at the state level. For example, assuming that you live in Nebraska, enter www.Nebraska.gov. You will find many different departments and a listing of jobs at different locations throughout the state. Follow the instructions for applying online, and then visit the office personally, repeating the procedure you used at the local level.

You cannot circumvent the application rules for government jobs, because legislation governs the employment process. Always try to use a referral source for government jobs.

FEDERAL GOVERNMENT JOBS

The federal government is the largest employer in the country and offers a variety of interesting jobs spanning every possible occupation. The employment process here becomes a bit more complicated, because the federal government employs over 16 million workers, according to the statistics released by the US Office of Personnel Management. A common misconception is that federal government jobs are located primarily in Washington, DC. Once again, the BLS statistics set us straight. Eighty-seven percent of federal government jobs are located outside of Washington, DC. There are federal government jobs in every state.

The processes for finding work with the federal government are often complex and even contradictory. Go to the BLS website and read Olivia Crosby's article titled "How to Get a Job in the Federal Government." The information and instructions in this article will demystify the federal government employment process, save you time, and possibly lead to employment. Not all government jobs are permanent positions. There are elected government jobs, and they come and go with periodic elections. However, other jobs exist regardless of the political party in power. They are called civil service jobs. These jobs keep the wheels of government turning and offer attractive salaries and excellent benefits. You will never find government jobs posted on Internet job boards or with corporate recruiters, so check out all government department websites to see what is available.

Government is something that touches every citizen, veterans and non-veterans, and your participation in the process is a significant responsibility. Government jobs in a country with a population of 315 million offer the opportunity to do something meaningful and long lasting. Here's an example of what one person did that affects all of us living in the United States. It happened because she applied her intelligence, energy, and passion to get the job done. This example flies in the face of the media gurus who have nothing but criticism for our elected officials. When you read her story, note well what she did for veterans, both female and male.

Congresswoman Patricia "Pat" Schroeder

Mrs. Schroeder was a mother of two young children when she decided to make a difference and run for political office in Colorado. She had no family history in politics, no one to pave the way for her through political connections, and no family money to pay for her election campaign. After a hard-fought campaign, she was elected to the United States House of Representatives and went on to serve twelve consecutive two-year terms. Few elected politicians serve for twenty-four years at the federal level.

During her tenure in the House, she became the Dean of Congressional Women, co-chaired the Congressional Caucus on Women's Issues for ten years, served on the House Judiciary Committee, the Post Office and Civil Service Committee, and was the first woman to

> *serve on the House Armed Services Committee. As chair of the House*
> *Select Committee on Children, Youth and Families from 1991 to*
> *1993, Mrs. Schroeder guided the Family and Medical Leave Act and*
> *the National Institutes of Health Revitalization Act to enactment in*
> *1993, a fitting legislative achievement for her lifetime of work on*
> *behalf of women's and family issues. In addition, she was active on*
> *many military issues, expediting the National Security Committee's*
> *vote to allow women to fly combat missions in 1991 and working*
> *to improve the situation of military families through passage of her*
> *Family and Medical Leave Act (FMLA).*

When you are in need and the FMLA comes to your support, think of Congresswoman Schroeder and say a prayer of thanksgiving that she had the courage, intelligence, energy, and passion to do something good for all Americans. Her story proves that one person can make a difference. If she did it, so can you, as an elected politician. Involvement begins by joining and working for political and community groups, by speaking and writing about issues, and by forming networks and alliances.

HELPFUL RESOURCES FOR EXPLORING FEDERAL GOVERNMENT JOBS

There are many sources of information and help for men and women veterans seeking employment with the government. Before you begin your exploration of federal government jobs, carefully review all of the sources listed below.

Veterans Employment Initiative. Executive Order 13518, signed by President Barack Obama in November 2009, grants veterans priority in federal government employment. The act names twenty-three federal government departments and agencies participating in this initiative. The easiest way to find the bill is to google "EO 13518."

USA Jobs, www.usajobs.gov/veterans. This site is the federal government's official job site. It provides general information about working in a federal government job and specific advice about how to begin your search. In addition, this site provides location-specific federal government job postings.

US Department of State, www.state.gov. On the home page, enter "veterans" in the search box, and you will reach the Veterans Program Office, a treasure trove of information and job opportunities. Prepare to spend several hours on this site exploring the various job opportunities available at the State Department, one of the most important and interesting departments within the federal government.

Feds Hire Vets, www.fedshirevets.gov. This source provides case studies of veterans who have transitioned to civilian government jobs, in addition to providing relevant general information. It also provides links to various federal government websites where you will find job information and job postings. This site will help you navigate the various branches of the federal government that are active in recruiting veterans transitioning from military to civilian employment.

Military.com, www.military.com/veteran-jobs. This comprehensive site provides information and postings for both government and non-government jobs. You will find practical advice in their article "Ten Steps to a Federal Job for Veterans."

US Office of Personnel Management (OPM), www.opm.gov. Think of this department of the federal government as the office of human resources. It manages all hiring procedures including recruiting, training, and benefits. In addition, it conducts background checks on all job candidates. Over the past several years, 40 percent of OPM hires were women and men veterans, including 18 percent who were disabled. When you are on this site, click on "Veterans Employment" for practical information. In addition, this site provides the name and contact information for the Veterans Employment Program Manager, a valuable link to an influential person who can steer you in the right direction.

Department of Veterans Affairs (VA), www.va.gov/jobs. The VA Career site lists all of its job openings, including specifics like location, salary, and benefits. This agency is committed to adding and retaining veterans in the workforce. The VA has come under attack recently for mismanagement of the medical benefits program for veterans, particularly at VA hospitals. However, a new secretary is making progress cleaning up the medical benefits problems that have plagued the VA for decades. The VA has always been a valuable and efficient source for helping veterans secure civilian or government employment. Check out this website frequently for timely information.

Veterans Preference, www.vaforvets.va.gov. This federal government initiative gives veterans preference over non-veteran job applicants. The goal of Veterans Preference is to make the federal government the leader in promoting employment for veterans.

Veterans Recruitment Appointment (VRA), www.federaljobs.net/vra. Determining the purpose and goal of VRA can be challenging, so we will quote directly from the website:

> The VRA is a special authority by which agencies can appoint an eligible veteran without competition. The VRA is an excepted appointment to a position that is otherwise in the competitive service. After 2 years of satisfactory service, the veteran is converted to a career-conditional appointment in the competitive service. (Note, however, that a veteran may be given a noncompetitive temporary or term appointment based on VRA eligibility. These appointments do not lead to career jobs.) When two or more VRA applicants are preference eligible, the agency must apply veterans' preference as required by law. (While all VRA eligibles have served in the Armed Forces, they do not necessarily meet the eligibility requirements for veterans' preference under section 2108 of title 5, United States Code.)

For instructions on applying for a VRA position, go to the website. You will find a number of interesting jobs that cover the entire span of employment, from skilled trades to executive banker. VRA appointed jobs are available for disabled veterans, too.

Veterans Employment Opportunities Act (VEOA). This is another initiative that has its own set of rules and regulations. You will find bits and pieces of information on VEOA in a number of different places, but we suggest that you begin with the Department of Veterans Affairs (www.va.gov). On the home page search box, enter "VEOA," which will take you to "Hiring Programs and Incentives."

United Service Organizations (USO), www.USO.org. This nonprofit private organization is best known for sponsoring live entertainment for troops in overseas locations since 1941. Few veterans know, however, that the USO provides help to those transitioning to a civilian job through its USO/Hire Heroes USA Transition Workshop. The program provides workshops on resume writing, interviewing techniques, and other job-related issues. Contact your local USO office for more information.

The Book of US Government Jobs. This book is in its eleventh edition, which tells you what a valuable resource it is. It is available from Amazon, Barnes and Noble, and the publisher. It has won numerous awards and is the best on the market for understanding how the federal government employment process works. For particulars, see this listing under **THE VETERAN'S LIBRARY** at the end of this chapter. The rules and regs for government employment can be onerous, and this book will clarify the process and save you much time. It includes a special chapter for veterans.

MOVING FORWARD

Veterans transitioning to the civilian workplace frequently overlook government jobs. Do not make that mistake. Jobs at all government levels, especially those at the state and federal levels, can offer rewarding careers that pay well, provide attractive benefits, and provide work satisfaction.

CHAPTER TAKEAWAYS

- Government jobs pay well and provide attractive benefits.
- Most government jobs are *not* political.
- Applying for government jobs can be challenging, so allow extra time to explore the process.
- Government jobs are not posted on Internet job boards or with civilian recruiters.
- Government officials hold veterans in high esteem and will take extra measures to help them find employment.
- Elected political jobs offer the opportunity to make a significant difference.
- Networking is an important factor in winning government jobs.

THE VETERAN'S LIBRARY

Dennis Damp. *The Book of US Government Jobs*. Bookhaven Press, 2011.

Chapter 6

Continuing Your Education in College, a Job Training Program, or a Job Apprenticeship Program

The workforce expects all workers to continue their education. It makes no difference if you have a high school diploma or a PhD. All workers in every conceivable job must continually update their knowledge and skills in order to remain productive (and employed). Those who think they have arrived because they hold a college degree and no longer need to continue their education are living in a dream world. Job requirements change and workers must grow with this change. Technology is responsible for this state of affairs.

So where do you start, now that you are discharged? The short answer is to continue where you left off in the military or in your pre-deployment civilian life. If you have a high school degree, aim for the next level, an AA degree from a community college or a BA from a four-year college or university. If you have a BA, consider moving on toward an MA. If you have an MA, consider working on a PhD or professional degree. All the data indicate that the higher your level of education, the more money you will make, and the greater your job security will be.

A COLLEGE DEGREE IS NOT FOR EVERYONE

What if you are not inclined to pursue additional formal college-level education? That is understandable, because college courses are not for everyone. If that is where you are, pursue training programs for jobs in a market niche that offers continual opportunities. Many veterans will find these opportunities in the skilled trades.

WORKING IN THE SKILLED TRADES

Jobs in the skilled trades are plentiful in the three major survival industries: food, shelter, clothing. Let's focus on the shelter industry. For example, if you want to pursue a career in one of the home/commercial trades, one option is to focus on heating and air conditioning systems by taking an HVAC certified training program. You will find HVAC training schools by going online and googling, "HVAC training." Your chances of finding employment in the HVAC field with a reputable contractor will be greatly enhanced if you have training and certification.

The Construction Trades. The same applies for those seeking employment in other building trades: plumber, electrician, painter, bricklayer, mason, boilermaker, plasterer, carpenter, roofer, ironworker, wood flooring/carpet installer, etc. All are noble career paths, and if this is where your interest lies, go for it. Even veterans who have military experience in one of these trades should seek civilian training and certification because it will increase your chances of finding work with a reputable company.

You will find brick-and-mortar trade schools and online courses in every location. Just google "trade and training schools" and add your area of interest. The trades offer incredible opportunities for satisfying lifetime employment. Ask any carpenter who has worked on a $2-million home what the rewards are in addition to money, and the responses you will get are "pride in creating something functional and beautiful" and "knowing there's a little piece of me standing there."

Transportation Jobs. Veterans with military transportation experience are in demand by companies both large and small. For example, I noted a Walmart posting for truck drivers that carried a base salary of $75,000, plus excellent benefits. Other military friendly large corporations, like Lowe's, pay similar wages to their transportation workers. However, you do not just walk into a company and expect to find a job with an ordinary driver's license.

Working in the commercial transportation business requires completion of tests for certification and a Commercial Driver's License (CDL). The Federal Motor Carriers Safety Administration (FMCSA), a division of the US Department of Transportation, is a required destination for learning about the various types of certification required for driving commercial vehicles of all types. Check out the website, www. FMCSA.gov, to learn about all of the rules and regs governing this line of work.

Apprenticeship Programs. Another approach to finding the right training program is to contact trade unions in your area to explore apprenticeship programs. Several years in an apprenticeship program taking classroom courses and working with a master-level worker almost guarantees a full-time high paying job in a particular skilled trade. Make no mistake about it, though. You must put in your time to reap the reward you are seeking.

SOURCES OF INFORMATION FOR THE SKILLED TRADES

Where do you go to learn more? Here are some online sources to get you started.

AFL-CIO, www.aflcio.org. On the home page, enter "training and apprenticeships," which will take you to a number of locations to explore your area of interest.

Union Apprenticeship, www.jobsgalore.com. This site will direct you to many nationwide apprenticeship programs in many different trades. Plan to spend a few hours here to explore all of the information.

Women and Apprenticeship. The International Organization of Operating Engineers (www.iuoe.org/jobs/women-and-apprenticeship) offers programs incorporating both classroom instruction and hands-on learning in a variety of settings for both women and men. Successful completion of an IUOE apprenticeship program virtually guarantees a job paying excellent wages and benefits.

The United States Department of Labor (DOL), www.dol.gov. The Employment and Training Administration (ETA) of the DOL operates the Registered Apprenticeship program to help veterans make the transition to the civilian workplace. The ETA works in conjunction with all states, so you will always be working in your local area.

Registered Apprenticeship is highly active in traditional industries such as construction and manufacturing, but it is also instrumental in the training and development of industries such as healthcare, energy, and homeland security. The program has trained more than 130,000 apprentices each year. It is an effective program, and veterans so-inclined should review this site for exciting job opportunities. It is there for the asking. Don't pass it up.

In addition, this program offers special opportunities for veterans under the Post-9/11 GI Bill Apprenticeship Program, which offers many attractive benefits, like allowances for housing.

BEGINNING OR CONTINUING COLLEGE LEVEL COURSES

Veterans who choose to work toward a BA, MA, or PhD will find much support from military friendly colleges and universities and from professional schools like Fordham Law School in New York City and the Cleveland Clinic in Cleveland, Ohio.

There is an interesting body of data regarding college graduates. For example, only 35 percent of the US population has a college degree. Of those with a BA or higher, the unemployment rate is always lower than it is for those without a college degree. Over a lifetime of work, college grads generate total income that is higher than the remainder of the non-degreed population. However, it is not all good news for those with a college degree, particularly *recent* college grads. During the past four years, over 65 percent of recent college graduates in the millennial category have not found a job nine months after receiving their diplomas. What's happening?

Contrary to what you hear from the media, the "no job" problem is not with the economy or the current administration in Washington; rather, it is because most college graduates, veterans and non-veterans alike, have no idea about how to find a job. Their college courses did not prepare them to enter the world of work after graduation. And for veterans specifically, the pre-discharge transition classes concentrated mainly on resumes and interviewing skills. As a result, veterans and non-veterans alike just sit at a computer and send resumes to postings on the job boards and company websites, never realizing that companies do not hire resumes, Tweets, or LinkedIn profiles. Finding a job requires building a personal relationship with a living breathing human being, like a human resources director or chief financial officer.

We will address these problems and provide solutions in Part V, VI, and VII. For now just remember that you send your resume only to a named person with a title and company affiliation, never to a box number or a job title.

CAVEATS FOR VETERANS PURSUING A COLLEGE DEGREE

Here are a number of tactics veterans can use to ensure that their college experience will be a productive and interesting venture.

1. Pursue a college major aligned with your interests and abilities. If your interest is teaching, pursue a degree in Education. If business is your thing, major in Business Administration or Finance. If you wish to pursue a degree in science or technology, select one of the STEM majors: Science, Technology, Engineering, Mathematics.

2. If you are not yet sure where your true interests lie, we recommend pursuing an associate's degree at a community college. Here you will learn about many academic disciplines. Surely, one of them will appeal to your interests.

3. Avoid going into debt. Going to college with financial help from a student loan has inevitable consequence; you will be obligated to repay that loan after graduating. There are many government tuition reimbursement plans available for veterans. Take advantage of all of them before tapping into the student loan program.

4. Begin your job search as soon as you enroll in a college degree program. Many students wait until they graduate to begin job hunting, and this is just plain dumb. Job hunting is a job in itself, and you cannot expect to walk away with your diploma one fine day and have a job the next. I suggest that the first resource to explore in your beginning year is my book *WELCOME TO THE REAL WORLD, A Complete Guide to Job Hunting for the Recent College Grad.* See **THE VETERAN'S LIBRARY** at the end of this chapter for additional information.

5. State colleges and universities offer academic programs on par with private institutions. The value of attending an undergraduate Ivy League school (or similar) has been greatly exaggerated. For example, one of the best small state schools is the College of New Jersey located in Trenton, NJ. It offers a quality academic program at a reasonable price, and the living costs are reasonable, too. In-state tuition is $15,000 and out-of-state is $25,000. Compare that with Dartmouth, where just the cost of tuition for one year will take more than $48,000 out of your pocket. For a ranking of the colleges and universities across the country, consult the *US News and World Report*, www.usnews.com/best-colleges. The annual rankings include tuition costs and other useful data.

6. Explore the military friendly list of colleges and universities, which you can find online at www.militaryfriendly.com/

school-list. These colleges and professional schools offer preferential terms for veterans.

GI BILL EDUCATION BENEFITS. PAYMENTS FOR COLLEGE TUITION

There are many programs for veterans that pay for college tuition and living expenses, as well as for certification and apprenticeship programs. The best source for information is the Department of Veterans Affairs (VA) GI Bill, www.benefits.va.gov/gibill. Learn about the numerous benefits waiting for you under the popular Post 9/11 GI Bill Yellow Ribbon Program. Many benefits fall under the rules and regs of this iteration of the GI Bill, which became effective in 2014. It is the Montgomery GI Bill. This bill provides monthly benefits that are adjusted each October 1, so you need to keep abreast of the program by going online each year to determine what the benefits are.

However, like all government programs that dispense money to veterans, the Montgomery Bill can be a challenge to navigate. The amount of reimbursement depends on a number of variables, like your time in service, the level of education you are seeking, and your veteran status. If you participated in an Army, Navy, Coast Guard, or Marine education funded program, your benefits under the Montgomery Bill will be altered.

The benefits are generous, and we advise pursuing them as the first step in planning your continuing college education. For example, you can receive close to $40,000 per year for tuition, books/supplies, and living expenses. In addition, veterans can by law receive in-state tuition at any state college or university, regardless of where they live.

I have spent countless hours researching this topic and advise veterans to seek help from colleagues, the VA, and VFW, for navigating the complex set of rules and regulations. You are entitled to these benefits, and there are well-informed people who can help you. Also, go online for additional help and updates on the status of these programs. The good news is that you are entitled to and will receive generous tuition and living expense benefits once you correctly complete the application process.

MUST-KNOW FACTS ABOUT THE GI BILL

Military.com has listed the five must-know facts about the GI Bill, which will help pave the way for learning about this program. They are:

1. Veterans have 10–15 years to use GI Bill benefits.
2. Many colleges and universities do not consider GI Bill payments financial aid because the payments are made directly to the veteran, not the school. This leaves the door open for veterans to seek additional financial aid from other sources, such as private or corporate scholarships.
3. Veterans can stop and start the GI Bill as needed making it possible to earn a master's degree or PhD over the 15-year eligibility period.
4. A "month" of benefits does not always mean 30 days. Once again, "government-speak" has special meaning. Go to the website for more information.
5. GI Bill payments are tied to your academic credit load.

GI BILL SPOUSE AND FAMILY ASSISTANCE PROGRAM

Often overlooked is the GI Bill Post 9/11 Transferability Program. It allows veterans to transfer a portion of their benefits to spouses and family members. Once again, it is a complicated process, but you can learn how it works by going online to the VA.

JOB OPPORTUNITIES FOR COLLEGE GRADS

A college degree opens the door to thousands of job opportunities. Exploring all of them would take a separate book of a thousand pages, but fortunately, there is just such a beast and we call it the *Occupational Outlook Handbook (OOH)*. It was developed by the US Department of Labor and is published by JIST Publishing Co. This one thousand-page book is updated every two years and provides the latest information about thousands of occupations spanning hundreds of industries. The book provides information about jobs by title and includes salary ranges, job forecasts, and academic requirements. This is a must-read book for all veterans. You can purchase it online from the publisher (www.jist.com), from Amazon, or from Barnes and Noble.

Many veterans enroll in college without the slightest idea of the job opportunities associated with a certain major. They believe that "something" will just happen after they earn that college diploma. To get you thinking about what you might do after college, here are some college majors and the doors they will open to certain job opportunities. We will explore just four to get you started: Arts and Humanities, Education, Business, and STEM (Science, Technology, Engineering, and Mathematics).

Arts and Humanities Majors

Arts and Humanities majors could have a difficult time breaking into the civilian world of work because there so many options. If you are not sure what path to follow, it is probably because you are not aware of the thousands of jobs available in many different industries.

So what interests you? There *is* something that you must like better than anything else, but it may be buried deep in your psyche. How do you reach down and discover what this is? A starting point, once again, is to read the latest edition of the *Occupational Outlook Handbook,* because it lists every job by title in every industry in the US and provides salary information, education requirements, and projections for job growth in a particular field.

Consult the *Occupational Outlook Handbook* to learn what kinds of jobs require a major in one of the Arts or Humanities, like Sociology or English. Those who are majoring in these interesting subjects may be wondering what you do with such majors. Here are two real life examples of what you can do with them.

Sociology. You do not have to be a social worker to use the concepts and skills you learned as a Sociology major. You can apply the content and related skills to many occupations, like those in television. An example is the famous Fox Business Network Channel reporter and anchor, Maria Bartiromo. Her major, Sociology, was instrumental in taking Maria to a top job in the industry. Google her name and you will get the picture. Remember to view her programs, and you will learn what the civilian world of work is about very quickly. In addition, she will teach you how to evaluate companies and how to invest in the stock and bond markets.

English. What can you do with an English degree other than teach? Exceptional written and verbal skills will take you anywhere you want to go. A good example is the co-founder and CEO of Bain Capital, former head of the Olympic Committee, governor of Massachusetts, and 2012 presidential candidate. His name is Mitt Romney, and he did it with an English major.

One thing Arts and Humanities majors might do to enhance their chances for employment is earn business and technology certification from an organization like HigherNext, which you will learn about later in this book.

Business Majors

In years past, Business majors had a relatively easy time finding jobs, but today that is not the case. Business majors may know how to read a balance sheet and know the meaning of acronyms like EBIDTA, but employers are looking for more than that. Business majors need to add more bullet points to their resumes, like exceptional written and verbal communication skills.

Having a working knowledge of business relationships is vital, because every job involves dealing with customers. Why? Because every product and service produced by a company is sold to customers. How many times have I been stunned by MBAs who know nothing about their customers?

Business majors with knowledge of the human side of business are marked for success. You might consider bypassing traditional jobs in accounting and finance and opt for a job in sales, marketing, or business development. These are exciting places because jobs of this type involve dealing with people outside of the office.

By the way, Business majors, if you are thinking about pursuing an MBA, note that admissions directors do not accept every veteran who submits an application. Now, one of the most important criteria universities use in assessing MBA candidates is potential employability. Your candidacy will be assessed not only by the admissions staff, but also by the career counseling staff. They will want to know if your career goals are reasonable and coordinated with your undergraduate degree, your military skill sets, and your future MBA. This is important because the schools are judged by the employment rate for their MBA graduates. If you go to an interview for MBA admission knowing little or nothing about the job market, your chances of gaining admission are greatly reduced. In today's world, MBA candidates should consider the admissions process comparable to the process for securing a job with a private sector employer.

There are many career choices for business majors, ranging from an accounting job with a local entrepreneurial employer in your neighborhood to employment as a financial analyst with Wall Street behemoths like Goldman Sachs, J.P. Morgan Chase, Wells Fargo, or Bank of America. Exercise due diligence evaluating these companies, however, and look closely at their ethical behavior in addition to their performance record. The last thing you want is to be part of a company that manipulates the numbers for the benefit of a handful of executives or a select list of clients.

Reputable Employers for Business Majors. OJS Faves

The banks listed here are frequently cited by financial rating firms as being the best of breed. I am giving you their URLs so you can review their career pages as you read this book. If you like the feel, smell, and look of money, you may find the Promised Land with one of these companies.

Sun Trust Banks Inc., www.suntrust.com, Atlanta, Georgia. This company traces its roots back to 1811, operates in all Southern states and Washington, DC, and employs 30,000 workers.

Regions Financial, www.regions.com, Birmingham, Alabama. This bank has 1,700 branches operating across sixteen states in the South, the Midwest, and Texas, and employs close to 30,000 workers.

Fifth Third Bank, www.53.com, Cincinnati, Ohio. Its history extends back to 1858. The company has more than 1,200 full-service banking centers and operates in the South, the Midwest, and Pennsylvania.

US Bancorp, www.usbank.com, Minneapolis, Minnesota. This is the country's fifth largest bank, and it employs approximately 60,000 workers. The company operates in twenty-five Midwestern and Western states. Interestingly, US Bancorp financed Charles Lindbergh's history-making flight across the Atlantic Ocean. This bank has an excellent reputation for hiring women into what was once exclusively a man's world and has been cited frequently for its quality service to its customers.

First Niagara Bank, www.firstniagara.com, Buffalo, New York. First Niagara was founded in 1870 as the Farmers and Mechanics' Savings Bank. Its footprint covers New York, the Mid-Atlantic states, and New England. The company posts many of its job openings on LinkedIn.

Columbia Banking System, www.columbiabank.com, Tacoma, Washington. This bank operates 157 branches in Washington and Oregon and employs 1,200 workers. It was founded in 1988.

Frost Bank, www.frostbank.com, San Antonio, Texas. Frost was founded and chartered in 1868 and operates 110 service centers across Texas. Frost employs more than 4,000 workers and is noted for its involvement in community affairs. It really is a good neighbor serving the community. Frost has seven human resources offices across Texas, and if you go on their website, you will find these locations and the phone numbers. All you need to do is call, ask for the name of the human resources director, and begin to build a relationship.

Education Majors

Finding a teaching position is not as easy today as it was just a few years ago. Budget cuts at the state and local levels have resulted in local school districts reducing staff or consolidating.

Most likely, you will receive help finding teaching opportunities from your college career counselors and education advisors. Many education majors take substitute teaching jobs as they look for permanent assignments, and I believe that to be a good way to get your foot into the world of school employment.

Your search activities should begin with a personal visit to your county or district superintendent's office of education. Dress appropriately; this means no jeans, sneakers, sweatshirts, or other casual dress. You are looking for a job and the unwritten rules of conduct apply to teachers as well as corporate workers. This example illustrates our point.

Nancy from North Carolina

I attended an education industry conference recently in Baltimore and met a vice president for sales with an educational technology company. I was evaluating his candidacy for a position, and in the course of our conversation, he mentioned that his daughter, Nancy, had just found a teaching job in a very interesting way. She put aside her digital gadgets and began calling on individual elementary schools during the summer months. Her plan was to meet school principals personally instead of just making a phone call or sending a resume to the district office. She drove to Washington School, parked her car in the near empty parking lot, and made her way toward the building. Unbeknownst to her, the school principal was looking out the window, saw her walking toward the building, and commented to his administrative assistant about how unusual it was to see a well-dressed young woman coming to the building. When Nancy arrived at his office, she received a warm welcome and learned that a job was available because a teacher had recently resigned due to pregnancy. The principal was so impressed with her demeanor and dress that he hired her on the spot after reviewing her resume and teaching credentials. How did Nancy's father know this? The principal told him this story when he was visiting the school on parents' night to see his daughter's classroom.

Recruiters for Education Majors

Another source for finding teaching positions is to contact recruiters who specialize in placing teachers. Conduct an Internet search for education recruiters in your area and check out the following as well:

Cal/West Educators Placement, www.calwesteducators.com (800–390–4737). This recruiter is located in Encino, California, and places teachers in California and the West.

Carney, Sandoe & Associates, www.carneysandoe.com (617–542–0260). This Boston-based company places teachers in the US and abroad.

The Education Group, www.educationgroup.com (800–369–9102). The Education Group is based in Dallas and places teachers and administrators in Texas and across the entire US.

Educational Directions Inc., www.edu-directions.com (800–647–2794). This firm is located in Portsmouth, Rhode Island, and places teachers across the US and internationally. They specialize in placement for independent and private schools.

Educator's Ally, Inc., www.educatorsally.com. Educator's Ally was founded in 1975 and is located in Bedford Hills, New York. This firm places teachers and administrators in private and public schools.

Social Networking for Educators

The premier social networking site for educators is EdWeb, www. edweb.net, a professional online community. EdWeb will keep you updated on the latest trends and research in education and provide leads for teaching and administrative positions in education, especially in the Mid-Atlantic area. In addition, you can participate in frequent webinars at a great price—free. There is no charge to sign up for EdWeb. Do it now.

What Else Is There for Education Majors?

As an alternative to teaching, Education majors might consider pursuing a corporate job. Human resources directors always like candidates with a degree in Education because workers attracted to the teaching profession usually have a good sense of values and mission. Add to that your military experience, and you will rise to the top of the candidate list. As a former teacher from Chicago, I can tell you how highly my candidacy was respected when I decided to change my career path and seek employment in the corporate world. I targeted educational publishing companies for positions in sales and three months into my search, I was offered sales positions with three major publishers.

The Education Industry

If you want to work in the broadly defined field of education but are not keen on being a classroom teacher, there are many jobs with companies that produce instructional materials and provide services for

K-12 and higher education. A recent Association of Education Publishers (AEP) newsletter lists four good reasons for pursuing a career on the corporate side of education. They are:

1. You believe that literacy and learning is the birthright of every child.
2. You have a passion for providing the educational tools that will help today's students fully develop their creative and intellectual potential to become tomorrow's productive, engaged citizens.
3. You believe that there is an urgent need to develop effective learning solutions in all subject areas for students of all talents, skills, and ability levels, and that these solutions must motivate them to be lifelong learners so that they can adapt and compete in a global economy.
4. You view the digital transformation as an opportunity to equalize education for all students and to support teachers in meeting the classroom challenges of the future.

Common Core Standards and NCLB

Education employers, whether they are from a school district, a state department of education, or a company in the education industry, will require that you have a working knowledge of the Common Core Standards and the No Child Left Behind Act, which you can learn more about by going to www.NEA.org, one of many sites that will give you the history and content of this landmark piece of legislation. Do not go into an interview without first doing your research on NCLB.

The same is true for Common Core Standards, which were designed to reform and unify instruction for English/Language Arts and Mathematics education across the country. Common Core is not a federal program, so the adoption of these standards rests with each individual State Department of Education (DOE). So far, almost all states have signed on. To learn about Common Core generally, go to www.NEA.org. To learn about Common Core in your state specifically, go to your state's Department of Education website.

Education majors, do not sell yourselves short. Your military experience and your major will open many doors to a multitude of interesting and fulfilling jobs. You bring much to the table, and employers will respect your candidacy, regardless of industry. You are off to a good start, and we are confident you will find your place in the civilian world of work and have a rewarding career.

Science, Technology, Engineering, and Mathematics. STEM Majors

If you have a degree in one of the STEM majors (Science, Technology, Engineering, Mathematics), you will find many job opportunities, but you, too, will profit from the advice in this book. The process of finding a job in the civilian workplace is the same for all veteran college graduates regardless of major.

The USA provides jobs for 155 million workers right here in America. More than half of all workers are in STEM-related positions. Huge manufacturing companies like General Motors, Ford, Chrysler, Boeing, John Deere, and Caterpillar are waiting for you with a variety of jobs located all across the US and abroad. Get your STEM degree, pursue military friendly companies, follow the job-search rubrics in **OJS**, and you will have no trouble finding civilian employment.

Do not buy into the hype that we are no longer a manufacturing country. It's just not true. Manufacturing is still alive and well in America and accounts for 12 million jobs and over 75 percent of our exports. Manufacturing jobs are always available and always in demand by employers. For example, two of America's premier heavy equipment and farming implement manufacturers are Caterpillar and John Deere. Both companies employ hundreds of thousands of workers in America and around the world.

Recently, I viewed an interview on CNBC with the CEO of Caterpillar. He was begging STEM majors to apply for jobs at his company, which employs more than 125,000 workers worldwide. Review the website (www.Caterpillar.com) to see what is available. Go to

"Careers," and you will see a multitude of jobs not only in the US but in other countries as well. In addition, Caterpillar is a military friendly company, one of the best.

Next, look at John Deere (www.Deere.com). On the home page, click on "Our Company" to reach the Careers page. You will be surprised at what this great American icon has to offer. Deere, too, is a military friendly company.

MOVING FORWARD

Continuing education is not an option for veterans in transition. It makes no difference if you are looking for a career in the skilled trades or a career that requires a college degree. Education is the name of the game if you are seeking a civilian career instead of just another job to carry you to the next paycheck. In the next chapter, I will tell you about military friendly colleges and professional schools. Stick around.

CHAPTER TAKEAWAYS

- Continuing your education is not an option. It is a requirement in our workplace.
- The GI Bill is your go-to place for benefits relating to education.
- Take advantage of every available government program that provides funding for continuing your education.
- Combining education with military experience is a powerful way to gain the attention of potential employers.
- A college degree is not a requirement to make it in America. Veterans with training in a skilled trade will find an abundance of job opportunities.

THE VETERAN'S LIBRARY

John Henry Weiss. *WELCOME TO THE REAL WORLD, A Complete Guide to Job Hunting for the Recent College Grad.* Skyhorse Publishing Inc., 2014.

Thomas Ricks. *The Generals*. Penguin Press, 2012.

Colin Powell. *It Worked for Me: In Life and Leadership*. Harper Collins, 2013.

Chesley Sullenberger. *Making a Difference*. William Morrow, 2013.

Chapter 7

Military Friendly Colleges

Many colleges and universities across the USA are sensitive to the challenges faced by veterans and have instituted substantial financial aid and counseling programs. When you contact the admissions department at colleges you are exploring, always inquire about the programs offered specifically for veterans and their families. You will be pleasantly surprised to learn about the substantial benefit programs offered to veterans.

MILITARY FRIENDLY COLLEGES AND COMMUNITY COLLEGES

Military Friendly, www.militaryfriendly.com, has completed its annual evaluation of colleges that are dedicated to enrolling and supporting military veterans. Go to the website for a listing of these colleges in all fifty states, plus Puerto Rico and the District of Columbia.

The colleges are scattered throughout the country and include some of the best names in higher education. For example, I clicked on Illinois and found seventy-eight listings, including renowned institutions of higher learning like DePaul University, The University of Illinois, Bradley University, DeVry University, and Columbia College. In addition, the list included a number of community colleges such as Illinois Valley Community College, Kankakee Community College and Shawnee Community College. The Illinois list is typical of the listings you will find in other states, a good mix of universities, four-year colleges, and community colleges. To learn about a specific college, look at the *GI Jobs Matchmaker*, www.GIjobs.com.

What exactly is a "military friendly" college? Generally, it is a school that is cognizant of the challenges faced by veterans and their spouses and has developed programs to provide solutions. For example, the University of Nebraska Omaha has a VA counselor on campus to provide orientation and counseling to veterans and their spouses.

On their website, UNO provides descriptive literature and numbers for tuition, room and board, and miscellaneous items. The listed charges for in-state students is $11,070, and for out-of-state students, $21,080. However, all veterans now qualify for in-state tuition, regardless of where they might live. When you are calculating the cost for your college education, first determine your GI Bill benefits, and then speak with the college counselor on campus to learn about additional benefits available to you and possibly your spouse.

Help for a veteran comes on a professional level, too, particularly at some of the nation's finest law schools. The following law schools have made special provisions to help veterans with tuition, room, and board. Do not overlook these opportunities.

MILITARY FRIENDLY LAW SCHOOLS

Many law schools work with the government-sponsored Yellow Ribbon programs that provide qualifying veterans with additional money to supplement GI Bill funding. I urge you to explore these opportunities even if you do not have the educational prerequisites for law school admission. Contact all or some of these schools to learn what it takes to gain admission and to learn what aspects of the legal field spark your interest. Act on the advice you get from counselors. One day you may be arguing cases before the Supreme Court!

A law degree can translate into jobs in the insurance industry, law enforcement, and business, in addition to jobs in the traditional practice of law. Here are some of the military friendly law schools:

1. Stanford Law School, www.law.stanford.edu
2. New York University School of Law, www.law.nyu.edu
3. Columbia Law School, www.law.columbia.edu
4. Duke University School of Law, www.law.duke.edu
5. Northwestern University Law School, www.law.northwestern.edu
6. UC Berkeley School of Law, www.law.berkeley.edu
7. Harvard Law School, www.law.harvard.edu
8. Fordham Law School, www.law.fordham.edu

SOURCES OF INFORMATION ABOUT MILITARY FRIENDLY COLLEGES

The best way to learn more about a college or professional school that sparks your interest is to contact the admissions office and request specific information. In addition, the following online resources will lead you in the right direction:

College Money from the US Military, www.gocollege.com. This website will help you navigate the education benefits you are entitled to receive for education. This should be your first step.

Military Friendly, www.militaryfriendly.com. There is no doubt that this is one of your best sources for up-to-date information about anything military in the workplace or in education.

Recommended List of Military Friendly Online Schools, www.guidetoonlineschools.com. This site recommends seventy-five online schools that it considers military friendly. Go to this site and click on one of their recommendations. You will find a wealth of information that includes course and degree offerings, costs, and special assistance programs for spouses. This site is one of our favorites because it helps shorten the evaluation process.

Military.com, www.military.com. This all-purpose military site includes instructions on how to complete a college application. This is important information because the application process can be detailed and confusing. Moreover, completing the application improperly could result in rejection. In addition, this site provides information on how to find a scholarship.

CHAPTER TAKEAWAYS

- One of the cardinal rules in the civilian world of work is that workers must continually update their knowledge and skills.
- Target those schools and colleges that are military friendly.
- Monitor all government websites periodically to determine changes in veteran's education programs and benefits.

Chapter 8

Female Veterans Transitioning to the Civilian Workplace

Civilian job-searching rubrics are much the same for females and males. However, there are unique challenges faced by female veterans. I will address these in Chapter 21, "Employment Challenges and Solutions for Female Veterans."

Being military veterans, you know that an operation is a multi-step process that involves defining the objective and the strategies required to accomplish the mission. The strategies could go on forever, but in order to accomplish the objective, finding a civilian job in a timely manner, I have distilled the literature to what I consider the most important action items.

FIFTEEN ACTION ITEMS FOR SUCCESSFUL JOB SEARCHING

Here are fifteen essential job-searching initiatives, each of which I address in detail in this book. Implementing them faithfully will pave the way to an understanding of the civilian workplace and a successful job search:

1. Define your interests, aptitude, and experience.
2. Plan your work. Work your plan.

3. Create an operations center (OC), a place where you can work your plan.

4. Activate a network of employed friends, relatives, and acquaintances.

5. Leave your OC to meet hiring managers at conventions, office and industrial parks, and job fairs.

6. Select and purchase suitable business attire. In an interview with *Redbook* in 2014, First Lady Michelle Obama said this about suitable clothing for female veterans, "They're used to being in uniform, and they need to understand the uniform of the civilian world. I think it gives them confidence to know, 'Okay, I'm properly dressed.' Knowing how to dress and feeling comfortable is huge."

7. Create an error-free resume and career profile.

8. Prepare for a successful interview.

9. Use social media creatively.

10. Communicate in civilian-speak, not military jargon.

11. Learn how to translate your military job experience into civilian terms.

12. Continue your education by reaching for the next level.

13. Interpret job descriptions accurately.

14. Negotiate all job offers.

15. Evaluate the company and the boss.

Implementing these fifteen steps in the job search process is essential for success. You cannot reach the Promised Land with just a "dynamite resume" or by "acing the interview." Finding a job is an operation, the kind you faced in the military.

ADVICE, GUIDANCE, AND SUPPORT FOR FEMALE VETERANS

Everyone in transition needs a hand now and then, but where does a female veteran find it? **OJS** recommends the following government and other organizations that offer support to female veterans. I have reviewed some of them in other parts of this book, but here I include additional information that female veterans may find useful.

The American Legion, www.legion.org. The Legion, founded in 1916, provides numerous benefits for female veterans. Go to the website and click on "Career Center," "Women Veterans," and "Veteran Employment." There is a Legion post in almost every town across the USA offering support and a place for networking. Among its members you will find almost every president, high-level military personnel, and female members of Congress.

The Department of Veterans Affairs (VA), www.ebenefits.va.gov. The VA is a veteran's most valuable resource during the transition to civilian employment. Rosye Cloud, Senior Advisor for Veteran Employment at the Department of Veterans Affairs, suggests that all veterans take advantage of the many benefits available through the VA, including tuition reimbursement, and help writing a resume in civilian language. She strongly advises female veterans to take advantage of the many services available through the Veterans Employment Center. As you begin your job search, make your first action item a trip to this link.

Disabled American Veterans (DAV), www.dav.org. DAV is an "organization of veterans helping veterans." It was established over ninety years ago and boasts 1.2 million members. It makes significant efforts reaching out to female veterans. DAV states, "Research reveals that America's nearly 300,000 female veterans are put at risk by a system designed for and dominated by male veterans."

DAV provides help on a variety of fronts for all veterans, but particularly for those with any kind of disability. Its services include assistance making the transition to the civilian workplace. DAV addresses these issues for female veterans: healthcare; unemployment; homelessness; military sexual trauma; mental health; physical and psychological disabilities. For more information, including the location of your closest DAV office, visit the website and join this nonprofit organization.

Veterans of Foreign Wars (VFW), www.vfw.org. The VFW is one of the best local organizations reaching out to veterans. Unlike government organizations, which are frequently difficult to reach, VFW Posts are located in almost every community across America. VFW Commanders and members are generous with time and advice and welcome newcomers. Most have an appointed chaplain who is always on call.

Transition Assistance Program (TAP), www.dodtap.mil. This is the Department of Defense program to help veterans make the transition to civilian life in general and to the civilian workplace in particular. It is a mandated training program for all military personnel before discharge, but many veterans miss the program for any number of valid reasons. In 2013, DOD launched the *TAP Virtual Program* through the Joint Knowledge Online (JKO) initiative, which enables veterans to take this course online.

The TAP program has been highly criticized for being outdated for female veterans because it was written more than twenty-five years ago, when the military was exclusively "a man's army." Fortunately, TAP has been revised a number of times, most recently in 2013, and has been transformed into a gender-neutral program. Go to their website for updates about the latest TAP assistance programs.

Corporate America Supports You (CASY), www.casy.msccn.org. CASY is devoted to one cause . . . veterans' employment. Deb Kloeppel and Rear Admiral Dan Kloeppel, USN (RET.) founded the organization in 2010. Deb is a military spouse and has won numerous awards for her work with veterans, including the Department of the Navy's Meritorious Public Service award. Admiral Kloeppel served in many active duty flag billets, and his last naval assignment was Commander, Naval Air Force Reserve. These two illustrious founders have a staff of twenty-seven active professionals, all with military credentials. Twenty-three staff members are women, some of whom work exclusively with female veterans on employment matters.

We highly recommend CASY and encourage you to contact one of their employment recruiters. When you log on to their website, go to "Job Seekers" and then click on "Female Veteran Program."

Military.com, www.military.com. This is one of the most celebrated and helpful sites dealing with veterans' causes, including employment issues. Go to Military.com at least once a week for current information on employment matters. Under "Veteran Jobs," you will find much helpful advice. Check out the following: "Military Skills Translator," "Attend a Career Expo," and "Military Friendly Jobs."

Joining Forces,www.whitehouse.gov/joiningforces. This is a national initiative to provide support and solutions for problems encountered by veterans. It is spearheaded by First Lady Michelle Obama and Dr. Jill Biden, wife of Vice President Joe Biden. Together they have enlisted the help of numerous private organizations and companies to reach out to veterans, particularly in their search for employment. Participating organizations include the American Association of Colleges of Nursing, the USO, The American Academy of Family Physicians, The American Nurses Association, Oracle, CVS Caremark, Northrup Grumman, J.P. Morgan Chase, and many others. Check the websites of each participant to learn about their programs for female veterans. When you are on the website, see "Joining Forces Mentoring Plus" for valuable information on transitioning.

The Business and Professional Women's Foundation, www.bpwfoundation.org. BPW has acquired a sterling reputation for helping female veterans find job opportunities. It partners with Joining Forces and a number of highly regarded companies throughout the country. On their website, go to "Women Veterans in Transition Research Project" for the latest information on what is being done to help female veterans make the transition.

Veteran Jobs Bank, www.veteranjobsbank.com. This organization grew out of a federal government initiative called The Vow to Hire

Heroes Act of 2011. VJB links your military experience with a civilian career and matches your profile with thousands of jobs from participating companies. Submit your military profile, including your MOS, and VJB will translate your experience into a number of civilian job opportunities.

Veterans Employment Center, www.ebenefits.va.gov/ebenefits/jobs. This is the federal government's authoritative center for connecting transitioning military veterans and their spouses with employment opportunities. This is a department in the VA devoted exclusively to matching veterans with civilian career opportunities. It has made a commitment to helping female veterans navigate the world of civilian work.

Vet 2Tech.Org, www.vet2tech.org. The purpose of this organization is to connect veterans with job opportunities in the manufacturing and technical industries. Vet2Tech has a network of 1,000 companies nationwide eager to find veterans for positions in fields such as information technology, customer service, supply chain management, logistics, sales, welding, assembling, fabricating, equipment repair, tool and die making, manufacturing engineering, electrical engineering, quality control analysis, and many others.

The Founder and CEO of Vet2Tech is Carol Multack, who possesses a passion for helping veterans, especially female veterans, find civilian employment in the manufacturing industry. Interestingly, Carol received a BA in English from Northern Illinois University. She is a good example of what one can do with a college major thought to be of little value in the workplace.

Contrary to what you might hear from the media, *manufacturing is still alive and well in America and provides millions of jobs that pay well and give job satisfaction.* The manufacturing sector faces a shortage of skilled workers, and who better to fill them than female veterans?

LinkedIn, Veterans Employment Center, www.veterans.linkedin. com. Go to this top-rated site and watch the video hosted by Evan

Guzman, director of military programs and military affairs for Verizon. He tells how LinkedIn helps veterans find jobs. Veterans are eligible for a free one-year subscription to LinkedIn and can become part of the LinkedIn user group called the "Veteran Mentor Network." Of all the social media sites, **OJS** places LinkedIn at the top of the list. If you have not joined LinkedIn, do so now. It could very well be your ticket to civilian employment.

Redbook Magazine, www.redbookmag.com. Review not only the *Redbook* print magazine but also the website. *Redbook* provides helpful information for women generally and, occasionally, for female veterans in particular. For example, in the November 2014 issue, *Redbook* ran an enlightening article about female veterans in transition to civilian employment. Included in this issue were bios of women who were in process of transitioning, and an interview between the *Redbook* Editor-in-Chief, Meredith Rollins, and First Lady Michelle Obama. You will find this article on the *Redbook* website.

Pierce IT and Technology Recruiting, www.pierce.com. Pierce is a recruiting firm that specializes in recruiting candidates for information technology positions. It has been in business since 1995 and has placed thousands of candidates in meaningful and well-paying positions. In 2015, Pierce launched Operation Veteran, a special division dedicated to placing transitioning veterans. This is a two-tier program. One is the *Management Track*, which offers veterans positions in technology driven careers. The other is the *Technical Track*, which places veterans with technical skills and military operational experience.

For female veterans with technical expertise and technology acumen, Pierce is a recruiting firm that could place you in an interesting civilian position.

The Lucas Group, www.lucasgroup.com. The Lucas Group is a national recruiting firm with a special division dedicated to recruiting and placing military veterans. All recruiters in this division are veterans and they walk the extra mile to be helpful. For example, Lucas conducts recruiting campaigns at military bases throughout the country for veterans in transition. Their counselors are known for making a special effort to help female veterans in transition.

Recruit Military, www.recruitmilitary.com. This company is devoted primarily to the client's needs. I include this site because it conducts job fairs for females and males across the country throughout the year. Since 2006, it has conducted 500 job fairs, which attract companies seeking candidates from the ranks of military veterans. Go to the website to learn the time and location of these job fairs and attend the one closest to your location. Job fairs are where you will meet hiring managers in the flesh. Remember to bring your business cards and at least twenty resumes.

Craigslist, www.craigslist.com. This employment site is your best bet to find local jobs in a variety of industries. The site will link you to local job openings by company name. Many listings provide the name and contact information of the business owner or hiring manager or human resources director, who usually is a female.

MOVING FORWARD

Finding a job is a multi-step process. It does not happen sitting at home firing off resumes to the third ring of the planet Saturn. As you move forward in this process, the most important action item is to leave the house to meet hiring managers at trade shows held at convention centers and job fairs.

The next step in the job search process is finding reputable employers, a challenge facing every female veteran. Begin by contacting companies listed in Chapter 2 and Chapter 3.

In the next Part, **OJS** will guide you in the process of creating a viable job search plan. Stay with us.

CHAPTER TAKEAWAYS

- Finding a civilian job is a multi-step process.
- Follow the steps listed by **OJS** to help you transition to the world of civilian employment.
- There can be additional challenges facing female veterans, but there are also many resources available to make this transition easier. Use them!

THE VETERAN'S LIBRARY

US Department of Veterans Affairs. ***Federal Benefits for Veterans, Dependents, and Survivors.*** Skyhorse Publishing Inc., 2012.

Mechel Lashawn Glass and Scott Scredon. ***The Veteran's Money Book: A Step-by-Step Program to Help Military Veterans Build a Personal Financial Action Plan and Map Their Futures.*** Career Press, 2014.

Martha Shirk and Anna Wadia. ***Kitchen Table Entrepreneurs: How Eleven Women Escaped Poverty and Became Their Own Bosses.*** Basic Books, 2004.

Jamie L. Yasko-Mangum. ***Look, Speak & Behave for Women.*** Skyhorse Publishing Inc., 2007.

PART II

Making a Job Search Plan for the Civilian Workplace

Luck is what happens when preparation meets opportunity.
—*Seneca, Roman Philosopher and Statesman*

Chapter 9

Understanding the Civilian Workplace

In order to create a viable job search plan, veterans need to understand how the workplace really works. This means learning why companies exist, understanding workplace numbers, and having an awareness of the rules of business courtesy. These are all prerequisites for constructing a work plan that makes sense and that will be your guide to finding employment opportunities. In addition, veterans need a place to work, because you cannot construct a work plan sitting on a park bench or at Starbucks. In the military, you called that place an operations center. In the civilian world, we call it a home office.

Veterans entering the civilian workplace for the first time and veterans reentering the civilian workplace after discharge will find the variety and number of industries, companies, businesses, and available jobs interesting and maybe staggering. We are not talking about hundreds of potential employers, but literally thousands of companies hiding *within* industries. In addition, veterans may find the workplace difficult to understand, because there are few written rules. In the military, you had no problem learning how it all worked because there was a written rule for everything.

The civilian workplace is entirely different. While there are few written rules, the civilian workplace does have traditions, and companies expect workers to observe them. Tackling the civilian workplace on a wing and a prayer will bring you nothing but confusion and slow the pace of your job search. To put it all in perspective, I have identified some of the most significant characteristics of our workplace.

AMERICAN WORKPLACE CHARACTERISTICS

- **It's all about the numbers.** All employers, whether a school, hospital, church, tech company, car manufacturer, football team, or home builder, have one thing in common. They run by the numbers. All must generate revenue in excess of expenditures to remain in business.
- **The job basket of the world.** The USA employs more than 155,000,000 workers, making our workforce alone the eighth largest "country" in the world by population count. The US job market is the most robust in the entire world, in both good economic times and bad. There are always jobs available here, even during a recession.
- **The workplace is highly organized.** So where are all of these jobs? Where does one start looking? It is not just helter-skelter, although it may appear so to the casual observer. Rest assured there is organization in the workplace, and a closer look will make sense out of it.
- **The workplace includes industries and companies.** The US workplace is composed of industries and companies within those industries. Identify the industry and then identify the companies and businesses within that industry for an understanding of how the workplace is structured. For example, Ford Motors is a *company* within the automotive manufacturing *industry*. Even entrepreneurial businesses and franchises fall within this structure. For example, McDonald's is a *company* in the broadly defined *food industry*.

   Trying to get your head around the great number of companies and industries in the USA is quite a task. To get a better idea of the available options, I suggest that all veterans read the *Occupational Outlook Handbook,* published biannually by

JIST Publishing Co. It provides information on thousands of jobs spanning various industries. Here is what you can expect to find.

I just opened *OOH* at random to page 91 and found a job category titled "Mining and Geological Engineers." Median pay for these jobs is $84,300 per year. There are approximately 6,400 jobs in this category, which will grow by 10 percent over the next ten years. In addition, there is a job description and a summary of the typical work environment. In addition, the *Handbook* provides information on education requirements. To complete the picture, there is a listing of similar jobs and contact information for engineering-related resources in this field.

Armed with information about how the workplace is structured, you can begin organizing your job search and narrowing your focus. While sitting at the computer in your operations center (a.k.a. your home office), select three industries that you really like or that arouse your curiosity. Let's assume you have selected these three: Automobile Manufacturing, Education, and Insurance. Now go to the Internet and find companies in each industry. For example, assuming your top choice is Automotive Manufacturing, google "Automobile Manufacturing Companies," as I just did. As expected, there are thousands of hits. On the first page, I found a site called "Automotive Business Review" (www.manufacturing-automotive.business-review.com), which lists the top ten auto manufacturers. One of the top ten was Honda. I went to their website (www.honda.com) to get an overview of the company and the job listings. I found "Careers at Honda," and there were five pages of job postings spanning everything from Financial Cost Analyst to Quality Control Manager.

Organizing your job search by industry and then by companies within each industry will open the door to potential employers.

- **The workplace does not guarantee a lifetime job.** A job in America is not an entitlement. You own it, and you must find it yourself. Once you have that job, you cannot assume it will last until the day you retire.

    Company jobs, and government jobs as well, come and go with events taking place in the local and global economy. In the course of your working life in America, you can expect to have a number of jobs, and they may be in different industries. The day when a worker took a job with a company and stayed there for thirty years is over. Even tenure for teachers, which guarantees lifetime employment, is under assault, if not disappearing.

- **Continuing education is required to maintain all jobs.** The knowledge curve grows steeper each day. Every industry demands that you continually update your skills, in many cases on your own time and dime. Today, many workers hurry home from work to take online courses to update their job skills. It is no longer a daily stampede to the local watering hole when the clock hits 5:00 p.m.

- **Education level determines rank and wages.** If you hold a bachelor's degree or higher, you will make more money and hold a job of higher rank than those who have a high school diploma or less. Also, workers with higher levels of education will find themselves unemployed less frequently. This chart, recently released by the Bureau of Labor Statistics, tells it all:

Unemployment Rate by Education Level
Less than a high school degree . . . 7.9%
High School Degree . . . 5.7%
Some College, like an AA degree . . . 4.8%
Bachelor's Degree or Higher . . . 3.1%

- **The workplace does not guarantee rank or wages.** Some workers just do not get it. Here is a true-life example. Mary had a job as Regional Sales Director managing a staff of ten sales reps and covering fifteen states. She had been in that position for six years and had averaged $150,000 per year plus benefits. In year seven, the country plunged into a nasty recession. The company had to trim its expenses and fired Mary. Now she was job hunting and expected to find another Regional Sales Manager job paying the same wages or better. She turned down several jobs as District Sales Manager with compensation of $120,000 per year because she felt that taking anything less would be "going backwards." Sorry, Mary. That's not the way it works. In America, you take what you can get, even if that means taking a step back. Our workplace does not guarantee a continual increase in job rank and compensation.

- **The workplace is diverse**. Today's workplace is comprised of workers spanning four generations. First, we have traditional experienced workers who hold very traditional work values, and who are running the show. Following them are the Baby Boomers who are fast leaving the workplace and heading for retirement. Next are the Generation X workers, who are somewhat egocentric and expect instant results. Last are Generation Y and Millennial workers, who are digital natives and expect the use of technology to find every workplace solution. Included in that mix are male and female workers of every color, ethnic background, political background, and religious faith. The workplace is not one-size-fits-all as it may have been in your parents' generation.

In order to work successfully in this wildly diverse place known as the American Workforce, veterans must exercise tolerance and acceptance. Veterans are well equipped to meet this workplace culture because of their military experience, which reflected diversity. Make this a talking point during personal interviews. Hiring managers and human resources directors will be impressed with your understanding of a key characteristic of the American workplace.

- **The workplace expects and demands technology expertise**. Technology expertise is the driving force behind success in the workplace. Rank and job title make no difference. Every job requires knowledge of the basic three workplace tools: word processing, spreadsheet, and database, plus a working knowledge of social media like Twitter, Facebook, and LinkedIn.

    If you lack some of these technology skills, take an online course or go to a local bricks-and-mortar facility, like a community college. If you want to jump ahead of the pack, take a course in 3D printing, which is already making headway in the workplace. You can learn more about this technology by going to www.3dprinting.com.

- **The workplace is both demanding and rewarding**. Our American workforce is the most productive in the entire world. This did not happen by accident. In our country, every job has a specified set of requirements that you must meet to remain employed. If you are not performing up to the standards set for your job, you will be fired or placed on probation while you are coming up to speed. Companies will reward those who meet the requirements with increases in compensation and promotions to positions of greater responsibility.

- **Companies do not tolerate alcohol and drug abuse**. The rule applies across the spectrum of jobs in the corporate environment, small businesses, and skilled trades. If a company fires you because of substance abuse, you have no recourse to the law for clemency.

    Drug and alcohol tests for job candidates are commonplace, especially at large corporations. Your candidacy could be rejected if you have any prior record of alcohol or drug abuse, or if you fail a drug screening prior to employment. To play it safe, assume that a potential employer will conduct a drug and alcohol screening. You cannot hide behind time because controlled substances remain in your system for weeks or even months. If for some reason you have become addicted to alcohol or drugs, get treated as soon as possible at a VA center or a private facility. Why mess up your life in the workplace for a bit of transitory pleasure?

- **The workplace includes leaders and followers.** The civilian workplace is much like the Armed Forces, where you have a definite hierarchy of leaders and followers. We constantly hear about leadership skills and leadership roles, but seldom do we hear about followership. It takes brains and skills to be a good follower, and there is nothing wrong with being a follower for your entire career. Every veteran, either officer or enlisted, was a follower at one time in the military, so you know the two main qualities of a good follower: 1. Obey orders. 2. Support the commander. The same rules apply on the civilian side.

These are the main characteristics of our civilian workplace. You will be doing this thing called "work" for a long time. Accept the rules.

CHAPTER TAKEAWAYS

- The US workplace is organized by industries and companies within each industry.
- The *Occupational Outlook Handbook* is your prime resource for learning about the thousands of jobs in the US workplace.
- All companies, for-profit and nonprofit, work by the numbers.
- There is zero tolerance for present or prior use of alcohol or controlled substances.
- The workplace demands and rewards performance.
- Continuing education is required to update technology skills.

THE VETERAN'S LIBRARY

US Department of Labor. ***Occupational Outlook Handbook***. JIST Publishing Co., 2015.

Jocko Willink and Leif Babin. ***Extreme Ownership: How U.S. Navy SEALs Lead and Win***. St. Martin's Press, 2015.

Chapter 10

Numbers and Terms Used in the Civilian Workplace

In order to understand the civilian workplace, you need to know the meaning of frequently used numbers and terms like *the unemployment rate*. Where does this number originate? Is there really such a thing as *underemployment*? Who measures these terms? Do the numbers tell the whole truth and nothing but the truth?

This may be one of the most important chapters in this book, because finding a civilian job and navigating the workplace requires knowledge and use of business numbers and terminology.

TERMS AND NUMBERS YOU NEED TO KNOW

In this chapter, we will explore terms and numbers that make a significant impact on your understanding of the workplace in general. Both numbers and terms enable you to assess the job market and act accordingly. This information will affect your attitude about how robust the job market is at any given time. Attitudes, which are based on information, determine behavior, so it is important to get it right. For example, if you take your information from the popular media and political speeches, you will most likely believe that it is impossible to get a job when the unemployment rate hovers near 9 percent. That is false.

The fact of the matter is that jobs are always available in America because companies need employees in order to function. Jobs are available even during a recession, when you hear the media and the unemployed shouting, "There's nothing out there!" That is not reality. Jobs are always available because people leave companies at any phase of the economic cycle for a variety of reasons and need to be replaced.

WHY COMPANIES ARE ALWAYS HIRING

If you listen to the media wax not-so-eloquently about the workplace, you might come away discouraged because you hear only bad news. You might hear the media report that jobs are tough to come by, nobody is hiring, companies are always laying off personnel, and the country is on the verge of another recession. Nothing could be further from the truth. Jobs are always available and companies are always hiring for five main reasons:

- Workers *quit* their jobs and need to be replaced.
- Workers are *fired* and need to be replaced.
- Workers are *promoted* to higher-ranking jobs and need to be replaced.
- Workers *retire* and need to be replaced.
- Workers *die*, unfortunately, and need to be replaced.

Jobs may be harder to find during a recession, but they *are* there. It is up to you to find them. Remember, companies are not going to knock on your door and offer you a job.

THE EIGHTH LARGEST COUNTRY IN THE WORLD: THE AMERICAN WORKFORCE

Let's zero in on the number of US workers, commonly referred to as the workforce or labor force. The Bureau of Labor Statistics defines the workforce as the number of Americans, age sixteen and over, who are working or unemployed. That number is 155,000,000 workers. If you compare our workforce to the total population of the ten largest countries on the planet, *it would make our workforce alone the eighth largest country in the world* (excluding the total US population of 320 million). The size of the American workforce has ramifications that affect everyone, including entry-level candidates and veterans. Understanding what they are will help us navigate the world of work.

THE UNEMPLOYMENT RATE

Some believe that the unemployment rate released by the Bureau of Labor Statistics (BLS) on a monthly basis *truly* reflects what is happening in our workforce, but let's take a closer look.

The *rate of change* in the employment numbers, up or down, depends upon the size of the labor force and reflects the state of the economic cycle at any given time. The larger the workforce, the longer it takes for the rate of employment to change, particularly as an economy emerges from a recession or depression. The deeper the recession, the longer it takes for the rate of employment to increase. In fact, in the US it takes a minimum of nine to twelve months following the bottom of a recession for the rate of employment to begin rising. In a very severe recession, such as the one we experienced from 2007 to 2009, the rate of acceleration in the employment numbers took even longer. Turning around a labor force of 155 million is a task not completed quickly.

The Unemployment Rate for Veterans

The rate of unemployment for veterans historically has been higher than the rate for non-military civilian job seekers. At any given time, the unemployment rate for all veterans is 2.5 percent higher than that for non-veterans. In addition, alarmingly, the unemployment rate for veterans in the 18–24 age bracket over the past six years has been approximately 20 percent. Among post-9/11 veterans, 33 percent have been unemployed for longer than one year and 17 percent have been unemployed for more than two years. Here are some of the root causes for these higher rates:

- Veterans have had little or no civilian job-hunting training before being discharged from active duty.

- The nature of the job market has changed dramatically post-recession (since 2009).
- Veterans have been misled into believing that the use of technology generally and social media specifically will lead them to the promised land of employment.
- Veterans need time and education to learn how the civilian job market works.
- Employers are not aware of the fact that serving in the armed forces is truly work experience.
- Lack of funding for civilian workforce training at the Department of Veterans Affairs (VA).
- Lack of support from members of the US Congress, where less than 20 percent of its members have served in the armed forces.

The numbers show clearly that the veteran population needs help in the job-hunting process, and that is the purpose of **OPERATION JOB SEARCH.**

WHAT DOES FULL EMPLOYMENT *REALLY* MEAN?

Full employment does not mean that 100 percent of the workforce is employed. In the United States and most other developed countries there has never been a 0 percent unemployment rate. Some members of the workforce will always be unemployed regardless of fiscal or monetary policy and regardless of how robustly private sector business is functioning.

Seasonal Unemployment and Structural Unemployment

There are two major types of unemployment. The first is *seasonal unemployment,* which occurs when workers are laid-off because of weather- or holiday-related factors. For example, in the northern latitudes, outdoor construction workers face unemployment during severe winter weather. There is nothing that construction industry or the government can do to prevent that occurrence.

The second is *structural unemployment*, which is caused by the introduction of new technology to perform tasks ordinarily performed by workers. For example, computers and word processing programs eliminated the need for most secretaries whose major responsibility was to type documents for managers and executives on typewriters like the IBM Selectric that you see in movies from the 1970s. Technology has taken over many tasks, resulting in the elimination of thousands of jobs, which are *never* coming back. Neither the private sector nor the government can prevent structural unemployment from occurring.

The Constant Rate of Unemployment

The constant rate of unemployment in the US since the Great Depression averages approximately 6 percent. We might interpret that to mean that an employment rate of 94 percent is truly full employment. Since 1970, our lowest rate of unemployment was 4 percent (in 2000) and the highest was 10 percent (in 2009).

If we consider 94 percent full employment at all phases of the economic cycle, an unemployment rate of 10 percent can be interpreted to mean that the true rate of unemployment caused by a recession is 4 percent, which is not that bad considering that the US workforce numbers 155 million. However, a 4 percent unemployment rate means that 6 million people are unemployed, while an unemployment rate of 10 percent means that more than *15 million* people are out of work. That number has serious repercussions for our economy. It affects the amount of money not spent on consumer goods, and it increases the amount of money the government spends on related safety net entitlements like unemployment compensation, food stamps, and Section 8 housing.

Do not buy into the hype from the media and politicians who tell you the country is in terrible shape because the unemployment rate is 6 percent and that we will never be whole until we reach 0 percent unemployment. That is just not possible. We will never have an unemployment rate of 0 percent regardless of the political party in power and the state of the economic cycle.

WHAT IS A RECESSION?

Economists tell us that we are in a recession when there are two consecutive quarters of negative growth in the Gross Domestic Product, frequently referred to as the GDP. The Gross Domestic Product is the total of all goods and services produced at any given time.

We measure the beginning and end of a recession not by the unemployment rate, but by the rate of positive or negative growth in the GDP. When we have two consecutive quarters of negative GDP, we are at the beginning of a recession. Two consecutive quarters of growth in the GDP herald the end of a recession. When a recession begins, the unemployment rate always goes up. When a recession has ended, the unemployment rate always goes down.

It is interesting to note that the unemployment rate is the most lagging economic indicator. In other words, employment is the last metric to show positive gains when we come out of a recession. Numbers like consumer spending and municipal building permits issued for constructing new homes and commercial buildings always increase before the employment numbers make their charge upward.

UNDEREMPLOYMENT

Frequently, the media and politicians use the term "underemployment." This term means that people are not able to find jobs equal in compensation and rank to those they had before losing their jobs. Does this make any sense?

Who said that once you reach a certain level of income, say $175,000 per year as a vice president of marketing, you are entitled to remain at that income number and rank for the rest of your life? That is not how things work in America. Here is an example.

Joe Caveman Is Fired

After missing his sales revenue goal for three straight years, Vice President for Sales Joe Caveman is fired from his job at International Coconut Inc. Joe had slacked off and assumed his sales team would carry the load for him. Life had been good for Joe. He was making a base salary of $150,000 and another $50,000 in bonuses, plus benefits.

Now Joe is looking for another position at the same rate of compensation, but all he can find is a district sales manager position with United Antelope Meat Processing Inc., with a base salary of $125,000. If Joe reaches his revenue goal, his total compensation would be $150,000, which is not too bad for an antelope sales manager, or any worker for that matter. However, Joe rejects the offer from United Antelope and other companies as well, because they are below the rank and compensation of his job at International Coconut. Soon Joe begins to whine, "there's nothing out there," and collect unemployment checks.

What's wrong with this picture? For starters, who said that once you are employed as a vice president at $200,000 per year that you are entitled to that rank and compensation number for the rest of your working career? The Constitution? The President? Congress? Twitter? YouTube? CNN? The Secretary of Defense? Your Mother?

Where does that leave Joe, now that he has stopped looking for a job because he claims "there is nothing out there"? Collecting unemployment compensation and other safety net entitlements, which come out of everyone's pocket in the form of taxes. You could have been making $150,000 this past year, Joe, and life would have been good for you, your wife, and your two kids. Your mistake is that you do not know how the US workplace *really* works.

THE UPS AND DOWNS OF RANK AND COMPENSATION

It is unrealistic to believe that your job rank and compensation at any time in the work cycle will continue to go up. Here is a real life example of how it works and what you can expect as you navigate the civilian workplace.

Carol of Philadelphia

On a cold January morning, Carol came to my office and said she was fired from a computer hardware company because of a reorganization necessitated by the declining business climate. Carol was a sales representative covering three Mid-Atlantic states and had a total compensation package of $220,000 per year plus benefits. Some years she made over $300,000. She was intelligent, energetic, and passionate about the use of technology. I told her that in a business climate heading into a possible recession her chances of finding a comparable position and compensation were slim. She scoffed and said that that is what she was worth and would not consider a job that paid any less. I tried to reason with Carol but to no avail. She declined several jobs I offered because of the compensation. In a fit of self-righteousness, Carol told me that I just did not have the right connections and said good-bye.

Fast-forward twelve months, to December of that same year. Carol, still unemployed, returned to my office telling me that potential employers just did not realize how good she was. I felt sorry for Carol and wished her well as she headed out of my office. Carol's problem was that she believed that once you make a certain amount of money, you are entitled to make that or more for the rest of your life. Wake up, Carol! Job rank and compensation are not entitlements in America.

In our economy, you take what you can get in order to be self-sufficient. That's our system, and it has served us well for the past three hundred years. Careers do not always progress in an upward spiral until one becomes CEO or president. Rank and compensation fluctuate according to one's abilities and the economic cycle.

WHO'S HIRING?

Let's revisit the critically important reason to know how the numbers work. Information forms attitudes, which guide behavior. Understanding this important concept in your civilian career will help you over the bumps in the work cycle that you are sure to encounter.

Some workers consider an unemployment rate above 6 percent so egregious that they become discouraged about the prospect of remaining employed or finding new opportunities. As a result, they just sit waiting for "something" to happen while collecting unemployment compensation checks and food stamps. It is true that jobs during a recession are fewer in number, but there is always a company that is hiring. It is your responsibility to find out who it is.

Frequently, when a Fortune 500 company like General Electric announces that it has dismissed several thousand employees in a given week, most likely it has concurrently hired several hundred workers *that very same week*. But you will rarely hear that reported. Why? Because it is bad news that makes headlines, not good news.

Please Leave the House!

Companies large and small always need workers, which is why you need to call on companies in person every day until you hit pay dirt. The human resources director, whom you met personally on a cold call on Monday and who told you that there is nothing available, could very well call you on Thursday and say, "Unfortunately, Linda, our assistant director of marketing, was hit by a truck on Wednesday and didn't make it. Come in on Friday and we will talk more about that job." Say a prayer for Linda and thank the Job-God for looking after you. Also, give yourself a pat on the back because you had the sense to pull yourself away from home and the iPad to call on potential employers personally. You were not intimidated by the unemployment rate and media gurus telling you there are no jobs available. Congratulations!

Can I Really Find a Job When the Unemployment Rate Is Over 6 Percent?

That is a marvelous question, and the answer is a resounding "Yes!" It may take longer when the unemployment rate is above 6 percent, but there are still many jobs available. They may not fall into the "ideal" job category, but all work has dignity and value, regardless of the job title and compensation. America is still the best country in the world to find work, regardless of where we are in the economic cycle.

KNOW THE NUMBERS: SURVIVAL RESOURCES FOR VETERAN JOB HUNTERS

As you prepare to find that civilian job, keep abreast of what is happening in the economy generally so you can discuss business matters intelligently during interviews. The following resources will keep you updated on all employment matters and provide the numbers you absolutely need to know.

ADP, www.ADP.com. Automatic Data Processing is a company that tracks employment data. This company releases employment numbers each Thursday at 8:00 a.m.

Bureau of Labor Statistics, www.BLS.gov. This is the definitive site for all numbers relating to employment matters. Review this site for data updates before every interview.

CNBC. This TV channel produces financial programs that air from 6 a.m. to 11 p.m., Monday through Friday. Check it out frequently for information about the economy and to view interviews with executives of major companies, government officials, and economists. At 6 p.m. each evening, be sure to see Jim Cramer, whose program is both informative and entertaining.

Forbes, www.forbes.com. *Forbes* business magazine provides timely advice and exclusive interviews with people who know how the economy works.

Heidrick and Struggles, www.heidrickandstruggles.com. This is one of the largest executive search firms in the world. On the company website, you will find pertinent employment data. Many large companies use this firm to recruit high-level executives.

LifeBound, www.lifebound.com. This helpful website founded and hosted by a career coach, Carol Carter, is a site you do not want to miss. Carol gives practical advice about job hunting and financial management for all job seekers. While visiting the site, click on "Career Blogger" for information targeting candidates new to the world of civilian work.

National Labor Relations Board, www.NLRB.gov. NLRB is a government agency devoted to all things work related. Check it frequently for specific information pertaining to rules and regulations in the workplace.

Occupational Outlook Handbook, 2014–2015. I mention this resource frequently in **OJS**. This 1,017-page book produced by the US Department of Labor is a necessary read for all veterans. It details everything you need to know about specific jobs in the workplace. You can purchase the book from its publisher (www.jist.com), on Amazon, or at any Barnes & Noble store.

Pew Research Center, www.pewresearch.com. Pew publishes information on social issues, political issues, employment trends, and key demographics.

Wall Street Journal. This journal, available in print or online, is the gold standard for information about the economy generally and the stock market specifically. It has no political agenda. It is in business to help people make money. The Thursday edition has an entire section devoted to employment and the job market.

MOVING FORWARD

Terms and numbers are key to understanding the workplace. For example, the employment rate always increases as the GDP grows. If the annualized GDP is growing, consumers and businesses are increasing their spending for goods and services.

If first time unemployment claims have been steadily decreasing, it means that more jobs will be available. However, while slow but sustained increases in the GDP bode well for the economy, they will not precipitate a rapid increase in employment. Employment is the last sector to recover, but rest assured that the job market will continue to show positive gains as the GDP increases. Even after a severe recession, we will return to "full employment" (that is, an unemployment rate of 6 percent).

CHAPTER TAKEAWAYS

- The numbers tell the truth about the workplace and the economy.
- Don't buy into the hype. Tune out the many political agendas on TV, radio, Twitter, Facebook, YouTube, and so on. Make your judgments based on the numbers from reliable sources.
- An unemployment rate of 6 percent is really "full employment" in the United States. Seasonal and structural unemployment will always cause workers to be sidelined. We will never have a 0 percent unemployment rate.

THE VETERAN'S LIBRARY

Troy Adair, PhD. *Corporate Finance Demystified.* McGraw-Hill, 2011.

Chapter 11

Establishing an Operations Center for Job Hunting

Finding a job is a job in itself, and you will need a workspace to organize your search. This is an important and necessary requirement, and you should make it a priority. Job hunting is a detailed and time-consuming process that requires a dedicated space and tools to make your work productive. Getting out of bed and going to the kitchen table to make a couple of calls or send a few resumes into space while you have a cup of coffee is not the way to go about it.

Establishing a home office will serve another purpose as well. During the course of their careers, many veterans will be conducting business from their homes instead of going to an office each day. Even today, many companies encourage working from home, especially for those who can conduct their work without needing constant communication with their coworkers. For example, programmers, digital designers, editors, sales people, and researchers can accomplish their work objectives remotely. Learning how to work from a home office *now* will be good preparation for working remotely in the future.

Every veteran needs an operations center, or, as it is called in the civilian workplace, a home office. It makes no difference whether you are seeking a corporate job, a construction job, or starting your own business. You need to have your own space while conducting your search.

DISCIPLINE AND FOCUS

Working from home requires discipline and planning, and you cannot cheat. Establishing a home office is just the first part of a job-seeking plan. You will use your office primarily for planning, follow up, and research. Strategic job hunting begins when you leave the office to see hiring managers personally.

If you cannot work from home because there are unavoidable distractions, find another space, like a college career center or a public library, where you have Internet access and a quiet space to make calls and conduct your research. However, before taking this route, try your best to carve out a space in your residence. It could be a desk in your bedroom or a corner of the basement, some place that is quiet and where there are few distractions.

EIGHT REQUIREMENTS FOR A VIABLE OPERATIONS CENTER

If you have not gone through this drill before, setting up a home office could be a challenge. To get you started in the right direction, here is a guide that will help you complete your operations center:

1. **A quiet workspace**. Your office should be large enough to hold a desk or small table, a bookcase, a file cabinet, and a chair. You will make this space friendlier if you have a table lamp. Make sure there are no barking dogs or crying babies in the background. The quickest way to disqualify yourself from a potential job is to have your dog barking in the background while you are speaking on the phone with a recruiter, a human resource director, or a hiring manager.

2. **Computer and printer**. Without these two items, you will be dead in the water. Don't have a printer? Go to a Staples or Costco and buy an ink jet printer for less than $100. Alternatively, go online to find the best deal, and make sure that shipping is free. B&H Photo in New York City is a good place

to buy online, and they ship throughout the country. The representatives are knowledgeable, courteous, and helpful. In addition, their prices are competitive, shipping is free, and the return policy is liberal. Go to www.bhphoto.com.

3. **Office tools.** Your office life will be easier if you have items like note pads, pens, a stapler, paper clips, printer paper, postage stamps, envelopes, and a bulletin board to hang on the wall to post reminder notes. Do not forget the small bookcase, which you can buy at Staples for about $35. You will need this to store your growing collection of books and magazines pertaining to work. Also, purchase a small filing cabinet to store files on companies, specific jobs, work-related research, and network contacts. Contrary to the hype, print and paper are not yet dead.

4. **A smartphone or landline phone.** If you are using a smart phone, make sure reception is strong enough to talk in a conversational tone. If not, use a landline for all outgoing and incoming calls. The real world of civilian work is not like being in the armed services. Continual background noise will be a poor reflection on your sense of maturity, your unfamiliarity with the civilian world, and a breach of business courtesy.

   Make sure to clean up your voicemail message. Remember that hiring managers and others involved in the job-hunting process will be calling you. This simple aspect of business etiquette is neglected more often than you would think.

   If you want a brief, acceptable, universal voicemail message, try something like this: "This is Mary Jones at 215–825–1290. Please leave your name, phone number, and a brief message, and I'll return your call promptly. Thank you for calling." Do not under any circumstances disguise your voice or say something cute. In the civilian world of work, remember this rule: Nobody Likes a Smart Ass (NLSA). Do not have another person record your message. A hiring manager will interpret this as too cute and surmise that you do not have the maturity or confidence to act appropriately.

5. **A record-keeping book and a planning book or computer app**. You can buy a daily or monthly planner at Staples for a few dollars. Better yet, use a digital database like Sage ACT or Microsoft Outlook, a part of Microsoft Office. You will need to record all of your company contacts, references, and networking sources. When you are attending conferences and talking with hundreds of people over a two-day period, you will need to record names and contact information, including email addresses, phone numbers, and social media handles.

6. **A briefcase for important documents**. Purchase a briefcase to store and transport important documents, such as your resume or career profile, to interviews, conventions, and trade shows. Backpacks are not acceptable. You can buy a reasonably priced attractive faux leather briefcase at Staples (www.Staples.com) for about $30. Alternatively, you might consider the combination laptop/briefcase for about $45, also at Staples. If you have a few extra dollars, buy a leather one. It will last for the next ten years or more and make for a striking appearance.

7. **Business calling cards**. Calling cards are a necessity for job-hunting activities. You will need something to establish your identity, even though you might not have a job. For example, when you meet a hiring manager or networking contact, how are you going to present your contact information? Will you scribble it on the back of a napkin or a scrap of paper? That is not professional. Contrary to what some veterans believe, not everyone uses a smartphone to record data like your name and contact information. The exchange of business cards is a time-honored tradition and another tactic used in the civilian workplace.

   You can purchase business cards from any number of places like Staples or Sir Speedy, or you can buy them online at a steep discount from VistaPrint. Go to www.vistaprint.com and select a design from among hundreds of samples. You can customize your cards and order sizable quantities at the lowest price possible, $10 for 250 cards. Frequently, VistaPrint will have free promotions for your first order of 250 cards. We suggest that you order at least 500 cards, because you will distribute hundreds when you attend trade shows and conferences.

Select a conservative card with no more than two colors. Do not get cute and order cards with bizarre designs. The business card reflects your persona, and you need to make a good first impression. This is business, not entertainment.

Be sure to include the following information on your card: name, address, cell phone number, landline number if you have one, email address, and Twitter and Facebook handles. You do not need to identify yourself as a veteran, or English major, or Stanford graduate. Just your name will suffice. In addition to distributing your cards to people you meet personally, attach them to documents you send from your home office to potential employers by mail or FedEx.

8. **Control your digital tools. Unplug.** Working from your personal operations center requires focus and attention, and the best way to avoid distractions is to unplug, to turn off your smartphone and silence your email so it will not click every time a new message arrives. We live in a digital world and it is difficult to put the smartphone away, but who is in charge, you or a digital device? Think about it. Do you want a smartphone or tablet controlling your life? Instead, allot a certain number of minutes each day for scanning your smartphone, tablet, and computer. We recommend using the final ten minutes of each hour to interact with your digital tools.

Please note that we are not recommending that you toss away your digital tools and social media apps. Most likely, these apps are loaded with personal stuff that you would not like a hiring manager to see, but getting rid of them would be a problem. The solution? Open a new Twitter and Facebook account to use exclusively for your job search and professional life. Alternatively, go to Twitter and subscribe to only one category: business. Follow companies and organizations that will be beneficial to your job search, such as the *Wall Street Journal*, *Forbes*, *Fortune*, the *New York Times*, Jim Cramer, and CNBC. In Part III, I will discuss Twitter, LinkedIn, Facebook, and other social media in detail.

YOUR RECORD-KEEPING SYSTEM

Record and save job-hunting information in your office using a commercial app or one that you design yourself. If you do not want to bother with a database like ACT or Windows Contacts, create your own. It should look something like this:

A Sample Record-Keeping Template

Company Name: Ford Motors
Company Website: www.Ford.com
Company Address: 1234 Ford Blvd., Worcester, MA 17760
Contact Name and Position: Betty Murphy, Human Resources Director
Cell phone: 701–234–5634
Office phone: 617–456–9876
Email Address: B.Murphy@ford.com
Date and purpose of last message: On 1/12/2017 received email from Betty; she received my resume and cover letter. Scheduled personal interview for 2/18/2017, at 9 a.m. at her office. Bring resume, transcript, and reference letters.
Follow up: 2/13/2017, emailed appointment confirmation to Betty.
Other Ford Contacts: Betty's Admin is Ted Thomas; T.Thomas@Ford.com
Notes: Learned that Betty played soccer at Michigan State. Admires Picasso's art.

That is all you will need for your record-keeping work. A database or record-keeping system you establish now and store in your home office will be an integral part of your civilian working life going forward.

By the way, did you look at the Ford website? Do it now and then click on "More Ford." When you pull down this menu, click on "Careers." You can do the rest. Who knows, next month you might be working at Ford and qualify for a discount on a new hybrid Ford Fusion. At the bottom of the "Careers" page, click on "Auto Shows" to learn where the next convention is being held. If the next show is within driving distance, you must attend, because there you will find Ford hiring managers who can tell you about available jobs and about the corporate culture at this great American icon. In Chapter 20, "The Convention Connection. The Top Convention Centers and Trade Shows," I will provide much more information about attending trade shows, conferences, and conventions, because these are places where you meet hiring managers in person.

HOW MUCH TIME SHOULD YOU SPEND IN YOUR OPERATIONS CENTER?

The easy answer is *as much time as you need*. However, if you do not control your schedule, you will always find something else to do, like visiting your friends, shopping, surfing the Internet, or attending a sporting event. Schedule at least five hours per day working in your office once or twice a week. The other days you will be job hunting away from home, making cold calls on potential employers, attending trade shows, conventions, and job fairs, or interviewing on site. Your home office is the place where you conduct research, collect information, make and answer calls, send resumes to a living person (not a job number), and conduct follow-ups.

CHAPTER TAKEAWAYS

- An operations center is necessary for serious job hunting during your current search and those that inevitably will follow.
- Employers want to see that you have the smarts and discipline to work from home.

- A record-keeping plan is required for productive civilian job hunting.
- While working from your ops center, limit the amount of time you spend using social media.

THE VETERAN'S LIBRARY

Dirk Zeller. *Successful Time Management for Dummies.* Wiley, 2008.

Chapter 12

The Search Plan as an Operation and a Process

It is not rocket science. *Plan your work. Work your plan.* If you begin any venture without a plan, you will end up somewhere far from your objective. Creating a plan, a written plan, is not difficult, and **OJS** will tell you how to do it.

BEGINNING YOUR JOB SEARCH PLAN

A civilian work plan, which is similar to a military operation, consists of two parts: a written objective and written strategies for accomplishing the objective. Think back to your life in the military and you will get the point. Everything you did there was part of an operation that carried a specific name, like Operation Desert Storm, Operation Desert Freedom, Operation Enduring Freedom, which Afghanistan veterans know so well, and Operation New Dawn, the name for our involvement in Iraq. These strategies were not written one evening on a cocktail napkin at the local watering hole. They were years in the making by some of the best brains in the military.

Creating a civilian job plan is much the same, and if you want an easy handle to keep you on track, call it **Operation Job Search**. Now, let's examine each part of the operation:

The Objective

We will not get involved in a lot of flowery prose. In everyday language, the primary objective of your plan is *to find a civilian job that will provide income to become a self-sufficient human being, which means providing my own food, shelter, clothing, and other necessities.*

If you elect to focus your search on a specific job in a specific industry, you may write a more specific objective, which may read like this: *to find a civilian job as an electrician with a large residential homebuilder in the Northeast, like Ryan Homes or Toll Brothers, that will provide income to become a self-sufficient human being.*

Do not become sidetracked by the rhetoric of the media and academia, which goes something like this: "Work is something to make you feel good, to make you feel fulfilled, to make you feel like a worthwhile human being. Do what you love. Money is secondary." Tell that to the finance company holding your car loan or your home mortgage, and you will get a lecture about the real world of work, as well as a foreclosure on your home or a repossession of your car.

However, all job hunters want to find work that is interesting and in sync with their talents, background, and skill sets. That too is a no-brainer, but we must remember that the prime objective is to make enough money to become self-sufficient. For example, if you want to be a high school teacher, but the compensation is not sufficient to meet your needs, look for something else. A higher paying job in a different industry may not be exactly what you want, but it will pay the bills. Another alternative is to take the high school teaching job and supplement your income with a part-time job on weekends.

Today our working hours and personal hours are not what they were in the industrial age of America. In that period, workers reported for the job at 7 a.m. in the morning and left for home at 5 p.m. in the afternoon. After 5 p.m. and on weekends, life was their own. Today it is different. Time on the job and personal time work in harmony with no rigidly defined hours (with some exceptions, of course). Veterans know this model from their experience on active duty when they worked until they accomplished the objective.

The Main Strategy

The strategy part is where most veterans struggle. A good part of **OJS** is about how to design and employ strategies that will lead you to the promised land of civilian employment. Job-hunting strategies are multifaceted. It is not just one action item, like writing a "winner" resume or a "killer" cover letter. Here is an overall strategy that is necessary to find employment in the civilian world of work: *to meet hiring managers personally through networking, attending conventions, conferences and job fairs, making cold calls at company offices, and by utilizing all support offered to veterans by government and other organizations.*

Note that resumes, cover letters, and interviewing techniques are not in this strategy. Why? Because these are items that support the overall strategy. Meeting hiring managers in person is the key action item in finding employment. Nothing happens until you establish that relationship with the hiring manager.

But what about the many online job-hunting gurus who will tell you that it is all about writing the "perfect" resume or using "guaranteed" rules for answering questions during an interview? Sorry, Internet job-jocks, there's more to it than that.

Take resumes, for instance. You can write the best resume known to humankind, but if you do not deliver it to the right person, it means nothing. Sending a resume to Job #127 or Position # 586 is like sending your resume to planet Pluto. The guaranteed results will be the same: no response, no interview, no job.

Supporting Strategies

OJS clearly delineates action items that will help you accomplish the objective. Note that a work job plan is not a one-time deal like sending out a resume. It is a multi-step process that includes the following actions:

- Establishing an operations center
- Creating a career profile instead of a mere resume
- Communicating in error-free civilian English

- Learning the numbers and terms relating to the civilian workplace
- Using technology in meaningful ways
- Evaluating and responding to a job description
- Evaluating a potential employer
- Building a useful network
- Learning about military friendly employers and colleges
- Selecting and wearing proper attire for an interview

In the next chapter, I will give you eight action items for creating strategies that support your objective. Stick around, veterans. **OJS** will tell you how it's done.

CHAPTER TAKEAWAYS

- The first step in the job-hunting process is to make a plan. The second step is to work your plan.
- Your personal Operation Job Search has two written parts: stating your objective(s) and defining strategies to accomplish your objective(s).
- Strategies are multifaceted. Constructing only a resume or cover letter falls short of a true operation.
- Meeting hiring managers personally is necessary for landing a job.
- Your work plan is a process.

THE VETERAN'S LIBRARY

Colin Powell. *It Worked for Me*. Harper, 2013.

Chesley "Sully" Sullenberger. *Making a Difference*. William Morrow, 2012.

Chapter 13

Creating Your Custom Job Search Plan

Many veterans leave the military without the slightest idea about the kind of civilian work they want to do. In addition, most have no idea about how to go about finding a civilian job. The prevailing wisdom says it is only a matter of sending out a few dozen resumes to postings on Internet job boards and a job will automatically fall into your lap. With that in mind, veterans begin looking for a job with no plan whatsoever. Those who are technology gurus believe that Tweets and texts from friends, a survey of the job boards, and a lot of Facebook chatter will miraculously result in job offers. That is not the way it happens in the civilian world of work.

Recently I watched a *Sixty Minutes* program that devoted thirty minutes to job hunting and focused on recently fired and laid off workers. What I saw was startling and bore a close resemblance to what most unsuccessful job hunters do. The program host interviewed a number of experienced corporate workers, most of whom whined, "there's nothing out there; I've been at my computer every day for two years sending out resumes and can't find anything." A man named Bob said that he had only three interviews over the course of a year after sending out hundreds of resumes.

These people should have known that you do not get a job sitting at a computer. You find work by leaving the house and meeting hiring managers at conventions, conferences, job fairs, and industry trade shows, or by cold calling on them at their offices in industrial parks.

Nobody is going to hire a resume unattached to a living breathing human being. Moreover, nobody is going to knock at your door and offer you a job. That is not how the real world works.

STRATEGIES INCLUDED IN THE WORK PLAN PROCESS

In the last chapter, we established the *main* job search strategy. Here we will discuss *supporting* strategies. Is this beginning to look like an *operation*, similar to what you found in the military? Here is a list of eight strategies and activities you must employ to support your main strategy and accomplish your objective:

1. **Establish an operations center for job hunting**. This is an important but often overlooked part of the job-hunting process. You will need more than the kitchen table and a smartphone, more than a table at Starbucks and your iPad. You need a designated place where you have peace and quiet and the tools to get the job done. I consider this vitally important and wrote an entire earlier chapter dedicated to the process.

2. **Find your passion**. A job search is a major commitment of time and energy, not something that you do in your spare time. Work is not something that will make you smile or feel fulfilled every day. In fact, much of the work we do is boring but necessary to accomplish valid objectives. However, if you work in an industry you really like, your days at work will be happy, meaningful, and productive. A key factor is finding what you really like to do, what gives meaning to your life.

   How do you find your passion? It is not rocket science, and it is not necessary to take a battery of psychological tests to learn what your interests are and what you would like to do in the civilian world of work. You have enough life experience to know what you like. Begin by making a list of things that interest you. Sports? Food? Clothing? Housing? Government?

Politics? Charitable foundations? Education? Cars? Airplanes? Boats? Teaching? Art? Music? Web design? Home construction? Digital marketing? Make a list of what you like in rank order, even if you feel you know what you like. Put it in writing.

The *Occupational Outlook Handbook* will help you uncover your passion. This book lists almost every job in the world and will surely help you uncover a hidden passion. Schedule several hours or maybe even a few days to review this book. It not only lists jobs by title, but also provides salary information, requirements, specific job projections, and other interesting and pertinent information. For more information about self-assessment, mission, and fulfillment, review Chapter 1 of this book.

3. **Find the companies specializing in your passion**. Let's assume that your main interest is music and that you have an aptitude for it, having played in the Marine Corps Marching Band. Go to the Internet, search for "companies in the music industry," and you will come back with two days' worth of hits to research.

    Repeat the process for your top three fields of interest and see what you get. Before you do, however, be prepared to spend the next several hours, or days, online, because you will learn much about yourself, the companies in your field of interest, and what jobs are available to satisfy your passion (and make you money to become self-sufficient).

4. **Search job boards for companies in your passion industry**. Search the various job boards for companies catering to your passion. Assuming it is music, go to LinkedIn and under the "Companies" menu enter "music." I did just that and found that the Universal Music Group has a number of job openings for marketing and sales people across the USA. Continue your online search until you have a list of twenty companies in your field of interest.

5. **Make a target list of twenty potential employers**. After making a list of twenty companies in your top industry, rank them using your own criteria for evaluation to supplement what you

find online. Also, use the rules for evaluating companies in Chapter 33.

6. **Create a resume and a career profile**. The most common mistake job hunters make is spending days or weeks constructing the *perfect* resume. Some veterans may have used VA resources or paid a professional resume writer to construct their resumes, only to learn that thousands of veterans have done the same thing. The result? Thousands of resumes will look just like yours, or like that of Mary from Topeka, Jose from San Diego, and Rebecca from Boston. You need to distinguish yourself by constructing a personal career profile where your resume is only one of several documents.

   In Part V, you will learn how to create your career profile and package yourself for employment. There is more to your persona than a mere two-page look-alike resume.

7. **Learn from online resources**. The Internet offers thousands of resources for job-hunting veterans of every stripe. Some of these resources are very good and others are mediocre. Much of what you find is redundant. How many ways can you write a resume or a cover letter?

   However, if you feel compelled to go to the Internet for resume and general job-hunting advice, go to Career Confidential. It is one of the best in the business. This Texas-based company provides webinars on all aspects of job hunting, from resume writing to phone interviews. In addition, the company provides online and phone coaching—for a charge, of course. However, most of their webinars are free, and podcasts are available for a nominal charge. Check it out: www.CareerConfidential.com.

   In addition, veterans can always find help and advice from the VA, the VFW, Military.com, and the American Legion.

8. **Create a written plan**. Let us assume that you have accomplished steps 1–7. Is it finally time to leave the house and go job hunting? Not really. What we need first is something that

every business pro needs, a written plan. That is what Hans from Minneapolis did, and it resulted in a lucrative business. Here is his success story.

Hans from Minneapolis

Once I met a very successful car dealer in Minneapolis. He started his business with just one dealership selling Chevrolet automobiles. Soon he had a Chrysler dealership and then came Honda and Subaru. Can you imagine that, owning four automobile dealerships in a major metropolitan area like Minneapolis-St. Paul, Minnesota? What did Hans do right? What was the one thing that propelled his business to the top of the pack?

Well, I hope you are sitting down, because the answer will knock you off your feet. It is that obvious. Hans attributed his success to his firmly held belief "Plan Your Work. Work Your Plan." How incredibly simple, yet how insightful. You cannot run a business without a plan, and that piece of advice applies to finding any type of job as well. You cannot run a job search without a plan.

PLAN YOUR WORK. WORK YOUR PLAN

When you land your first job, you will learn that companies do not plan the day's activities at 7:00 a.m. every day. They do not delete everything on the server at 5:00 p.m. and reprogram the following morning. Companies plan three to five years ahead, and everyone follows the plan each day. Most likely, your boss will give you the work plan for your position on the first day of work. Let's follow Hans's road to success and write a job-hunting plan that will take you to the promised land of employment.

Before you even begin to make your plan, make a firm resolution to carry out this task in your operations center. This is serious stuff, and trying to write it on a Word doc or a sheet of paper in the TV room during half-time will not be productive. Let's get into it, step by step.

Beginning Your Plan

Let's assume that you have decided to seek a position in the insurance industry and that you are interested in sales. As a backup, you want to explore marketing positions for insurance companies because that niche provides many opportunities for entry-level positions.

Next Step. The Phone Directory

The next step includes a number of proactive initiatives to learn where you can find insurance companies in your local area. One strategy is to look in the print or online phone directory for insurance companies within a 90-minute drive of your residence. (Do not expect job locations to be a few blocks from home. Sometimes they will be across town or 75 miles away. If driving 90 minutes a day to work seems like too much of a burden, stop your job search immediately and go on welfare.) Some consider using a phone directory for job hunting "so yesterday," but this method has a high rate of success, over 60 percent according to reliable sources.

Next Step. Convention Centers

In Chapter 20, I provide the names, phone numbers, and URLs for every major convention center in the USA. Why attend these venues? Because there you will meet hiring managers personally. Your plan must include time for attending these conferences.

Next Step. Activate Your Network

Activate your network of employed individuals. Almost everyone has a salesperson for purchasing life, medical, homeowners, and automobile insurance. Ask your network contacts for their names and contact information and plan to visit them personally.

Next Step. Let's Write!

Use the weekly calendar on your computer or construct a paper weekly calendar. Make sure the calendar provides writing space for each day. You are going to plan a week in advance for now, but soon you will expand that period to a month, and then to three months. If you connect with a job during the first three months, you can say good-bye to the second quarterly plan.

In the space for each day, write the activities you will perform come hell or high water. Beginning with Monday, fill in all of the blanks for each day of the next week. Take it one week at a time. Your plan for the first week should look something like this:

A Job Search Plan for the Week of June 23, 2017

Monday

8:00–10:00 a.m. Visit ABC Auto Insurance Company regional office and ask to see the sales manager, marketing manager, and human resources director for an interview. (This is a cold call, which is making a call when you do not have a scheduled appointment.)

10:00–11:30 a.m. Cold call Prudential Life Insurance Company home office. Learn the name and contact information for the human resources director and ask for an interview.

11:30–1:00 p.m. Lunch. Have a sandwich and review what happened during your morning calls. Record your plans for sending follow-up emails or personal notes when you return home to your Operations Center. Select a restaurant where you see people wearing business attire. These are most likely hiring managers, so make an effort to meet them.

1:30–2:30 p.m. Visit your personal local insurance agent(s). Request his/her advice for landing a job in the insurance industry in sales or marketing. Ask for the names of hiring managers and their contact information. This is a scheduled appointment.

3:00–4:30 p.m. Visit United Health Insurance district sales office. Learn the name and contact information for the sales director and ask for an interview. Cold call.

5:00–6:00 p.m. Return home and send follow-up emails or write personal notes to people you saw or did not see today. Begin planning for next week.

Tuesday

8:00 a.m.–5:00 p.m. Attend insurance trade show at McCormick Place in Chicago. Visit each booth and ask to see the hiring manager for sales and marketing. Bring plenty of business cards and career profiles or resumes. Continue planning for next week.

Wednesday

8:00 a.m.–5:00 p.m. Attend insurance trade show at McCormick Place. Repeat of Tuesday activities. Continue planning for next week.

Thursday

9:00 a.m.–5:00 p.m. Work at your Operations Center conducting trade show follow-up. Continue planning for next week.

Friday

8:00–9:00 a.m. Coffee at Starbucks with the automobile insurance agent of a relative or friend. Informational interview. This is a scheduled appointment.

9:30–11:30 a.m. Scheduled appointment with the human resources director at Ajax Life Insurance Co. Bring career profile.

11:30–1:30 p.m. Lunch at Chipotle. Make notes about your meeting at Ajax and plan follow-up when you return home. Sit next to someone in business attire and strike up a conversation.

1:30–3:00 p.m. Cold call at Allstate auto insurance district sales office. Learn name and contact information for the district sales manager. Request an interview. If the district sales manager is busy or out of the office, ask to see the assistant sales manager and the human resources director.

4:00–6:00 p.m. Return to your Operations Center and write follow-up emails and personal notes. WRITE YOUR WORK PLAN FOR NEXT WEEK, and then knock it off and meet a friend at the local watering hole for a drink and dinner. Discuss your job-hunting activities this week.

Saturday and Sunday
Take the weekend off unless there is a trade show, conference, or job fair to attend. Do not miss an opportunity to meet potential employers personally, even if the show falls on a weekend. Make time to work on your plan for the next three weeks.

Who said job hunting would be easy? This was a tough week, but look back at the number of personal contacts you made. You could not have met that many potential hiring managers sitting at home firing off resumes into space.

Over the weekend, complete your plan for the following week. Finalize your work plan for the coming week just as you did for the week above. Repeat that over the next two weeks, and you will have a one-month plan. Nice, but it does not stop there. Repeat that operation for the next two months, and you will have a quarterly plan just as the big guys do in businesses across America. Welcome to the world of work!

THE PAYOFF. YOUR QUARTERLY NUMBERS

Let's review the results of your activities on your work plan, assuming the following:

- You have attended two trade shows, conferences, or job fairs each month and personally met with fifty company representatives, most of whom were hiring managers.
- You have made an average of five personal calls on potential employers each week.
- You have spoken to one referral contact each week, as you did on Friday when you had coffee at Starbucks with your father's automobile insurance agent.

Here is what you will have accomplished in one three-month period, or as they say in the corporate world, in one quarter:

- Six trade shows and/or job fairs attended where you spoke with representatives of more than 300 potential employers
- Sixty personal meetings with information sources or hiring authorities, apart from trade shows, conferences, or job fairs
- Twelve personal referral meetings for informational or job interviews

The number of people you spoke with personally could go up considerably depending upon the number of people you saw at trade shows, conferences, and job fairs. Our experience has been that if you attend a medium to large show where there are anywhere from 300 to 600 exhibitors, you will average approximately twenty-five meaningful personal contacts per conference. If you multiply that by the number of trade shows you attended in one quarter (six), you will have spoken with 150 potential employers. If you include the number of personal meetings you had apart from trade shows (sixty), your total personal contacts could exceed 300. Job hunting does not get any better than that!

CHAPTER TAKEAWAYS

- A job search begins with a written plan. Only *written* plans have meaning and usefulness.
- Plan your work. Work your plan.
- Written work plans generate contacts with hiring managers and interviews.
- Find your passion before creating your plan.

THE VETERAN'S LIBRARY

Richard Walsh. *The Start Your Own Business Bible*. F&W Media, 2011.

PART III

Technology in the Civilian Workplace

The number one benefit of information technology is that it empowers people to do what they want to do. It lets people be creative. It lets people be productive. It lets people learn things they didn't think they could learn before, and so in a sense it is all about potential.

—Steve Ballmer, Former CEO, Microsoft

Chapter 14

Technology Is Changing the Civilian Workplace

This may be the most important chapter in **OJS** for those forward-looking veterans who want to be in sync with the workplace of the future. However, before envisioning the workplace of the future, let's take a good look at work today.

Traditional civilian work goes something like this. You get up in the morning, eat breakfast, and then report to a building where you do something called work for the next eight to ten hours. You report to someone called a boss who defines the tasks you perform and how you are to do them. You take time off for a morning and afternoon break and for lunch. At the appointed hour, somewhere between 5:00 and 6:00 p.m., you stop working, say good-bye to your boss and coworkers, and head out the door to go home. Occasionally, you might stop at a local pub for a drink with your friends, or you might go shopping. Some of you might go directly from work to perform community outreach activities for which you are not paid. Others will go home to work online toward a degree program or to a bricks-and-mortar school for continuing education.

Employers structure work for you and your coworkers to maximize productivity. Whether your job is entry-level or managerial, it will be structured until the day you retire. That's the way it is today, but as you read this book, changes are taking place below the radar, changes that will alter the traditional work paradigm. The main driver of workplace change? Technology. In the military, you experienced a technology-driven workplace, and that will work in your favor as you begin your transition to civilian employment. Significant changes are taking place in the civilian workforce as you read this book. One of them is working from home.

WORKING FROM YOUR OPERATIONS CENTER (a.k.a. HOME OFFICE)

This is an exciting time to be a worker in America because your workplace guarantees one thing: change. Your job today will not look the same five years from now because technology is changing the way tasks are accomplished. For example, technology in many companies no longer depends on servers located on company premises.

Companies like Salesforce.com, www.salesforce.com, store data for companies on their servers, which may be located thousands of miles away. (Before we move on, did you go to the website and check out the "Careers" pages? This company is in hiring mode, so review it now.)

If what pops up on your monitor is coming from a server thousands of miles away, why do you need to report to a certain location every day? Couldn't you perform your assigned tasks working from *your* location, your home office? The answer is obvious.

But who works from home? If working from home is appealing, how do you find companies who encourage this practice? Where are they located? What industries are most likely to permit working from home? There is a timely article in the "Personal Finance" section of the January 17, 2014, issue of *Forbes* that lists the top 100 companies that permit and encourage working from home. The list includes a number of insurance and technology companies, but generally, the industries represented are quite diverse and include both for-profit and nonprofit companies. Here are the top ten in the "work from home" list:

The Top Ten Work-from-Home Companies

1. ADP

2. Adobe

3. Aetna

4. American Express

5. Dell

6. First Data

7. Humana

8. United Health Group

9. Westat

10. Xerox

Other high visibility companies on this list are Apple, General Electric, Hartford Financial Services, Salesforce.com, Microsoft, Lockheed Martin, CVS Caremark, The American Heart Association, the US Department of Transportation, and Pearson Education. Interestingly, many companies on the top 100 list are also military friendly.

Who Works from Home?

Here is some interesting data about home workers from the US Census Bureau:

- About 25 percent of home workers are in management, business, and finance.
- Half of home workers are self-employed.
- Colorado has the highest number of home workers.
- The number of STEM (science, technology, engineering, and mathematics) home workers increased 69 percent between 2000 and 2010.

Corporate and Government Home-Office Workers

The Census Bureau tells us that home-based workers are more likely to work in the private sector than in government jobs. In addition, people working in finance, sales, and STEM positions are more likely to work from home. As for worker productivity and job satisfaction, a study by Cisco Systems found that employees working from home experienced an improvement in both productivity and quality of life.

THE CHANGING WORKPLACE

There is no reason why most corporate workers should spend their time in cubicles or, as we call them, *people kennels*. During your lifetime, many multistory office buildings may become grain silos or call centers, as offshore work returns to America. For the most part, today's office environment is depressogenic and contributes to worker dissatisfaction and low productivity.

Most companies still cling to the traditional depressing workspace model, however, and lose productivity every day. The reason? Company executives are hesitant to change. I believe that once veterans like you take over the executive level positions, we will see people kennels disappear as workers are permitted, encouraged, and required to work from home.

There is also evidence that the civilian workplace is changing. Some companies, mostly technology companies, have re-created the work environment to make a more productive working space. Google is a good example of what a company can do to make the work environment more pleasant and productive, but do not let the TV ads for Google fool you. Even though there are refreshment kiosks and ping-pong tables on the work floor, workers are held strictly accountable for meeting objectives. Too many high-protein shakes and too much fun at the ping-pong table will reduce your productivity, and soon you will be looking for another job. The civilian workplace is not where you have fun. It is a place where workers produce.

Get used to the coming new paradigm, work-from-home, because you will see it in your lifetime, well before you retire and begin seeking a new career. Change, however, is painful and comes in fits and starts as we noted recently at one of our iconic technology companies, Yahoo.

Yahoo Bucks the Trend

In February 2013, the new CEO of Yahoo, Marissa Mayer, issued an edict requiring all home workers to return to the corporate office. That was 10 percent of Yahoo's workers. She said that having the entire team in one location made for better communication and increased loyalty and productivity. Yahoo reportedly had been in a state of dysfunction before she took over as CEO. However, was working from home the root cause of it? We will need to see how this plays out at Yahoo long term. Click on the website, www.yahoo.com, for the latest information. While you are there, check to see the available jobs.

MESSING WITH THE OFFICE FLOOR PLAN

Other companies have redesigned the workspace by lowering cubicle walls and eliminating private offices, all in hope of increasing human interaction, which some employment experts claim increases productivity. However, in a recent article in the *Wall Street Journal*, one writer claimed the opposite effect has been generated. Her research says that more open space results in frequent interruptions and distractions, which decrease productivity. It takes on average nearly half an hour to resume a task after an interruption. In fact, the interruption problem has become so acute that workers in the open environment wear signs saying Do Not Disturb. An obvious solution to these office environment problems is working from home.

EXPLOSIVE INNOVATION IN TECHNOLOGY

As a veteran who received significant technology training in the military, you know that technology is playing a more prominent role in all aspects of our lives. The world of work is no exception. As the use of technology expands and replaces human workers, there will be serious disruptions in the workplace. Many jobs will disappear causing widespread structural unemployment in some industries but new

employment opportunities in other industries. As you are reading this
book, someone is being fired because that person's job was eliminated
by a new software application. However, as one person leaves, another
finds work with SalesForce.com or another cloud company. As you
read these pages, someone is designing new technology products that
will influence what you do in your work cycle.

Listen to Peter

Peter Diamandis is chairman of the XPRIZE Foundation, www.xprize.
org, a nonprofit company that awards large prizes to foster technological innovations. XPRIZE partners with organizations like the Bill and
Melinda Gates Foundation, the $35 billion nonprofit founded and
funded by Bill Gates, founder of Microsoft. Diamandis predicts eight
significant technological breakthroughs that will change the world of
work for everyone. You will experience all of them in your work cycle,
so listen carefully. What you read in the next few paragraphs will affect
your job five years from now. Here are the "explosive eight" as reported
in the January 22, 2013, issue of the *Wall Street Journal*.

Peter's Predictions:

1. ***Bacteriology***. *Biologists are making rapid progress thinking of life
   in terms of a programming language. This will result in the cre-
   ation of many new billion-dollar companies.*
2. ***Computational Systems***. *This technology gives us the ability to
   model almost anything, resulting in many new industries requiring many new workers.*
3. ***Networks and Sensors***. *This technology will give us large amounts
   of data that will enable us to do anything data related, such as
   earthquake forecasting, in fractions of a second.*
4. ***Artificial Intelligence***. *This is the stuff of which science fiction is
   made. AI will transform every industry in your work cycle.*
5. ***Robotics***. *This exciting technology is one that all workers should
   explore for job opportunities. Robotics will create many new jobs*

during your work cycle and may even change how you perform your work. Soon robotics may replace everyone's most dreaded job, cleaning the house. Can you envision your own business called "Terry's Robotic House Cleaning Service"? It is coming, so stay tuned. Or get ahead of the curve and think about a business you can create using robotic technology.

6. ***Digital Manufacturing****. It is here already in the form of advanced barcoding techniques and 3-D printing. Think about how exciting this will be in the world of clothing design and manufacture.*

7. ***Medicine****. Remote medical diagnosis is already on the scene but in rudimentary form. Within five years, there will be hand-held devices that will record and transmit data about your body functions directly to your physician. After reading your data, your doctor may very well call and say, "Joe, get in here ASAP. You have elevated T1 and TSH readings, indicating you have a thyroid problem. I have to treat it now." In fact, we have already begun down that path with the Apple iWatch, which provides data on a variety of your own body functions.*

8. ***Nanotechnology****. It works at the atomic and molecular level and has widespread applications, such as increased battery energy and storage capacities. Most interesting is the use of DNA to replace traditional technology storage devices. There is no doubt that you will look back upon the "cloud" as primitive. Nanotechnology companies are springing up like mushrooms across America and the world. Google "nanotechnology" for a look at the present, the future, and, most importantly, job opportunities.*

A CLOSER LOOK AT THREE GAME-CHANGERS

Robotics

It is fascinating to explore the use of robots, particularly in manufacturing and medicine. The best way to see how robots work is to visit a manufacturing company like Ford or General Motors.

Another example is robotic surgery. Using this technology, the surgeon sits at a computer console a few feet away from the patient and manipulates probes inserted into the patient through very small incisions. The result is better outcomes for the patients, new jobs for the professional staff, but fewer jobs for the traditional surgical nursing assistants. On the Internet, you will find a number of videos showing robotic surgery using the da Vinci Surgical System.

Many civilian robot applications are adaptations of technology used in the military. Drones are a good example. When you are in an interview, let the hiring manager know that you are up to speed on technology applications because of your military work experience.

RFID Technology and 3D Barcodes

New barcode technology is eliminating thousands of jobs previously done by hand. For example, retail companies like Walmart used to conduct a physical count of every item in every store for inventory purposes. With thousands of stores worldwide, this was a huge undertaking requiring millions of worker hours to complete.

Now inventory workers have been replaced by a technology called Radio-frequency Identification, RFID, a system that uses 3D barcodes to track inventory. The system tracks each individual product from the time of manufacture until the time it leaves the store. When you buy a product, it is removed from the store's inventory automatically. When the inventory for that specific product goes down to a certain level, an order for additional products is sent to the manufacturer.

Before this technology came on the scene, workers physically counted each item on a shelf and recorded that number in a notebook. It was a laborious error-ridden process costing the company millions of dollars in human labor. RFID will continue to change the way we live and eliminate many more jobs.

This technology can process information of all kinds, eliminating tedious tasks like airplane ticketing. Importantly, it is also used in manufacturing, saving money for both companies and customers. You have probably seen the 3D barcode on your smartphone or tablet, as well as the packages of many consumer products.

There is no doubt this technology will affect you in some personal way in your work cycle. It may provide additional job opportunities, or it may eliminate existing jobs.

Big Data Analytics. The Salesforce.com WAVE

Recently the world's foremost CRM cloud company, Salesforce.com, launched its innovative WAVE program. It permits business technology workers to use and transport data anywhere, anytime on mobile devices. There is no doubt that the new WAVE will change the way we use and access data. Here is how the company advertises this product:

> Measure. Group. Filter. View. Share. Five actions let you unlock limitless insight. The only platform that lets you easily navigate every data set right from your phone. Get answers and share findings — no desktop required. Have a conversation around data, answer any question with everyone on your team, and present your findings from your phone.

Before you walk into any interview, be sure to review the Salesforce.com website, www.salesforce.com, to learn about the new WAVE. Winning that job could be contingent upon your knowledge of technology and your ability to articulate that knowledge to the hiring manager.

WHAT KINDS OF TECHNOLOGY JOBS ARE OUT THERE?

Here is an example of what you can expect to see as you search for a civilian job. This is real life in today's world of work. I am part of a LinkedIn group called the Education Sales & Marketing Network and receive daily updates on industry trends, career matters, and job openings. A recent posting included the following nine job openings:

1. Marketing Manager. Online and End User Marketing
2. Digital Analytics Manager

3. Senior Enterprise Technology Products Sales Executive
4. Senior Account Manager for Higher Education Technology Products
5. Senior Solutions Engineer I
6. Solutions Engineer II
7. Systems Analyst
8. Search and Display Group Manager
9. Pre-Sales Senior Solutions Engineer

Look closely at this list. All nine positions are technology related. That is where the job market is heading, and you must be prepared to constantly upgrade your existing technology skills and acquire new ones, like web programming.

MOVING FORWARD

By now, all veterans should get the picture. Going forward, technology will play a more prominent role in every industry and every job. You must have up-to-date technology skills in addition to whatever degree you hold or whatever technology experience you have from the military. It makes no difference whether you are going to teach in a third grade classroom or work in investment banking with Goldman Sachs. Teachers are now grappling with the transition from print instructional materials to sophisticated digital products, and bankers are using big data to better serve their customers and improve the bottom line.

We're not talking about ho-hum technology skills like knowing how to use Excel, PowerPoint, and various social media. Nobody really cares if you can knock out twenty Tweets a minute. Your world of work will require more, much more than that. You need to update your skills constantly by taking refresher courses online or at bricks-and-mortar facilities.

A technology worker that we highly respect, Eric Schmidt, Executive Board Chair of Google, says it better than anyone else in his book *The New Digital Age: Reshaping the Future of People, Nations & Business*. The book begins like this:

Soon everyone on Earth will be connected. With five billion more people set to join the virtual world, the boom in digital connectivity will bring gains in productivity, health, education, quality of life, and myriad other avenues in the physical world . . .

Need we say any more about what technology will do in your work cycle? Listen to Eric. Read his book, and you will come away with a better understanding of the role of technology in the workplace.

CHAPTER TAKEAWAYS

- Technology moves at lightning speed. Before an interview, search the Internet for the latest technology innovations and learn how they will impact the workplace.
- Speaking intelligently about technology with a hiring manager is a must.
- Continuously update your technology skills by taking online courses or classroom courses at your local college.
- Working from your home operations center is productive and economical. Explore companies that permit this practice.

THE VETERAN'S LIBRARY

Maynard Webb and Carlye Adler. *Rebooting Work*. Wiley, 2013.

Jared Cohen and Eric Schmidt. *The New Digital Age: Reshaping the Future of People, Nations and Business*. Random House, 2013.

Laszlo Bock. **Work Rules!:** *Insights from Inside Google That Will Transform How You Live and Lead*. Hachette Book Group, 2015.

Peter Diamandis. *Abundance: The Future Is Better Than You Think*. Simon & Schuster, 2012.

Peter Diamandis. *BOLD: How to Go Big, Create Weather and Impact the World*. Simon & Schuster, 2015.

Chapter 15

Using Social Media for Civilian Job Hunting

Veterans have come to rely on digital devices for every purpose under the sun. Given that you used social media in the military for a variety of personal and possibly military purposes, it *seems* to make sense that you can use social media for job hunting, too. Right? We are living in a digital world, so why not go to the social media from the get-go instead of creating a work plan first? It seems to make good sense. Or does it?

WHAT THE "EXPERTS" ARE SAYING

There is an increasing amount of media hype about the use of social media and digital devices for job hunting. It's a hot topic, and while reporters are always looking for a good story, they frequently ignore the *rest of the story.* Sure, you can use *some* of the media to find job leads, but what happens after that? Your smartphone may have been instrumental in finding the job lead for the customer service position at AT&T, but that is just the beginning. As you move forward in the employment process, it becomes more personal, like knowing the name of a hiring authority inside of a company and then establishing a personal relationship.

The noise on the street considers social media the panacea for finding a job. What you frequently hear is that face-to-face communication, shaking hands, and having a cup of joe with a hiring manager are passé. As Phyllis Korkki wrote in an article in the *Wall Street Journal*, "Old-fashioned personal networking can still be an effective way to land a job but online networking now supplements it in many fields." I do not agree with Phyllis, because the evidence shows that using digital media exclusively is the least effective method of finding a job. Sorry, Phyllis. Try job hunting using social media and you will come away with a different point of view.

An article published in a recent issue of the *Wall Street Journal* caught my attention. The headline was "Job Hunting Moves to Mobile Devices." This cleverly written article used several examples of workers who found *job leads* by accessing job boards using social media on mobile devices. Finding job leads on job boards is nothing new. It has been going on ever since job boards and desktop computers came together decades ago. However, the article is misleading, because it gives the reader the impression that the use of social media *per se* is the new way to go job hunting. Nothing could be further from reality.

BREAKFAST IN THE DIGITAL WORLD

Can using social media lead to a civilian job? Can Twitter lead you to the Promised Land? Facebook? Pinterest? I'll cut through the rhetoric and begin by relating what happened recently while I was having breakfast at a local restaurant. A real-life example is always the best teacher.

Breakfast at Fred's Restaurant in New Hope, Pennsylvania

I was sitting at the counter having breakfast at this neighborhood restaurant, when a man in his late twenties dressed in jeans, a purple t-shirt, and sneakers occupied the empty seat next to me. His natural red hair was very long but becoming, and his beard was full but attractive. He reminded me of a young Zeus. He placed his iPhone on the counter. Not to be outdone, I placed my Droid 4G Razor beside

my plate. He ordered an omelet with bacon and rye toast, and I had
my favorite: blueberry pancakes and sausage. After a few bites, we
began talking about the use of technology, and what he told me was
fascinating.

Zeus said that he was a software developer for a local company.
He used the various social media but in a very controlled way for both
personal use and work productivity. He had two technology jobs since
earning his bachelor's in computer technology several years ago. When
I asked how he secured his first job, he said he had used LinkedIn,
Twitter, and Facebook extensively, but those media did not land a
job, even though LinkedIn did provide networking opportunities. He
found employment through personal networking, especially through
meeting people at trade shows and conferences. He went on to say,
with conviction, that the only way to land a job is through meeting
people personally. He added that the best way to find hiring managers
is to attend conferences and trade shows, not bang away on social
media 24/7.

There you have it, a real-life story from a worker familiar with many
aspects of social media. I agree with Zeus. You need to contact living
human beings with a name and a title. Zeus will go a long way in his
career because he knows how to navigate the world of work by using
digital technologies creatively.

The point of this story should be obvious. Even though many
veterans are married to the various social media sites and use them
throughout the day, social media is not the universal answer to finding
a job. Using social media creatively as a tool in your plan for securing
employment places it in the proper perspective.

CLEAN UP YOUR ACT

All of us have done interesting, funny, and stupid things using social
media. Remember that picture you posted on Facebook of you and

your friends slugging down some Bud Lites and cheap wine in a bar somewhere in the world? And you might recall the YouTube video that you made before joining the military. You know, the one of you and some friends having a food fight at Mickey D's when you were a high school senior. Images and text that may have been hilarious just a few years ago are not viewed the same way in the civilian world of work, even at a company like Google or Facebook. The corporate world is a serious place, so you must follow the rules of business, which include proper and creative use of digital devices and social media. Play this game according to the rules of business.

Before you submit a resume or talk with a potential employer, delete every picture and message on your social media that reflects immaturity. Do it now, because hiring authorities vetting your candidacy are looking at Facebook, Twitter, YouTube, and other social media to learn who you *really* are. Even if you use Facebook only with family and close friends, get rid of the bad stuff. If you do not, you are jeopardizing your chances of finding your civilian job.

The primary use of social media is to locate potential employers, find job opportunities, and learn the names and titles of hiring managers so you can communicate with them and build a personal relationship. You can click away on your digital devices night and day, but nothing happens until you see the hiring manager face to face. Make that part of your work plan.

To illustrate the point, here is a true story about my recent encounter with a college senior who was about to receive her bachelor's degree.

Fiona of Florida

I was evaluating Fiona's candidacy and was impressed with both her resume and LinkedIn profile. She did a superlative job on both. Grammar and spelling? Perfect. Style and formatting? Perfect. Then I went to Twitter and found a picture that made Fiona look like a sophomore. When I advised her to get rid of it, she countered with, "The business world has become more informal. Pictures of candidates in crazy poses are just the way the world is. It's okay to be informal because that's the way work is today." Are you sure, Fiona? Tell that to a hiring manager, and you will receive a pleasant smile and a polite dismissal. Enjoy the sand in Cancun. You will be spending a lot of time there making crazy videos and banging away on your iPad instead of working to become self-sufficient and paying off your student loan.

In all fairness to Fiona, I can understand how this well-qualified candidate could have become confused about the world of work. Social media seems to have triumphed over reason. It is controlling the lives of many job candidates, both veterans and non-veterans. Don't fall into that trap.

EVALUATING SOCIAL MEDIA SITES

Let's get specific and examine social media sites by name, remembering that technology moves fast. Changes are always in the works. Stay updated, because *creative* use of social media could get you where you need to go—to the personal interview with a hiring manager who has the authority to say, "You're hired!" I'm limiting our discussion to the social media that I believe are most useful for job-hunting purposes.

Google and Bing

Google, Bing, and other search engines are powerful sites for learning where the jobs are. Some pundits liken them to social media. Creative use of these search engines can lead to niche job boards, names of hiring authorities, and company job postings. Begin by experimenting with various search strings until you find your target.

Google and Bing are tools for employers, too. When human resources directors are vetting your candidacy, the first thing they will do is enter your name on Google or Bing. Your name appears on the screen and they begin to learn who you really are. Next step? They go to LinkedIn, Twitter, Facebook, YouTube, Pinterest, and others.

Twitter, www.twitter.com.

For all the hype it receives, one would think that Twitter is the god of social media. It seems that everyone is using Twitter, from your friends all across the USA to the talking heads on CNN, Fox, CBS, NBC, and ABC. But how many people *really* use Twitter every day? According to statistics released by the Pew Research Center, only 8 percent of American adults who use the Internet use Twitter. That's a wakeup call for job seekers who think that *everyone* is on Twitter, even hiring authorities at Fortune 500 companies. The hype is greater than the reality. In addition, what happens when you post something stupid on Twitter? Here's an example that illustrates the importance of cleaning up your Tweets.

Ms. Seattle

Jean-Sun Hannah Ahn was twenty-two years old when she was crowned Miss Seattle in 2012. Following the crowning ceremony, she made some nasty postings on Twitter, such as "I seriously am hating Seattle right now" and "Ugh can't stand cold, rainy Seattle and the annoying people." The media latched on to these Tweets immediately, and despite her sincere apologies, the damage did not go away. It jeopardized her chances for winning future pageant competitions, like Miss America, to say nothing of her future job opportunities.

Twitter in Proper Perspective

Messages on Twitter are limited to 140 characters, just enough to tell your friend in San Diego, "I've responded to 400 tweets and sent out 300 resumes, but I still don't have a job. There's nothing out there!" The communication medium used most frequently by adults in the world of work is email, and the number one medium for gathering information is still the Internet search engines. Twitter's use for job searching is limited, but companies have found it a tool for marketing and customer service.

Using Twitter Creatively for Job Hunting

The problem with Twitter is that it can become addictive. You can receive and send Tweets all day and come up with little helpful information for your job search. Twitter will suck up your time like nothing else. To use it effectively, first develop a plan similar to Kara's.

Kara from North Carolina

Kara graduated from a North Carolina college with a degree in Communications. Kara used Twitter in a very creative manner. First, she created a job-hunting plan for Twitter; then she worked her plan. She targeted local corporate presidents and CEOs, and in doing so, found the president of a local company and learned that he made frequent visits to his company's district and regional offices. In addition, she learned that he attended trade shows across the USA. He used Twitter to keep his constituents apprised of his whereabouts. Kara bought into his network and began responding to his Tweets that highlighted his itinerary. She tweeted her interest in his travels, his company, and his mission, all of which caught his attention. Kara was, in effect, building a relationship. One of her Tweets to the president focused on her college experience and her search for an internship. He responded by requesting that Kara call his administrative assistant to schedule a personal interview at the company home office. Kara's interview was a hit and she landed her internship.

The Internet and various media provide much advice for using Twitter. So does your next-door neighbor. In addition, so does your veteran friend in Edina, Minnesota. However, Twitter itself provides timely advice for using its product, so start there. The landscape is always changing, so check the Twitter website periodically. Most of what you read online has limited value, and some information is just plain misleading. For example, Twitter can send you a stream of jobs, but few will match your background and experience.

If you must use Twitter, create a separate Twitter account exclusively for job-hunting purposes. Do not load your new Twitter account with sophomoric images. Make sure it jibes with your resume and LinkedIn profile. Finally, do not use a cutesy handle like @CityDudeJoe, or @ hotwiremary.

Sina Wiebo. The Chinese Answer to Twitter

Twitter may be a topic of conversation during interviews, so learn all you can about its function as a *marketing tool* in business. You might even want to show how current you are by telling the interviewer about what is happening in China. Why China? Because it is the second largest economy in the world (which soon may overtake the USA as number one), and chances are good that your future employer will be working with the Chinese.

China's version of Twitter is Sina Wiebo, and more than 260,000 companies use it, primarily for marketing and damage control (like making apologies to consumers for poor service or gaffs that customers find offensive). The term itself literally means "New-wave Micro-blog." The messages are called micro-blogs and can include videos, images, and hyperlinks. It has over 500 million users, about 30 percent of all Chinese Internet users. More than 100 million messages travel over Sina Wiebo each day. The Chinese version is www.wiebo.com and the English version, launched in 2014, is www.wieboenglish.com.

Fastweb, www.fastweb.com.
This site provides useful information for job searching with Twitter. The advice is displayed in non-technical terms, so everyone can understand and apply the basic and advanced rules.

YouTube, www.youtube.com.

Can a video lead you to a job? Yes, it can, but you must be judicious when using a video as a tool for job hunting. First, remove anything from your archives that will make you look foolish and immature. If you have a video that presents you in a good light, submit it to a potential employer as an addendum to your digital resume. The video does not replace the resume or career profile, contrary to what you hear from video aficionados.

Employers like to see evidence that you were able to initiate a project and see it through to a successful conclusion. As a veteran, you have that experience. You might even have a YouTube video illustrating that qualification. Refrain from submitting a video with marginal value. There is nothing more harmful to your candidacy than a video that lacks mature subject matter and competent production. Peggy McKee of Career Confidential specializes in job-hunting strategies, one of which is producing videos. For more information, access her website, www.CareerConfidential.com.

Facebook, www.facebook.com.

Some social media sites, like Facebook, include job postings by companies, both large and small, some of which include the names of their executives, hiring managers, and human resources directors.

Facebook has a reputation for being a hangout for high school and college students to have fun and post pictures of themselves doing things that adults consider immature. Once you have had your Facebook images blasted all over the world, how do you recover? We all know that once your images are out there, it is difficult to get rid of them. For help, go to the Facebook site and check the Internet for other sources that will help you clean up your Facebook page. Also, consider creating a new Facebook account for job-hunting purposes only.

Indeed, www.indeed.com.

Indeed came online in 2004 and ranks high among social media job-hunting sites. Indeed is really a job aggregator that lists thousands of job postings from competitors' websites, job boards, company career pages, newspapers, and any other source that posts job opportunities. Enter a job title, a specific company if you wish, and a location. Indeed will provide job listings that match your criteria.

However, there is a yellow flag with Indeed job postings. Most do not provide the name of the hiring manager. Sending a resume off to a job number is a waste of time. To be productive, you must send your resume or career profile to a named person with a title. You can find those names on LinkedIn or by calling the company customer service department and asking for the name of a specific department's hiring manager or human resources director.

Indeed works the other side of the job search business as well. You can upload your resume at no charge. Also, the advanced search option permits you to focus on a specific job by title.

Simply Hired, www.simplyhired.com.
Simply Hired is a job aggregator similar to Indeed. However, it not only posts jobs but also provides job trend information, including the latest on salaries. It has a convenient "jobs by category" list for quick access to specific jobs in a specific location. For example, I clicked on "accounting" and found a multitude of accounting-related jobs world-wide. Under "healthcare," there were job listings for support personnel, professional personnel such as doctors and midwives, and for health-care administrators.

Employment trend information is a valuable feature of this site. It compares specific job trends using metrics derived from Simply Hired's database of users. When I clicked on "accounting," I learned there has been virtually no increase in the number of accounting jobs available during the past two years.

Craigslist, www.craigslist.com.
I'm surprised that many job seekers ignore Craigslist, the number one place to find *local* jobs. Small businesses employ more than 50 percent of American workers and most search for local workers using

local media. The postings on Craigslist are interesting and cover the full gamut of industries and jobs. For example, I checked Craigslist recently and found a retail sales consultant position with AT&T in Flemington, New Jersey. What an interesting entry-level position with a great American name in the communications industry! Also, I viewed a sales position for a family owned and operated fencing company in New Jersey. The posting included a phone number. You know how convenient that is. All you need to do is call the number and ask for the name and contact information of the hiring manager to begin building a personal relationship.

I suggest that you set aside ten minutes each day to check Craigslist for job postings in your local area. Craigslist jobs have a tendency to come and go quickly because of the local listing feature. Act quickly when you see something interesting.

Pinterest, www.pinterest.com.
This site has been attracting millions of visitors, but it is not by any means your ticket to the Promised Land. Pinterest is a site where users share their special interests by posting or pinning photos on a pin-board. It is clever, cute, and entertaining but has little value for job hunting. However, some companies are now using Pinterest, and they may begin pinning job opportunities on their company pinboards. Check this site occasionally for changes that could target job hunters more actively.

LinkedIn, www.linkedin.com.
The most valuable social medium in your search for employment is LinkedIn. LinkedIn is a site designed exclusively for the workplace, and if used properly, it can be one of your most important job-hunting tools. After you sign up, you will be able to post your photo and your profile, which will be seen by thousands of workers and hiring managers.

Both companies and individuals can post their profiles on LinkedIn. For example, I just entered the name of an American corporate icon,

Harley-Davidson, www.harleydavidson.com. I learned that this motor-cycle manufacturer has been in business for one hundred years, is based in Wisconsin, and has regional offices and dealerships in every state in the US. Here's what else I did when I was on LinkedIn. I conducted a search for the name of the Harley-Davidson human resources director and got it immediately along with her photo and contact information. The entire process took less than a minute and gave me the name of a key player in one of our most respected companies. Check the Harley website for career postings. They may have something just for you.

I find LinkedIn a valuable source for finding both job candidates and client companies. Each day, I receive several invitations from work-ers at every level to join their LinkedIn network. After viewing their online profile, I either accept or decline, depending on several criteria I use to sort out workers who will be valuable members of my network.

LinkedIn has several levels of membership. The higher the level of membership, the higher the cost. As you go up the chain, you will have access to more information and more details about the individuals or companies you want to reach. I suggest that you take the lowest level of membership, which is free. Take the time now and sign up, because LinkedIn is the one social media/networking site dedicated exclusively to the world of work.

LinkedIn members hold positions from entry-level support workers to managers, directors, vice presidents, presidents, and CEOs. Once you become familiar with LinkedIn, you can become a member of a sub-group dedicated to one specific area of employment, such as marketing, sales, or information technology. Once you connect with such a group, you can view job openings across the entire spectrum of businesses. For example, recently I received notices from the International Society for Technology Education (ISTE) for the following job openings:

- Editorial Director, Victoria's Secret
- President, Connecticut Audubon Society
- President, Columbia Consulting Group
- Business Development Director, Simply Hired

These are jobs for experienced workers, but LinkedIn has not forgotten entry-level job candidates. For example, they have created a special group called "Recent College Grads." This group is a must for veterans seeking entry-level positions or above. Once you are in, you will receive daily reports about the state of the job market generally and job postings specifically. Here are just a few of the jobs I saw recently:

- Business Analyst
- Technical Customer Support Specialist
- Business Intelligence Trainee
- Sales Representative
- Java Developer Trainee

In addition, a number of recruiters belong to this group and post jobs frequently. You cannot go wrong accessing LinkedIn every day.

LinkedIn for Veterans, www.veterans.linkedin.com.
This site offers a free one-year premium account to all veterans who complete the online application. It provides advanced tools for contacting hiring authorities and collaborating with groups helping veterans in transition, like the Veteran Mentor Network (VMN). Incorporate this site into your daily work plan.

WRITING A DIGITAL PROFILE TO USE WITH SOCIAL MEDIA

The digital profile is a document used with social media sites like LinkedIn. It is a condensed version of your resume with modifications required by the site posting it. The key point to remember is that your digital profile must be consistent with your resume. Most social media will define the format of your profile and even limit its length. When constructing your profile, have your written resume at your side to use as a guide. For more information about creating a digital profile and to see a sample, refer to Chapter 25.

MOVING FORWARD

One of the key messages of this book is that company hiring authorities do not hire resumes, Tweets, YouTube videos, texts, or emails. They hire warm, living human beings, like you, who take the time to find their names and contact them personally. Social media sites are not replacing personal communication. They are simply tools for job hunting and will be helpful in your search . . . if used appropriately.

CHAPTER TAKEAWAYS

- Use social media as a tool, not a panacea, for job hunting.
- LinkedIn is where the hiring managers hang out.
- Your resume and digital profiles must say the same thing.
- Clean up your social media profiles.

THE VETERAN'S LIBRARY

Joshua Waldman. *Job Searching with Social Media for Dummies*. Wiley, 2013.

Chapter 16

Online Technology and Business Certification

In the civilian world of work, technology skills and business knowledge are necessary components for an attention-getting career profile. Many veterans hold an advantage over non-veteran civilians because of the technology skills learned in the military. However, all veterans need to update their technology skills periodically by completing online courses and tests that offer a written certificate of completion. The same applies for business certification, even for those veterans with military experience that involved using business applications.

There are hundreds of online courses for technology and business certification. Some of them are inexpensive or even free; others are very costly. Many providers are no-name organizations, while others are known entities like Microsoft and Cisco. Completion of specialized courses may take one or two years. Rudimentary or introductory courses may take only weeks or months.

TECHNOLOGY AND BUSINESS SKILLS

There are general technology skills that everyone must have to conduct work productively. These include a working knowledge of word processing, databases, spreadsheets, and online research. Some of the common apps for traditional business applications are Microsoft Office Suite, PowerPoint, Adobe Creative Suite (especially if you are in marketing or design), and Adobe Muse, which is used for HTML design. In addition, social media are finding their way into business as companies are increasingly using these products in their marketing initiatives.

An increasing number of jobs require specific skills that go beyond those mentioned above. Carefully read the requirements in every job description to learn what you will need to compete for that position.

WHERE TO GO FOR TRAINING AND CERTIFICATION

There are many options for training and certification and we suggest that you go online to find courses that fit your needs. Remember that your employer, or potential employer, may offer its own proprietary business and technology courses that could be mandatory or optional.

There are many options available for veterans, and **OJS** has identified some of the best online sources:

The Department of Veterans Affairs (VA), www.va.gov. The GI Bill provides funding for veterans taking certain online entrance examinations, certification and licensing tests, and correspondence courses under the Veterans Educational Assistance Program (VEAP). To learn more, go to the VA website and enter "VEAP" in the search box.

Army and Navy COOL Programs, www.cool.navy.mil and www.cool. army.mil. The Department of Defense COOL (Credentialing Opportunities On-Line) programs help veterans find information about certifications and licenses related to their Military Occupational Specialties (MOS). COOL explains how veterans can meet civilian certification and license requirements and provides links to numerous resources to help get them started. Education, career, and transition counselors provide guidance on education, professional growth, and career requirements and opportunities. COOL contains information about credentialing and licensing and can be used to:

- Find background information about civilian licensure and certification in general, as well as specific information on individual credentials, including eligibility requirements and resources, to prepare for a credentialing exam

- Identify licenses and certifications relevant to your MOS
- Learn how to fill gaps between military training/experience and civilian credentialing requirements
- Discover resources available to veterans that will help them gain civilian job credentials

When you transition back to civilian employment, credentials help you translate your military training and experience into something civilian employers can easily recognize.

HigherNext and *ProctorU,* www.proctoru.com. HigherNext, recently purchased by ProctorU, offers a flagship standardized business and technology skills exam that enables job seekers to demonstrate their business and technology skills to employers in uniform and measurable ways. Upon successful completion of this online course, HigherNext awards a written certification called the Certified Business Laureate (CBL) degree. It is an impressive document to present to a prospective employer as part of your career profile package. The cost for the CBL certification is low, and it is a valuable job-hunting tool. This is how it works:

1. Students take each test online, and they are proctored via the webcam.
2. Certification bundles are generated upon completion.
3. Test time: 15 minutes each.

Coursera, www.coursera.org. This online company offers courses spanning many curriculum areas, including business and technology, at attractive prices. However, it does charge a small fee for a written certification of course completion. It describes itself as "an education company that partners with the top universities and organizations in the world to offer courses online for anyone to take, for free." Coursera boasts over four million users and offers 389 courses. This California-based company was founded in 2012 by Dr. Daphne Koller, a professor in the Computer Science Department at Stanford University, and Andrew Ng, an associate professor of Computer Science at Stanford. Its Advisory Board consists of Chancellors and Provosts from major universities across the USA such as Princeton, Duke, and the University of Michigan. Course offerings include:

- Creative Programming for Digital Media and Social Apps
- Computer Networks
- Foundations of Business Strategy
- An Introduction to Financial Accounting
- Introduction to Data Science
- Internet History, Technology, and Security

In an article from the June 16, 2015, issue of the *Wall Street Journal*, Dr. Koller stated, "Online learning gives people the opportunity to pause and reflect and grapple with the material." Veterans, listen to Dr. Koller.

Alison, www.alison.com. This online company offers courses and certification free of charge, a very attractive price. Their many courses fall under major categories such as:

- Digital Literacy and Skills
- Business and Enterprise Skills
- Information Technology
- Entrepreneurial Skills
- Presentation Skills
- Financial and Economic Literacy

Association for Talent Development, www.astd.org. ASTD offers a business certification degree, which is something that you must explore. Here is an excerpt from the ASTD website about their certification course: "The ASTD Certification Institute's Certified Professional in Learning and Performance Certification (CPLP) equips you with the tools to be the best in the field and lets employers know that you have real world, practical expertise that can be readily applied to the current work environment." Download the CPLP Candidate brochure to find out more.

UMASSOnline, www.umassonline.net. This site offers the UMASS Lowell Information Technology Certificate. This is a very user-friendly site that offers a sample course before you buy into the program. Courses vary from three to six credit hours. UMASSOnline is an outstanding gateway to information technology and has won a number of prestigious awards.

Tom's IT Pro, www.tomsitpro.com. Tom's is a valuable site for exploring the best online IT courses that award certification. On the website, you will find descriptions of numerous IT online programs by category. For example, under the category "System Administrator Certificates" you will find the names of numerous organizations and companies offering this kind of certification. Included are Microsoft, Linux, and Red Hat. Explore Tom's. It will save you hours of time and lead you to the best information technology programs available.

Penn State Online, www.worldcampus.psu.edu. Pennsylvania State University offers many online courses leading to certifications. One of these is an online certificate course in Information Sciences and Technology. It is a four-course program offering thirteen credit hours of study. For details, check the Penn State Online website.

Many other colleges, universities, and independent entities offer technology and business certifications. Select one or more that align with your interests, academic background, and level of expertise. Do not select a course that is too advanced or too elementary. Do your homework and you will find the right program that matches your interests, aptitudes, and MOS.

REQUIRED CERTIFICATIONS

Certifications are required for workers holding positions in the building trades, transportation, insurance, medicine, food services, and many other industries. State and federal laws require these certifications and licenses for certain positions that may involve public health and safety. If you are exploring these careers, learn about the requirements first and make sure that the school you attend is qualified to issue the certifications you need.

Some positions require taking an examination for licensure as well. For example, lawyers and medical personnel must pass a state-issued exam in order to obtain a license to practice law or medicine in that state.

You can easily check the requirements for all certifications and licenses in your state by going online and entering a job type and the name of your state.

PROFESSIONAL CERTIFICATIONS WILL SET YOU APART FROM THE CROWD

Be assured that potential employers will assess your business and technology skills. Candidates who can prove they have these skills by presenting a written certification will have a distinct advantage over those who present only a resume. Presenting a written certification as part of your career profile will make you stand out from the rest of the pack. The civilian workplace is highly competitive, even with companies claiming to be "military friendly."

MOVING FORWARD

All jobs require technology and business skills, some of which you already have from your military work experience and other sources. To stand out from your competition, complete technology and business courses that carry certification. Incorporate the written certification document into the career portfolio you present to hiring managers. If you suspect that jobs you are planning to pursue may require certification and/or licensing, go to your state for more information. If your research indicates that these credentials are required, take immediate steps to obtain them. Why apply for jobs if you know ahead of time that you do not meet the requirements?

CHAPTER TAKEAWAYS

- Technology skills are a requirement in today's world of work.
- Written technology and business certifications will enhance your candidacy.
- When job hunting, you are in competition with thousands of candidates. Do everything you can to make your candidacy unique.

THE VETERAN'S LIBRARY

Lisa Guerin and Amy DelPo. *The Essential Guide to Federal Employment Laws*. Nolo, 2013.

Robert Kiyosaki. *Why "A" Students Work For "C" Students and Why "B" Students Work For the Government*. Plata Publishing, 2013.

PART IV

How and Where to Find Civilian Employers

There is no challenge you can't overcome. Never stop trying!
—*Kevin Treiber, Medic 91A, Veteran, Operation Desert Storm/Shield*

Chapter 17

How to Find Employers through Networking, Print Media, Cold Calling, Trade Shows, and Job Fairs

Employers do not come looking for you at home while you are sitting at your computer sending resumes to job boards and career pages. You must seek them out yourself. If this sounds like a daunting task, fear not, because here are certain tried and true methods for finding employers and their workers responsible for hiring. The people you need to contact personally are hiring managers and human resources directors. These are the people in large companies or small businesses who decide who is hired and who is not.

If you are seeking a job in sales, the person you need to reach is the sales manager. If you are pursuing a marketing job, the person you should see is the marketing director. If technology is your focus, the person you need to see is the chief technology officer (CTO) or chief information officer (CIO). If you are seeking a position in finance, the person you need to reach is the chief financial officer (CFO). If you are not sure what role you would like and are seeking opportunities generally, the person you need to see is the human resources director.

Sometimes people at the highest departmental rank will refer you to a subordinate who handles entry-level positions. That happens frequently. See the person to whom you are referred, and do not consider this a put down. Be assured that the department head always approves every person hired at every level. For every position, but especially for entry-level positions, the first interview is usually with the human resources director, who will then send the best candidates to the hiring manager, who will make the final decision.

FINDING THE DECISION MAKERS

How do you go about finding the people who have the authority to hire you? How do you learn their names and contact information? You may have had the experience of calling a company and asking for the director of sales to apply for a job only to have the receptionist tell you that all job applicants must go through the human resources department. Take it to the next level by asking for the name and contact information of the human resources director. You can learn the name and contact information for the human resources director or department head by using several methods:

- Googling the company and the department head title (i.e. "VP Sales for Walmart")
- Reviewing the company website for the names of executives
- Networking with friends, neighbors, and relatives who are employed
- Calling the company customer services department and asking for the name of the person you want to contact
- Using LinkedIn and entering the name of a company and a position
- Leaving the house and attending conferences and trade shows that take place almost every day in most large and medium-sized cities across the country
- Making cold calls at companies located in office and industrial parks

- Using "old-fashioned" methods like the *Yellow Pages* and newspapers

THE PROACTIVE JOB HUNTER

People who have the authority to hire you are lurking everywhere. You can find them in airports, on airplanes, in restaurants, bars, tapas joints, Starbucks, sports events—any location where people gather. However, just being in a crowd is not enough; you must be proactive.

When you're at Starbucks ordering a grande cappuccino, most likely the first thing you will do is look for a table that is unoccupied so you can whip out your smartphone or iPad and begin texting or Tweeting with your friends. This is not the way to find your potential boss. Select a table occupied by a person dressed in business attire because they are the people you want to know. Instead of Tweeting your life away, begin a conversation with the woman who is dressed for success and pounding away on her laptop. How do you begin the conversation? Begin with that all-time favorite, the weather. "It's really hot out today. Good thing this place has air-conditioning. By the way, you look like the president of a company. What do you do?" You have just opened the door, and who knows what is inside.

A CEO in my circle of business acquaintances found many entry-level employees for his sixty-million-dollar company that produced science supplies for schools and colleges in what may seem like an unorthodox way:

Paul from Buffalo

Paul started his business, Science Kit Inc., by purchasing a failing mom and pop company that produced a hobby kit of science materials for kids at the elementary school level and sold it in department stores. He transformed that kit into a major product in the school science supply business because he always found the right workers to get the job done. When I visited the company's home office in Buffalo, New York, I noticed an unusually high number of young adults, probably in the twenty- to thirty-year-old age bracket. Paul told me that he made a practice of hiring millennial age candidates who were smart, energetic, and passionate about finding their niche in the world of work. They did not have to be college graduates. Paul even paid tuition for promising workers to continue their formal education. I asked, "Where do you find candidates with such potential?" He responded that he traveled frequently by air and made a practice of getting to the airport early for candidate-hunting purposes. When he saw a person who was acceptably dressed and not texting or jabbering away on a smartphone, he began a conversation, which was really the beginning of an interview. If he liked what he saw and heard, he requested a resume and often scheduled another interview at his home office. His method of recruiting had a very high success rate because it began with a personal meeting.

HIRING MANAGERS ARE DRESSED FOR SUCCESS

One never knows the status of the person in business attire, but it is your job to find out. What's that you say? "Nobody really dresses up any more. The world of work has gone casual." Don't drink the Kool-Aid. Business executives on the job always dress in business attire. Even in the technology world, executive level people are dressed a cut above the people working in the trenches. Look for the people in business attire and you will find hiring managers and even people like Paul, the CEO. Here is a real-life example about how people of different rank dress in the business world.

Long Hair in Boston

I had an appointment with the CEO of a successful educational technology company in Boston to discuss a search for a director of marketing. I entered the building wearing a suit, tie, and leather shoes . . . all traditional business attire. What I saw was close to mayhem. There were workers everywhere in a large open space. Some were chatting animatedly with colleagues; others were sitting in a corner banging away on a laptop; still others were drinking sodas and looking into space. All had one thing in common: very casual dress and long unkempt hair. (Don't get me wrong. I have nothing against long hair, but I think there are some unwritten work rules that govern how we look and what we wear under certain circumstances.)

When I entered the executive offices, the scene changed dramatically. The CEO wore traditional business attire and so did the human resources director, and so did the vice president for marketing. All of these executives had the authority to hire job candidates.

There are three takeaways from this example:

1. When you see people dressed in business attire, they are usually managerial-level people who have hiring authority. You want to meet them personally.
2. Always dress in business attire when you go for a personal interview. After you are hired, you can dress as the culture dictates. The exceptions are outside sales people who always dress in traditional business attire because they are out meeting customers with purchasing authority.
3. Seek out people who are dressed for business at any venue and begin a conversation that can turn into an interview.

LOOKING FOR EMPLOYERS AND HIRING MANAGERS IN THE *YELLOW PAGES*

Another way to find employers may shock you. It is using the good old *Yellow Pages*. Prior to 1990, people used print books to find just about everything, including employers. One of the most useful books was the *Yellow Pages* phone directory. It is still being published for every location in the US, and it is a fascinating book to review. As all of you know, the *Yellow Pages* are online too. The directory for a large city like Chicago, Dallas, or New York City could run over a thousand pages. It lists all businesses alphabetically under industry headings.

For example, I just clicked on www.yellowpages.com and then entered "cosmetic companies, New York." The result? There were 799 hits, almost every single one a company dealing in cosmetics, from manufacturing to retail sales. Each company is a potential employer.

How to Use the *Yellow Pages*

Using the *Yellow Pages*, a mere phone directory, to look for a job in the digital age? What is this, some kind of joke? Before you write off the *Yellow Pages*, consider this real-life example:

Alan from Chicago

Alan was a middle school teacher in Chicago when he decided to explore alternate career opportunities. A friend of his was a sales rep for a textbook publishing company and suggested that he explore this line of work. Bright guy that Alan was, he went to the Chicago Yellow Pages and found the major heading "Publishers." Under that heading, he found dozens of publishers listed by type, and he found twelve companies that published textbooks. He called each company and asked the customer services representative for the name of the sales manager for the Chicago Metro Area. He scored every time. Armed with these twelve names he began a search for his first job in

> *the private sector. He called each manager and asked for a personal interview. The result? Five personal interviews and three job offers. He accepted an offer from a prominent publisher at a base salary that was twice what he was making as a teacher, plus a commission plan that yielded 50 percent of his base salary for meeting revenue goals, plus a company car, plus benefits. Thank you,* Yellow Pages!

Are the *Yellow Pages* for Real?

Could anything sounding so *yesterday* really help you find a civilian job in today's digital world? In the latest edition of the classic job-hunting book *What Color Is Your Parachute?* Richard Bolles lists the five best ways to look for a job. Guess what number three is? Using the *Yellow Pages*. Bolles's research revealed candidates using this method had a success rate exceeding 50 percent.

If you know the industry you want to explore, just go to that major heading and find the firms listed under that heading. If you are not sure what you want to do, flip through the *Yellow Pages* and note the major industry headings. One of them might be your cup of coffee. Finance. Education. Banking. Publishing. Retailing. Agriculture. Automobiles. Insurance. Healthcare. It's all there . . . in the *Yellow Pages*.

BACK TO THE FUTURE . . . AGAIN. FINDING EMPLOYERS USING THE NEWSPAPER

Reading the print or the digital versions of local, regional, or national newspapers is still one of the most productive ways to reach potential employers. One of the best newspapers is the *Wall Street Journal*. I call this daily newspaper America's most honest publication because its agenda makes no bones about helping people make money. Certain issues of the *Journal* have ads for jobs and advice for job seekers. I suggest that you subscribe to the *Journal* if you want an education about how the civilian workplace *really* works. Here is an example of what you will find there.

Recently I was reading the *Journal* and found the following quote in an op-ed written by Brad Smith, Executive Vice President and General Counsel of Microsoft:

> Many American companies are now creating more jobs for which they cannot find qualified applicants. At Microsoft, we have more than 6,000 open jobs in the US, a 15% increase from a year ago. Some 3,400 of these positions are for engineers, software developers and researchers.

Smith goes on to say that colleges need to try new methods for educating students so they will be better qualified to meet the needs of companies in the digital age. Executives in companies across the USA agree with Smith. Unfortunately, some veterans who are new to the job market believe that sources like newspapers and phone directories are of little value when you are job hunting. Well, think again and start reading traditional media.

By the way, the Microsoft URL is www.Microsoft.com. A couple of clicks will tell you what's happening there. It is a great employer, and it might have a job for you. And you do not have to be a whiz-bang techie to get a job there.

What else can the newspapers do for you? The local newspaper is where local employers will advertise local jobs. You will find their job postings in the classified sections of print and digital newspapers. Usually the weekend versions carry the most job postings.

FINDING EMPLOYMENT THROUGH INTERNSHIPS

Internships, paid and unpaid, are a great way to segue to permanent civilian employment in the public or private sectors. How do you find them? On the websites of employers you are exploring. Google "internships for veterans" and you will find much information about how to explore this route to permanent employment. I did just that and found a fascinating internship program for veterans at the New York Stock Exchange. It was listed by *Business Insider*, www.businessinsider.com. Veterans participating in this internship program work side by side with experienced NYSE workers. The human resources director for NYSE said, "We're not asking these vets to come in here and know everything about a certain job. They have leadership skills and motivation. We can train them on the technical skills."

This is an exciting beginning to a successful civilian job search and we urge you to get on board. The site provides the stories and photos of three recent veterans speaking about their internship experience here. What could be more exciting than working with the NYSE staff dedicated to helping veterans transition to civilian employment? Veterans, when you discover an opportunity like this, act right away. Such opportunities do not last long.

Other companies advertising internships for veterans were Disney, General Electric, and J.P. Morgan. The Veterans Administration (VA) has an active internship program for veterans, too.

NETWORKING

The primary purpose of networking is to connect personally with someone who can help you secure a job. Who are these people? Everyone who is presently employed by a company or who owns a business is a networking source. Where do you find them? They are as close as your next-door neighbor. Here are sources for connecting with a person who can steer you in the right direction.

Your Former Boss

Before joining the military, or while working part-time during college, you reported to someone familiar with your services. Your boss. Contact those persons and ask for the names of hiring managers at their present employer. Also, you might ask that person for a letter of recommendation. Do not overlook this obvious resource. Most people are willing to help veterans in their job searches. Here's an example of what happened when a worker solicited the help of a former boss.

Laura from New Jersey

When she graduated from Penn State with a BA in Communications, Laura thought the world was waiting for her with great jobs paying big bucks. However, her first job was a part-time stint running a Christmas show for a local department store in Philadelphia. When that job ended, she solicited help from her original networking source, her former boss, who gave her the name of a hiring manager at a video production company in Philadelphia. She was hired as a temp worker to stand in for the receptionist who was going on a three-month pregnancy leave. Laura worked the front desk and the executive staff took notice. Coincidentally, an operations manager position opened up, and Laura hit pay dirt. She landed a full-time job with a successful video production company and a year later was promoted to production manager. Laura says it is all about getting your foot in the door, even as a part-time worker, and that you can do that using networking sources.

Laura went on to have a successful career with her employer, all the result of networking. Here is another example of what a former boss can do for you.

Alice from Pennsylvania

When Alice graduated from James Madison University with a BA in Music Education, she was not sure about pursuing a career in the classroom and looked at other opportunities in the business of music. While working as a volunteer host at JMU's public radio station, Alice took advantage of radio industry job opportunities posted by NPR and the Corporation for Public Broadcasting.

It so happened that the station chief engineer, to whom she reported, noticed an opening for which he thought Alice would be qualified. He brought it to Alice's attention, and the job was right

> *up her alley. KCND, a start-up radio station in Bismarck, North Dakota, had a full-time opening for a classical music host/producer. Alice immediately submitted her resume, audition tape, and photo. After several phone interviews with the station's general manager and operations manager, she was offered an on-air, full-time afternoon hosting position, which she accepted. It could not have happened without a referral source, her boss.*

Breaking into professional radio in a specialized area like classical music is no easy task, but Alice applied her intelligence, energy, and passion and used her networking resource to her advantage. Although the pay was minimal, Alice received valuable working experience at her first job out of college. She has since gone on to work successfully for other public radio stations. Now she is the program director for WWFM, The Classical Network, in Trenton, New Jersey.

Referrals from a Company Employee

A candidate referred by an employee of the company has an excellent chance of getting the job. In fact, many companies give monetary rewards to employees who refer a candidate the company hires. Looking down the road a year or two after you are employed, you will see that an internal candidate has the best chance at winning a promotion. The networking continues even while you're employed. This does not ensure that the company always gets the best candidate, but that's the way it works. Fair or not, that is just the way it works.

USING THE COLD CALL METHOD TO FIND HIRING MANAGERS

Before we begin our discussion, we need to be mindful of the importance of people called "gatekeepers," those who control access to the people you want to see. There are gatekeepers in every company, one of the most important being the receptionist at the front desk. When cold calling, the receptionist is the first person you will meet. These individuals can make or break you, and you must treat them with respect and build a relationship quickly. Your appearance and introductory remarks are critical. The receptionist will dismiss anyone demanding, disrespectful, or dressed inappropriately.

The Cold Call Process

Some veterans may have had experience cold calling, but let's start from the beginning to make sure we are all on the same page. The process begins when you enter an office without an appointment. You tell the receptionist that you are seeking a position and would like to meet with the human resources director or hiring manager for a specific department. If you are focusing on a specific position, such as an associate marketing manager, ask to see the hiring manager in charge of marketing. If you are seeking a position in sales, ask for the sales manager. Your introductory statement to the receptionist, accompanied by a smile, might go something like this: "Good morning, Ms. Jones. My name is William Foster. I'm an Iraq military veteran and I'm seeking a position in information technology. May I please speak with your technology director?"

The receptionist will respond in one of several ways:

1. "Our technology director is Mrs. Deborah George and I'll see if she's available." Your response might be, "Thank you. I would appreciate only a few minutes of her time. I know she's a busy person."

2. "Our technology director is Mr. Adams, but he's out of the office today." Your response might be, "Thank you. In that case, may I speak with his administrative assistant to make an appointment to see him?"

3. "We do not have a technology director." Your response might be, "Thank you. In that case, may I speak with the human resources director?"

4. "I'm sorry, you need an appointment to see any of our staff members." Your response might be, "Thank you. May I please have the name of your human resources director and the email address and phone number? I'll call for an appointment as you suggested."

Note that your response should always begin with a "thank you." Also note that you never just say "thank you" and walk out. That is not the way it works in the civilian business world. You are calling there because this is a business deal. You are selling yourself and the company is always looking for new talent, like you. Be professionally assertive, but courteous, until you get what you want and need. In addition, always state your status as a military veteran.

Cold Calls Are Always in Style

Some consider making personal calls on potential employers without an appointment something out of yesterday's playbook. Wrong! The purpose of the cold call is to arrange a personal interview with a hiring manager.

Cold calling is not easy at first, but the more calls you make the easier it will become. Also, you risk rejection when you make a cold call, and that is not easy. Do not take it personally. Over time, your technique will improve and you will learn that rejection is not a personal insult but part of the business process.

The odds of something happening are in your favor, as the numbers will show. Assume that you make fifteen cold calls per week on potential employers in an industrial or office park. At the end of one month, you will have made sixty calls where you spoke with a real person, a receptionist, an administrative assistant, a human resources director, or a hiring manager. Assuming a success rate of only 10 percent, at the end of one month you will have met personally with six influential people. Compare that to the number of personal interviews you will have had if you stayed at home and fired off resumes to unknown entities.

What Do Hiring Authorities Say about Cold Calls?

Recently, I attended an education industry conference in Baltimore and spoke with several vice presidents in charge of sales, marketing, and product development. (By the way, the education industry consists of those companies that produce and provide instructional materials, supplies, and services to K-12 schools and post-secondary institutions. It has nothing to do with teaching. Some companies in the education industry are: McGraw-Hill, College Board, ETS, Pearson, Scholastic, and a host of other companies both large and small.) Their take on how job candidates go about job hunting was remarkable.

All said they would run to see a candidate who knocked on their door without an appointment (i.e. making a cold call). They consider resumes that come in through human resources or addressed to Box 29 just that, a document unattached to a living human being. Even if the cold call candidate did not connect on that first try, the vice presidents said they would place that candidate on a "must-see" list when they had the time.

HOW TO FIND EMPLOYERS AT CONFERENCES AND TRADE SHOWS

The best way to find potential employers in the flesh is to attend conferences, trade shows, job fairs, and conventions. Here you will find a multitude of potential employers, all under one roof. Attending conferences at major convention centers like McCormick Place in Chicago or the Javits Center in New York City is the best use of your job-hunting time. In fact, I so strongly believe in this method of finding a job that I have devoted an entire chapter to it. In Chapter 20, I will tell you where the convention halls are located and advise you what to do once you are there and faced with hundreds or thousands of booths occupied by potential employers. I know from first-hand experience that many candidates have met their potential employers on the floor of a convention center; in fact, candidates are sometimes even hired right there.

FINDING EMPLOYERS AT BUSINESS AND INDUSTRIAL PARKS

In every metropolitan area, you will find office, business, and industrial parks—places where hundreds of different companies locate their local offices, home offices, or regional offices. Some parks specialize in one particular industry while others host companies from different industries. For example, an industrial park in Langhorne, Pennsylvania, specializes in medical offices for both physicians and dentists. An industrial park in Portland, Maine, hosts a diversified group of companies including J. Weston Walch Publishing Company, a ninety-year-old educational publisher.

How do you contact companies in a business or industrial park? Easy. You leave the house at 8 a.m. in your business attire and armed with business cards and two dozen career profiles or resumes to distribute to hiring managers and human resources directors. You go from door to door and request a personal meeting with the hiring manager in charge of your field of interest.

One might ask, "Do I make a cold call on every business in the business park?" If you are job hunting for any kind of job regardless of industry or position, the answer is *yes*. If you are interested only in positions with insurance companies as an underwriter, sales representative, or claims adjuster, you narrow the cold calls to insurance companies. You determine who these companies are by checking out the names of the companies in the business or office park on the website beforehand.

Use the Internet to Find Business Parks

There are many business, office, and industrial parks in every area of the country and the best way to find out where they are is to google a phrase like "business parks in Denver, Colorado." I did just that and found the Denver Tech Center, an area along the I-25 corridor southeast of Denver. This business park is home to more than sixty companies spanning a number of industries. The list includes Agilent Technologies, Boeing, Cargill, Centex Homes, J.P. Morgan, Kodiak

Petroleum, Morgan Stanley, Nissan Motor Corp., Time Warner Cable, and Western Union. These are either home offices or regional offices and are potential employers. If you live in the Denver Metro Area, start cold calling at the companies located here to find your first civilian job.

Here is another example of what you will find. I googled "industrial parks in Houston, Texas" and found the Beltway Industrial Park, where light manufacturing companies are located. Industrial parks in other locations host large manufacturers as well as warehouses and regional offices.

Do you live in Seattle? Enter "Seattle business parks." I did that and found enough potential employers (and their locations) to keep me busy job hunting for the next six months.

No matter where you live in the US, you will find office parks, business parks, and industrial parks. Google using all three names, and you will find companies galore to explore for your civilian job.

FINDING EMPLOYERS AT JOB FAIRS

Attending job fairs is an excellent way to meet potential employers and their hiring managers. There are hundreds available throughout the year at a location within driving distance from your home. Some job fairs are general in nature and others are industry specific, job specific, and candidate specific. For example, some job fairs are exclusively for veterans. Select your area of interest and attend.

The managers you will meet have one thing in mind: to find the best candidates for job openings. It is all business, so you must go prepared, just as you would for attending a trade show. That means bringing a dozen resumes and calling cards, as well as dressing appropriately. How you dress could take you to the top of the heap or put you in the trashcan.

How do you learn where and when the job fairs are, particularly those for veterans? The best source I have found is Military.com. Go to the website, www.military.com, and then click on "Job Fairs." You will find a list of twenty to thirty veteran-specific job fairs by location and date. Click on a specific listing and you will find all the details. Truly, this is a treasure trove of information for veterans.

Other sources for job fair listing include:

- Recruit Military, www.recruitmilitary.com
- Hire Veterans, www.hireveterans.com/jobfairs
- US Chamber of Commerce Foundation, www.uschamber-foundation.org/hiring-our-heroes

GOING ONLINE TO MAKE THE RIGHT CONNECTION

Using online resources creatively can return positive benefits, but it is necessary to proceed with caution because online job hunting can chew up your time like nothing else. Studies show that using digital media is the least effective way to find employment, but I have found one exception, LinkedIn, which you may consider a networking place as well.

Using LinkedIn

The best employment networking site is LinkedIn. For those not familiar with LinkedIn, here is an example of how it works. If you are interested in the broadly defined area of information technology, enter that term in the LinkedIn search box and you will find the names and contact information for many people in that field. I did that just now by entering "sales managers" and came up with the names of 134 contacts, all of them networking sources and some of them hiring managers.

Using Job Boards

Job boards have yielded disappointing results for many job hunters. Candidates and companies using the boards have a success rate of less than 15 percent. My assessment of the boards is that most fail to connect you with a named person, a hiring authority, and in many cases even a named company. When you respond to a posting on a board, your resume goes to Job #234 or Position #456. You might as well send your resume to Jupiter, Mars, or the third ring of Saturn.

Reviewing Corporate Websites

If you want to see what is happening at consumer goods companies, like Procter & Gamble, it makes sense to review their websites and check out their career pages. However, do not assume that all available jobs are posted on company websites. Many jobs, entry-level as well as established jobs, are posted elsewhere or given to recruiters.

I suggest that you begin with the military friendly companies, which we discussed in Chapter 3. Before we move on, here is an example of how to reach the right person when you see a website posting:

Customer Service Workers

The publisher of the Occupational Outlook Handbook *is JIST Publishing Co. I accessed the website, www.jist.empc.com, and clicked on the "Careers" button. I found job openings in California, Texas, Tennessee, Kentucky, West Virginia, New York City, and New Jersey. If you see a position you like and want to apply, do not send your resume to "Employment at emcp.com" as the company requests. Instead, call the customer service number and ask for the name and email address of the human resources director. Too bold? I did just that and the customer service rep gave me the name and email address for the human resources director. No questions asked. What could be easier?*

While tracking down the human resources director at JIST, I learned about another valuable source of information: the customer service representative. These individuals are trained to be helpful, courteous, and just plain nice. If you want information about a company, always call the number listed for the customer service department, not the general company number. Alternatively, you can contact the customer service department online for help, but I recommend using the phone because it establishes a more personal relationship. When you reach this person on the phone, simply state your case like this: "I'm Barbara Smith. I'm a military veteran and want to contact your human resources director about job opportunities. Could you please give me her or his name and email address and phone number?" Enter the name, phone number, and email address of the customer service rep in your database and then follow up by contacting the human resources director to develop the relationship.

MOVING FORWARD

This chapter reviewed *how* we find employers using tried and true methods. The best method is leaving the house to make personal contacts at conventions, conferences, and trade shows. In the following chapter, we'll tell you *where* to find employers.

CHAPTER TAKEAWAYS

- Nothing happens until you leave the house to meet potential employers personally.
- Attending conferences is the best way to meet potential employers.
- Dress and appearance do matter, especially during the interview process.
- Treat the gatekeepers with respect.
- Business parks are fertile hunting grounds to locate employers.

THE VETERAN'S LIBRARY

Sheryl Sandberg. *Lean In: Women, Work, and the Will to Lead*. Knopf, 2013.

Standard and Poor's. *Standard & Poor's 500 Guide 2013: America's Most Watched Companies*. McGraw-Hill, 2013.

Michael Faulkner and Andrea Nierenberg. *Networking for Veterans: A Guidebook for a Successful Military Transition into the Civilian Workforce*. Pearson Learning Solutions, 2012.

Chapter 18

Where to Find Employers. Who Is Hiring?

It all sounds so easy: find counseling at the VA, scour the job boards, send out a few resumes, and a job will follow. All veterans wish it were so simple. You know jobs are out there, but where? And how do you tap into our vast job market? Does it make any difference where you work? Isn't working as an associate director of marketing with a manufacturer like Ford Motors the same as working as an associate director of marketing for a technology company like Apple? Marketing is marketing. It makes no difference, or does it? Are there significant differences between working for a *service producer* like Mass Mutual Insurance Company and working for a *goods producer* like Pepsi Cola? The short answer is yes. There is a difference. But how do you decide what sectors and what companies to explore for potential employment? Where are all of these jobs?

The American economy is so large and varied that we need a road map to learn how it breaks down into its component parts. Knowing something about the components will provide direction for your search and save you time and energy. In addition, knowledge of the differences between a *service producer* and a *goods producer* will help you to understand where to locate employers of interest to you.

THE SCOPE OF THE AMERICAN ECONOMY

The scope of the American job market is vast, so vast that it can be confusing listening to the financial experts on CNBC, Bloomberg, and Fox as they speak glibly about the world of work, sometimes using vocabulary that leaves you in the dark. Occasionally you will hear them talk about the size of the American workforce and how that relates to employment. Rarely will they tell you *where* you can find employers at any given time in the economic cycle.

To begin learning where the jobs are, let's divide the workforce into bite-size chunks for easy understanding. There are two broad divisions in our economy, which can be broken down into numerous subsections.

AMERICAN JOB SECTORS

The Bureau of Labor Statistics divides the American economy into two main parts or job sectors: the *goods* producing industries and the *services* producing industries. What will it be for you, event planning manager for Hyatt, a *services producing* company, or customer service representative for California-based Callaway Golf Company, a *goods producing* company? (By the way, both have jobs available. Go to their websites, www.hyatt.com and www.callawaygolf.com, and click on "Careers.")

Let us examine each sector, keeping in mind that most veterans will probably be working in one of these two sectors. (Others might be working in government jobs, something entirely different.) Learning about these two sectors will also give you time to think about your interests, your work aptitude, what you would like to do with your life in the world of work.

THE GOODS PRODUCING SECTOR

Any industry that produces something tangible in a factory, plant, mill, or mine falls into this category. These are industries like food, shelter, clothing, technology hardware, manufacturing, chemicals, coal mining, petroleum, and the like. There are many subsets in each category but we will examine just one of these industries, manufacturing, in more detail because this sector produces millions of jobs.

The Manufacturers

Contrary to what you might hear, the US is still the number one manufacturing country in the world. True, much US manufacturing has moved overseas in the past fifty years, mainly because of the demands for high wages and benefits by unions, but we have not abandoned manufacturing to become a services producing country.

The world's largest manufacturer is the Texas-based gas and oil producer, Exxon Mobile Corp. Exxon's 2015 revenues were approximately $450 billion, and the company employs almost 88,000 workers. Other American manufacturers in the top twenty worldwide are Chevron and Conoco Phillips (both oil and gas producers), Boeing, Caterpillar, General Motors, and General Electric. So much for "manufacturing is dead in America."

Who Are the Manufacturers and Where Are Manufacturing Jobs Located?

In addition to those listed above, manufacturers are companies like Dow Chemical, Ford, John Deere, Kellogg, Procter & Gamble, US Steel, and Nike. Manufacturing in the US is not dead by any means. In fact, more than 12 percent of our GDP comes from manufacturing. The manufacturers employ millions of workers in a variety of jobs like sales, marketing, finance, human resources, information technology, and finance. Working for a manufacturing company does not always mean working a strenuous job requiring muscle and sweat. In fact, most jobs in manufacturing are "clean-hands" jobs.

You do not have to live near the headquarters of a large manufacturer to work there. While a large company like Ford has home offices in Detroit, Michigan, it maintains manufacturing plants and regional offices scattered in dozens of locations across the US and abroad. There are job opportunities at every location.

Is the manufacturing sector right for you? If you get a kick out of seeing a Boeing 747 defy gravity and lift off the runway to a cruising altitude of 35,000 feet, you might want to look at airline manufacturers like Boeing and Lockheed Martin for civilian employment. Click on their websites and view their career pages at www.Boeing.com and www.lockheed.com.

The chemical industry is another goods producer providing jobs for tens of thousands of workers. Check out the website of one of the best in this industry, Dow Chemical, www.Dow.com, a military friendly company. This Fortune 500 Company, which produces chemicals primarily for the agriculture industry, is one of the best employers in America because one of its attributes is treating employees fairly.

There are millions of jobs in the American manufacturing sector and one could be tailor-made for you. Check them out.

THE BIG THREE GOODS PRODUCERS

I have always considered the big three—food, shelter, clothing—a cut above the other goods producers for an obvious reason. People need food, shelter, and clothing to survive. The big three will always provide an abundance of jobs regardless of the state of our economic cycle.

Food and Agriculture Companies

Do not wait to check out the food-related companies, because smart job seekers are all over their jobs like flies on honey. The food industry is almost recession-proof because people will always need to eat, hard times or not. These jobs are located everywhere in the country.

If you live in the Northeast and want to work with a first-class regional food company, check out Wakefern at www.Wakefern.com. It is the nation's largest retailer-owned cooperative and wholesale distributor of food products to supermarkets. The last time I checked the job board, I saw more than a dozen Wakefern jobs ranging from entry-level to managerial positions.

Agriculture is a frequently overlooked part of the food industry. It's a large booming industry employing millions of workers in jobs as diverse as driving a tractor on a soybean farm in Iowa or operating a computer that controls machines pouring ketchup into bottles at H.J. Heinz, the food company headquartered in Pittsburgh, Pennsylvania. The last time I checked the Heinz website, I noted that there were many jobs available. Check it out at www.Heinz.com.

Many veterans have had some experience in the food/agriculture segment of the military and all are welcome in the food and agriculture arena. The US is home to over 320 million people and all of them must eat every day to survive. You get the picture. America is a hungry country!

The job outlook in the food and agriculture industry is very promising. The Bureau of Labor Statistics forecasts robust growth and many new jobs over the next ten years, as you can see from this BLS chart:

Jobs in the Food and Agriculture Industry

Position	Projected Job Growth to 2020
Farm equipment mechanics and service technicians	13.4%
Animal, plant and food scientists	10.4%
Agricultural engineers	9.1%
Agriculture and food-science technicians	7.0%
Farm products buyers and purchasing agents	5.5%

The total number of new agriculture-related jobs through 2020 is projected to be *in excess of one million.* Veterans should have no problem finding jobs in one of our largest goods-producing industries, food and agriculture.

Clothing Companies

Like people, clothing companies come in different sizes and shapes. They offer millions of jobs across the country, most of them behind the scenes. Mistakenly, most people think of jobs in the clothing industry as those of the behind-the-counter salespeople. The reality is that most jobs in the clothing business are those you will never see on the store floor. These are jobs in marketing, finance, fashion design, purchasing, human resources, law, information technology, and web merchandising. Companies in this industry are basic clothing retailers like Macy's, JC Penney, Target, Walmart, Kohl's, and Sears.

Another category of companies in the clothing business consists of fashion producers like Talbots, Nordstrom's, Bloomingdales, and Brooks Brothers. Other clothing companies specialize in shoes and sporting gear and include Nike, Adidas, New Balance, Aeropostale, and Lululemon Athletica.

One of our favorites in this category is Lululemon Athletica, a Vancouver-based company that manufactures and sells high-quality fashionable yoga and running apparel, mainly for women. One of their brilliant marketing initiatives is conducting free yoga classes in public parks and in-store locations several times each week with qualified instructors. This company is a Wall Street favorite because it makes money for shareholders in a very competitive market. The former CEO, Christine Day, has built a great international company, and if you are smart, you will review the website now at www.lululemon.com. The last time I checked their career page, I saw assistant store manager positions open in Chicago and Palo Alto; human resources jobs at the home office; and support jobs at many locations across the US, Asia, and Europe. People who work with Lululemon consider it an interesting people-oriented company. Check it out!

To put the clothing industry in perspective, consider the numbers. According to research released by the NPD Group, revenue generated from sales of men's clothing at the beginning of 2015 reached $61 billion, and for women's clothing, $116 billion. The grand total is $177 billion! Where are the jobs? In the clothing industry.

Shelter Companies

Shelter includes houses and commercial buildings, and everything therein required to protect you from the elements and make your life more comfortable. It is a vast industry and includes companies such as Toll Brothers, a high-end residential homebuilder, and commercial builders like the Trump Organization, headed by Donald Trump. Included in this industry are furniture producers like Ikea and Ethan Allen and home improvement retailers like Home Depot and Lowe's. Here are examples of two shelter companies.

Ryan Homes. Ryan builds residential housing developments in the northeastern United States. Prices for individual houses are in the $300,000 to $800,000 price range. Ryan hires and trains workers for a variety of jobs in marketing, sales, information technology, finance, land purchasing, construction supervision, and customer service. Check out the website for current job opportunities at www.nvrinc.com.

Weyerhaeuser. This company says that it is *inspired by trees*, which is understandable. It produces wood products for residential and commercial buildings throughout the country. Annual revenues are approximately $9 billion. This Tacoma, Washington, company has been in business for over 100 years and offers job opportunities across the USA and abroad. Weyerhaeuser will be around long after you and I are gone, a reassuring fact when seeking a long-term career. In addition, the company maintains an excellent record of diversity recruitment. Check it out at www.weyerhaeuser.com to review a number of both hands-on and office-based opportunities.

THE SERVICES SECTOR

The Bureau of Labor Statistics defines this sector as that which has to do with *producing a non-tangible product*. Included in this group are educational services, health care and social assistance, government, finance, insurance, computer and information technology, entertainment, transportation, recreation, publishing, and many others. This sector is expected to grow at double-digit rates in the near future.

Service providers are companies like Microsoft, Adobe, Bank of America, Google, Wells Fargo Bank, Travelers Insurance Co., Pearson Publishing, McGraw-Hill Publishing, and Salesforce.com. Like manufacturers, large service producers have offices in locations all across the US.

Technology companies are always inventing new products and services and are likely places to find technical and non-technical jobs. Check out Microsoft, www.microsoft.com, and Salesforce.com, www.salesforce.com, two interesting technology companies in the services sector. Both have numerous job postings on their career pages.

The services sector is sometimes described as "the people sector." If meeting and greeting the public is something that appeals to you, explore the services companies. There are thousands of them across the country, both large and small, and one of them probably has an appealing job for you. Here's an example of an often overlooked job opportunity.

Reservations at Delta

A friend of mine recently landed a job with Delta as a reservationist working at the call center in Minneapolis, one of Delta's many reservation centers throughout the US. The position pays $11 per hour and carries a full benefits package. Annual salary at $11 per hour for a forty-hour workweek is $21,120 per year. Add 30 percent of your base salary for benefits (the value of vacation time, insurance, paid holidays and sick days), and your true compensation is $27,456. But that's not all. Spouses and family members can fly anywhere in the Delta network for free! In addition, after ten years of employment with Delta, the free airfare benefit becomes a lifetime benefit. Interested? Go to www.deltajobs.net. In addition, some reservationist and customer service jobs with airline passenger companies are "home office" jobs.

For a detailed look at the goods and services sectors, consult the Bureau of Labor Statistics, www.BLS.gov, and the latest edition of the *Occupational Outlook Handbook.*

FOR-PROFIT AND NONPROFIT COMPANIES

Our workplace is divided further into for-profit and nonprofit companies. The Bureau of Labor Statistics (BLS) defines the *nonprofit* category as

> Organizations that are neither for-profit businesses nor government agencies. Nonprofits are a subset of private industry. Nonprofit organizations may generate revenue, but this revenue cannot be distributed to owners or employees as they might be in a for-profit business. Nonprofits include hospitals, educational institutions, churches, and social welfare organizations and charitable organizations. More than one million charitable organizations work to benefit a variety of different causes, such as disaster relief, civil rights, community development, environmental advocacy, and the arts. Charitable organizations also include hospitals and private schools. More than half of all hospitals and almost a third of postsecondary educational institutions are nonprofit.

Nonprofit companies are frequently involved in charitable work, like providing medical care for the disadvantaged in the US and abroad, education services for certain socio-economic groups, and skills training for the unemployed.

Some nonprofits operate in much the same manner as for-profit companies because they must make money to pay their employees and support the corporate infrastructure. Two such companies are the College Board and Educational Testing Services (ETS). They produce and sell products for the K-12 and higher education markets. Check out their websites for job opportunities at www.ets.org and www.college-board.org. Both companies offer pay scales and benefit packages that are comparable to, or above, what you would find in the for-profit sector. The College Board is based in New York City and ETS in Princeton, New Jersey, but both have regional offices across the US.

Foundations

Some nonprofits are "foundations," like the Ford Foundation, the Bill and Melinda Gates Foundation, the Salesforce Foundation, and the Robert Wood Johnson Foundation. They employ thousands of workers in a variety of jobs ranging from sales representatives to marketing directors to chief technology officers. Compensation for jobs at these organizations is comparable to similar jobs in the for-profit world. However, the benefits are usually much better, the culture more stimulating, and the opportunity for long-term employment much greater. These organizations seek out workers who are passionate about doing good things for others and who care about having a rewarding, satisfying, and fulfilling career.

FOR-PROFIT COMPANIES

The workplace is vast and it takes time to determine where to start searching for a civilian job. Education, healthcare, insurance, and security are some of my favorite industries based on personal experience, research, work experience, and anecdotal information from a variety of sources. These are industries employing millions of workers and providing an opportunity to take home more than just a paycheck. However, workers in these industries find that monetary rewards are attractive as well. See Chapter 2, "Working for a Corporation or a Small Business," for information about specific companies.

THE TEN LARGEST EMPLOYERS IN AMERICA BY NUMBER OF EMPLOYEES

Where do you find companies that employ thousands or workers? If the word "big" has a certain appeal for you, target America's largest companies. Who are they? The *Wall Street Journal* recently published a list of such employers. Here are the top ten by number of employees:

1. Walmart . . . 2,200,000
2. United States Postal Service . . . 491,017
3. McDonald's . . . 440,000
4. International Business Machines (IBM) . . . 431,212
5. Kroger . . . 375,000
6. Target . . . 366,000
7. Home Depot . . . 365,000
8. Hewlett-Packard . . . 317,500
9. Yum! Brands . . . 307,230
10. General Electric . . . 307,000

Note that six of the top ten are companies in our "basic three" industries: food, shelter, clothing. They are Walmart, McDonald's, Kroger, Target, Home Depot, and Yum! Brands.

SMALL BUSINESSES CREATE MOST JOBS

In this chapter, we have concentrated on large companies to illustrate the American job sectors and to learn what kinds of companies fall into the various industries.

A common misperception about the market is that large companies like Costco, Coca-Cola, Starbucks, and Dow create most jobs. While it is true that large companies employ millions of workers, small businesses create most of the jobs in America. These are no-name companies that you might find in shopping malls, on Main Street USA, or in industrial parks. Their names might be Faulkner Toyota, Lincoln Tech Consulting, Kim's Hair Styling, or Maplewood Physical Therapy.

Where do you find job opportunities with small businesses? Take a stroll through your local mall or industrial/office park, and you will find them. Look through your *Yellow Pages* directory and check your local newspapers, and you will find them. Look on Craigslist and you will find them.

This segment of our workplace is so important that the federal government created a special department devoted to small business operations. It is the **Small Business Administration**. Review the website for additional information at www.sba.gov.

THE BEST WAY TO LEARN WHERE JOBS ARE LOCATED

The proven way to find a job is by doing a lot of hard work, such as knocking on doors of companies in your area to discover opportunities that are not posted on job boards or company websites. They can be with large companies, like Johnson & Johnson Pharmaceuticals, or small companies, like your neighborhood branch bank or a local car dealer. But can you really find a job that way? Well, consider this real-life example.

Jobs at Toyota

Recently, I took my Avalon XLE to the local Toyota dealer for service. While waiting for the service tech to complete the oil change and lube, I noticed a sign at the service manager's counter. It read: VALET NEEDED. FULL TIME. SALARY AND BENEFITS. *I didn't know what a valet at a car dealership did, so I asked the service manager and learned that this person drove cars from the service area to the waiting area, took cars to the car wash, and accompanied owners to their car's location when service was complete. The job paid $11 per hour plus benefits and possible overtime. That's $440 per week, $1,760 per month, and $21,120 per year. Add another 30 percent for benefits like insurance and vacation time, and the job is worth $27,456 a year. Not much you say? And why would any veteran want to drive cars around the service area of a car dealership? Well, here's the rest of the story. The service manager told me that the valet position was her entry-level job, and after twelve months she was promoted to assistant manager and then service manager at more than double the salary. In addition, she said that the valet position could be a stepping-stone to a sales position with Toyota, a reputable manufacturer with the best-selling cars in the US.*

Selling quality cars is an often-overlooked opportunity, and some consider it a "brainless" job. Think again. A good car sales representative can make a very good income, work flexible hours, and provide a necessary service to the public. If you want an interesting sales job with very high-income potential, sell cars like Mercedes, Lexus, BMW, or Volvo. You need high-level communication skills to sell high-level products, skills like those acquired in the military.

THE BEST LOCATIONS FOR JOB HUNTING

Certain metropolitan areas offer more job opportunities than others. For example, the following states and cities had high rates of employment opportunities according to the Brookings Institute:

Texas. Throughout the state, employment opportunities are plentiful, especially in the oil and gas industry. Six major cities showing the most robust job growth were Austin, San Antonio, El Paso, McAllen, Dallas, and Houston. Austin leads the pack with many job openings in state government and at the University of Texas. In addition, Austin has become one of the fastest growing high-tech areas in the country and provides many jobs in that industry.

Texas is the leading state in the country for job growth because of a favorable business climate. For this reason, many companies are locating their headquarters or regional offices in Texas. Texas is the best-run state in the entire country. Taxes in Texas are low, there are reasonable rules and regulations for businesses, and the climate is favorable.

If you are seeking a new location to begin your work cycle, think about relocating to Texas. Two of the best places are Austin and San Antonio. Both have an ideal semitropical climate and very favorable cultural and educational facilities.

Oklahoma City, Oklahoma. You will find many job opportunities here in the petroleum industry.

Omaha, Nebraska. For careers in agribusiness, this is one of the best places to be.

Salt Lake City, Utah. This area offers many job opportunities in the booming mining industry and the recreation industry.

Pittsburgh, Pennsylvania. Pitt has a robust education environment. Noted universities like Carnegie Mellon and Duquesne are located here and they provide many job opportunities. The area supports many manufacturers and as we know, they produce jobs by the bucketful.

San Jose, California. Did you ever hear of Silicon Valley? This is the heart of the technology industry. If you like bits and bytes, this is the place for you.

Knoxville, Tennessee. This city provides many job opportunities in healthcare and in education at the University of Tennessee. In addition, factories in Knoxville manufacture parts for Volkswagen, whose major US plant is in Chattanooga. Drive west ninety minutes to Nashville and you will find Vanderbilt University, known not only for academic excellence, but also for being a world-class medical center, which provides countless jobs for those interested in healthcare careers.

Charleston, South Carolina. This pleasant city is home to many manufacturers. One of the largest is the airplane manufacturer Boeing.

Upper Midwest. The upper Midwest, South Dakota and North Dakota specifically, is one of the hottest spots in America for job opportunities. The reason? This area has huge deposits of natural gas and oil, which are being extracted using fracking technology. If you like to work outside doing some heavy lifting in the gas and oil patch, you could make $90,000 per year or more. This area has one of the lowest unemployment rates in the country.

MOVING FORWARD

The American workplace has many different industries and companies where veterans can find employment. Matching your military experience with a certain job sector is sure to bring results. For example, if you were an Army 92G Food Service Specialist, you would be well qualified to work with one of our food and agricultural companies.

Military.com has constructed a useful tool to help veterans translate their military experience to an equivalent job in the civilian workplace. It's called the Skills Translator, which you will find at www.military.com/skillstranslator. This tool is easy to use and provides veterans with a good starting point. **OJS** advises you to try it before moving on.

CHAPTER TAKEAWAYS

- Jobs are located in one of two sectors: the goods producers and the services providers.
- Small businesses are where you will find most job opportunities.
- Manufacturing is alive and well in America and provides plentiful job opportunities.
- The "big three" industries (food, shelter, clothing) provide millions of jobs regardless of the economic cycle.

THE VETERAN'S LIBRARY

Dennis Damp. *The Book of US Government Jobs*. Bookhaven Press, 2011.

Rory Freedman and Kim Barnouin. *Skinny Bitch*. Running Press, 2005. The authors advocate a straight vegan diet, but what interested me most about this book was its analysis of the food industry, one of my faves. This book was on the bestseller lists in the US and UK for five years and has become a classic.

Robert Kaplan. *What You're Really Meant To Do*. Harvard Business Review Press, 2013.

Enrico Noretti. *The New Geography of Jobs*. Mariner Books, 2013.

Chapter 19

How to Work a Trade Show to Meet Hiring Managers

A trade show is a gathering of workers from companies in a specific industry. The purpose of a trade show is to give companies an opportunity to display their products and advertise their services in exhibit booths located on the floor of a convention center.

Trade shows go by different names—conventions, conferences, exhibits, expos, trade fairs, trade exhibitions—but all mean the same thing. Usually they are held at convention centers, which are located in major cities or state capitals. Sometimes they meet in hotels or resorts that have large rooms for hosting exhibits and smaller rooms to host "breakout sessions" where industry experts present new products or discuss research and industry trends.

Industry professional organizations host these shows, which are extremely costly to sponsor. Some of those costs are defrayed by member dues and by conference attendance fees.

An example of a trade show is the world's largest technology show called the Consumer Electronics Show (CES), which convenes every January in Las Vegas. In 2015, attendance at this show exceeded 150,000, including 35,000 people from foreign countries. More than 3,000 companies attended and hosted exhibits. Can you imagine 3,000 potential employers under one roof? If you are interested in technology, you cannot afford to miss CES. For more information and to register for the next show, go to www.cesweb.org.

Attending trade shows is the most productive method for job hunting. However, how do you know where to go and what to do once you find yourself in a convention hall? In this chapter, I will give you instructions for attending trade shows, as well as the names and locations of the major convention centers across the country.

PREPARATION CHECKLIST FOR ATTENDING A CONVENTION

One does not just show up at an exhibit and expect miracles to happen. In order to reap maximum benefits from attending a trade show, plan for it in advance. Here is a checklist and suggestions for planning purposes:

- Your primary purpose for attending these events is to visit the many exhibit booths where you will find hiring managers. Many shows hold exhibits only on specific days and at specific hours. For example, the dates listed for CES, the technology conference in Las Vegas, may be January 10–16, but the exhibits could be open only on January 11–15, from 10 a.m. to 6 p.m. You can find this information online, or by calling the conference center or the organization hosting the show. This is important because you are attending the conference primarily to visit the exhibit booths where you will find the hiring managers. There is no need to attend the conference on days when the exhibits are not open.

- The organization sponsoring the conference publishes a list of companies attending (online and in the printed conference program) and the names of the representatives who will be attending, along with their contact information. Obtain a list either online or at the conference center.

- Bring at least 100 business cards and 20 resumes to the exhibit each day. The exchange of business cards is the accepted way to build your list of networking contacts.

- When you enter the conference center to attend the show, first go to the registration desk to pay the exhibit fee, obtain your nametag, and pick up the conference program, which is usually tucked in a tote bag. Make sure you get the conference program, because it will provide the names of the companies attending, the names of company representatives, and their exhibit booth numbers. Always wear your nametag.

- Almost all shows charge a fee for attendance. Fees may vary with the number of days you will attend, your affiliation, and your work status. Sometimes there is a steep discount for veterans and students. Ask for this discount at the registration desk. Occasionally there is no charge for veterans or students.

- The attendance fees will vary. A technology education industry trade show called EdNET can charge up to $900 for admission, but the fee is worth it. The reason is that 600 hiring authorities, including CEOs, presidents, vice presidents for sales, marketing, and product development, chief technology and information officers, and human resources directors, attend this annual convention. During this three-day conference, you will meet keynote speakers and participate in breakout sessions. Also, you will have an opportunity to present your candidacy for two minutes in front of 600 hiring authorities. It does not get better than that. Negotiate the lowest entrance fee for this and every conference. Many large trade shows, which are open to the public, charge very low fees, in the $50 to $100 range.

- If you are coming from a distance and plan to stay overnight near the conference center, make hotel reservations well in advance. If the conference center is in a large city like Los Angeles, local hotel rates will be quite steep. Find a hotel or motel just out of town at a more reasonable room rate and then drive to the conference center each day. In addition, some conference organizations negotiate lower room rates with hotels and motels in the area, so always check this out online six months in advance.

- Dress at trade shows is usually casual, but you are there to sell your candidacy and you should dress with that in mind.

WHAT YOU DO AT A CONVENTION

Are you ready for a bit of fun? This is where you will have a good time in a very relaxed environment and meet hundreds of full-time company workers, many of whom will be hiring managers. Exhibit halls are usually crowded with customers who are there to get product information and visit company representatives. This is a place where workers conduct business in a pleasant way. Usually people working in the various exhibit booths will be dressed informally, many times wearing a casual shirt or top bearing the name of the company and the company logo. Remember, however, that you are not a worker here and you should be in business attire.

After you register and get your nametag, enter the exhibit hall and begin visiting each booth. You can start your booth visits in the first aisle and proceed around the hall until you have stopped at each booth. If there are hundreds of exhibits, this may take two or even three days.

What Do You Say After You Say "Hello"?

When you enter an exhibit booth, view the products on display and ask one of the representatives to explain what the company does. Establish a personal relationship by learning what the person's job is and how he or she likes working for the company. After you establish the relationship, tell the person you are job hunting and ask to speak with any hiring manager who may be there. If you are interested in marketing and the director of marketing is not there for some reason, ask for that person's name and contact information, and follow up with a phone call or email when you return to your home office.

If all of this is new to you, here is a script you might use to break the ice and get in the game, remembering that workers are always eager to help a person looking for a job. Establish the relationship by addressing the worker by name, which is always on the nametag: *"Hello, Justin. My name is Julia, and I'm here for two reasons and would appreciate your help. First, I would like to know more about your company and what you do. Second, I'm a recently discharged veteran seeking employment and would like to see the hiring manager for marketing, if this person is attending the conference. If not, would you please write his or her name and contact information on the back of your business card for me? Also, could you give me the name and contact information for the company human resources director? Thanks, Justin."*

Before you leave the exhibit booth, give your business card to your new contact and write on the back, "Military veteran seeking employment and would appreciate your help."

If a hiring manager you want to see is in the booth, request a few minutes for an informal interview and give that person your resume. The way to get this moving without feeling awkward is to say something like this: *"Bill, here's my resume, and if you have the time now, maybe you could take a minute to review it. I'm a recently discharged veteran looking for a job opportunity in marketing. If you don't have time now, could we make an appointment to sit down later and chat for a few minutes, maybe over a cup of coffee or lunch? My treat, of course."*

How to Recognize a Hiring Manager

In the exhibit booths and on the convention center floor, you will see people dressed in formal business attire. Most often, these are the company executives, the people you need to meet. Lacking an introduction, you just have to wing it. Walk up to that person and say something like this: *"I can tell by the way you're dressed that you must be running the show here. My name is Tony and I'm here job hunting. I'm a recently discharged veteran and looking for a sales position. Could you steer me in the right direction? I would really appreciate your help."*

This person will appreciate your sense of humor and your subtle note of respect and recognition. The odds of getting a positive response are in your favor because business execs remember when they were in your position and they are willing to lend a hand to a newcomer.

LUNCH AT A TRADE SHOW. A TIME FOR NETWORKING

On the convention center floor there will be restaurants, kiosks selling hot dogs and soft drinks, and sometimes bars selling alcoholic drinks. This is another place to meet people. After you buy a burger and a Coke, find a table that is partially occupied. Take a seat, introduce yourself to the person next to you, and go into your sales pitch. Lunch is not just lunch; it is a networking opportunity. You never select an empty table, whip out your smartphone, and begin texting. Never. Why waste your time and money Tweeting when you could be meeting potential employers?

Thirsty for a Cold Beer?

Bars and restaurants frequently sell alcoholic drinks. *Never* buy them. Do not even think of it. A cardinal rule is never to drink anything alcoholic while job hunting, even if others around you are. You are here on business, not to throw down a beer or a Chardonnay. Many of the people here are hiring managers, and they could be sizing up your personal habits. Company managers do not hire veterans who drink while job hunting. The same rules apply to using any form of controlled substances.

FINDING JOBS WITH CONVENTION CENTERS

When you review the conference center website, always check out the career postings. Convention centers, such at McCormick Place in Chicago, are profit-making organizations and employ many workers across all specialties. These are good full-time jobs in sales, marketing, technology, finance, and human resources. In addition, go to the conference center offices and inquire about job opportunities when you attend the conference.

WHERE THE HIRING MANAGERS HANG OUT

The big guys, the hiring managers, always attend trade shows and conventions in order to meet their key customers, keep up with industry trends, and to recruit workers for all levels of employment. Recruiters, too, often attend these shows to prospect for new clients, seek workers for open positions, or to look for qualified candidates to place in their database for future reference. I have attended hundreds of conferences to recruit job candidates and seek new clients. I have never been disappointed. In the job-hunting world, trade shows and exhibits *are* the Promised Land. Visiting these shows is the best way to begin your job search.

MOVING FORWARD

Working a trade show is another important step in the job-hunting process, once you learn where the convention centers are located. My state-by-state list of convention and conference centers is your key to learning where you will find hiring authorities, upcoming conferences, and exhibits. It's all there in the next chapter. Don't miss it!

CHAPTER TAKEAWAYS

- Finding Hiring Managers is a key step in the job-hunting process.
- Hiring Managers always attend trade shows.
- Never drink alcoholic beverages at trade shows.
- Attending trade shows is the best way to find a job.

Chapter 20

The Convention Connection. The Top Convention Centers and Trade Shows

Every city and state has convention centers that host trade shows and conferences, the best locations to find potential job opportunities and hiring managers. Managers and directors from sales, marketing, product development, technology, advertising, human resources, event planning, and finance work in the trade show exhibit booths. Stop at a booth, introduce yourself, and ask for help securing employment. Does it get any easier than that? Potential employers are not hiding under rocks; rather, they hang out at convention centers, the names and locations of which are just a couple of clicks away.

Go online and contact the convention centers on the list below. Each center will provide the dates and names of the trade shows for the entire year and in many instances will provide links to the names of the companies attending. In addition, you will find the price of admission and other pertinent information that will make your visit there more profitable.

US CONVENTION CENTERS BY STATE

Here is the list of convention centers in every state. Locate the one closest to you and access the convention center website where you will find a listing of upcoming trade shows and information about hours and costs. If the convention center website does not provide such information, go to the website for the sponsoring organization.

Alabama
Birmingham-Jefferson Civic Center
www.bjcc.org
2100 Richard Arrington Jr. Boulevard North
Birmingham, AL 35203
(205) 458–8400

Alaska
Anchorage Convention Centers
www.anchorageconventioncenters.com
555 West Fifth Avenue
Anchorage, AK 99501
(907) 263–2800

Juneau Centennial Hall Convention Center
www.juneau.org/centennial
101 Egan Drive
Juneau, AK 99801
(907) 586–5283

Arizona
Phoenix Convention Center
www.phoenixconventioncenter.com
111 N 3rd St.
Phoenix, AZ 85004–2231
(602) 262–6225

Tucson Convention Center
www.tucsonconventioncenter.com
260 S. Church St.
Tucson, AZ 85701
(520) 791–4101

Arkansas
Statehouse Convention Center
www.littlerockmeetings.com
#1 Statehouse Plaza
Little Rock, AR 72201
(501) 376–4781
(800) 844–4781

California
Long Beach Convention and Entertainment Center
www.longbeachcc.com
300 Ocean Boulevard
Long Beach, CA 90802
(562) 436–3636

Los Angeles Convention Center
www.lacclink.com
685 South Figueroa St.
(between Wilshire Blvd and 7th St)
Los Angeles, CA 90017
(213) 689–8822

San Diego Convention Center
www.visitsandiego.com
111 West Harbor Drive
San Diego, CA 92101
(619) 525–5214

Moscone Center
www.moscone.com
747 Howard Street
San Francisco, CA 94103
(415) 974–4000

Colorado
Colorado Convention Center
www.denverconvention.com
700 14th Street
Denver, CO 80202
(303) 228–8000

Connecticut
XL Center (formerly the Hartford Civic Center)
www.xlcenter.com
One Civic Center Plaza
Hartford, CT 06103
(860) 249–6333

Delaware
Delaware does not have a major convention center. Check the convention centers in Baltimore, MD, Philadelphia, PA, Atlantic City, NJ, and Washington, DC.

District of Columbia
Washington Convention Center
www.dcconvention.com
801 Mount Vernon Place, N.W.
Washington, DC 20001
(202) 249–3000

Florida
Fort Lauderdale/Broward Co. Convention Center
www.ftlauderdalecc.com
1950 Eisenhower Blvd.
Fort Lauderdale, FL 33316
(305) 765–5900

Miami Beach Convention Center
www.miamibeachconvention.com

1901 Convention Center Dr.
Miami Beach, FL 33139
(305) 673–7311

Orange County Convention Center
www.occc.net
9800 International Dr.
Orlando, FL 32819
(407) 345–9800

Tampa Convention Center
www.tampaconventioncenter.com
333 S. Franklin St.
Tampa, FL 33602
(813) 274–8511

Georgia
Georgia World Congress Center
www.gwcc.com
285 Andrew Young International Blvd. NW
Atlanta, GA 30313
(404) 223–4200

Hawaii
Hawaii Convention Center
www.hawaiiconvention.com
1801 Kalakaua Avenue
Honolulu, HI 96815
(808) 943–3500

Idaho
Boise Center
www.boisecentre.com
850 West Front St.
Boise, ID 83702
(208) 336–8900

Illinois
McCormick Place
www.mccormickplace.com
2301 S. Lake Shore Drive
Chicago, IL 60616
(312) 791–7000

Navy Pier
www.navypier.com
600 East Grand Avenue
Chicago, IL 60611
(312) 595-PIER

Indiana
Indiana Convention Center
www.icclos.com
100 South Capital Avenue
Indianapolis, IN 46225
(317) 262–3400

Iowa
Iowa Events Center
www.iowaeventscenter.com
730 Third St.
Des Moines, IA 50309
(515) 564–8000

Kentucky
Kentucky International Convention Center
www.kyconvention.org
221 Fourth Street
Louisville, KY 40202
(502) 595–4381

Louisiana
Ernest N. Morial Convention Center
www.mccno.com

900 Convention Center Blvd.
New Orleans, LA 70130
(504) 582–3023

Maine
Cumberland Convention Center
www.theciviccenter.com
One Civic Center Sq.
Portland, ME 04101
(207) 775–3481

Maryland
Baltimore Convention Center
www.bccenter.org
1 West Pratt Street
Baltimore, MD 21201
(410) 649–7000

Massachusetts
Boston Convention and Exhibition Center
www.bostonconventioncenter.com
415 Summer Street
Boston, MA
(617) 867–8286

John B. Hynes Convention Center
www.massconvention.com
900 Boylston Street
Boston, MA 02115
(617) 867–8286

Michigan
Cobo Conference/Exhibition Center
www.cobocenter.com
One Washington Blvd.
Detroit, MI 48226
(313) 877–8777

Minnesota

Mayo Civic Center

www.mayociviccenter.com

30 Civic Center Dr. SE

Rochester, MN 55904

(507) 281–6184

Duluth Entertainment Convention Center

www.decc.org

350 Harbor Dr.

Duluth, MN 55802

(218) 722–5573

Minneapolis Convention Center

www.minneapolisconventioncenter.com

1301 Second Avenue S.

Minneapolis, MN 55403

(612) 335–6000

Mississippi

Mississippi Coast Convention Center

www.mscoastconventioncenter.com

2350 Beach Boulevard

Biloxi, MS 39531

(228) 594–3700

Missouri

Kansas City Convention

www.kcconvention.com

301 West 13th Street

Suite 100

Kansas City, MO 64105

(816) 513-5071

America's Center Convention Complex

301 West 13th Street

Suite 100

Kansas City, MO 64105
(816) 513–5071

America's Center
www.explorestlouis.com
701 Convention Plaza
St. Louis, MO 63105
(800)–325–7962

Montana
Butte Silver Bow Civic Center
www.butteciviccenter.com
1340 Harrison Avenue
Butte, MT 59701
(406) 497–6400

Mansfield Convention Center
www.greatfalls.net/mansfieldcenter.com
4 Park Drive
Great Falls, MT 59401
(406) 455–8510

Helena Civic Center
www.helenaciviccenter.com
340 Neill Avenue
Helena, MT 59601
(406) 461–8785

Nebraska
CenturyLink Center
www.centurylinkcenteromaha.com
455 N. 10th Street
Omaha, NE 68102
(402) 341–1500

Nevada
Las Vegas Convention and Visitors Authority
www.lvcva.com
3150 Paradise Rd

Las Vegas, NV 89109
(702) 386–7100

New Hampshire
Check the convention centers in Maine and Massachusetts.

New Jersey
Atlantic City Convention Center
www.accenter.com
2301 Boardwalk
Atlantic City, NJ 08401
(800) 214–0663

Meadowlands Exposition Center
www.mecexpo.com
355 Plaza Dr.
Secaucus, NJ 07094
(201) 330–1172

Edison Conference Center
www.njexpocenter.com/eb&cc
97 Sunfield Avenue
Edison, NJ 08837
(732) 661–1205

Garden State Convention & Exhibit Center
www.gsec.com
50 Atrium Dr.
Somerset, NJ 08873
(732) 417–1400

Wildwoods Convention Center
www.wildwoodsnj.com/cc
4501 Boardwalk

Wildwood, NJ
(609) 729–9000

New Mexico
Albuquerque Convention Center
www.albuquerquecc.com
Second & Tijeras NW
Albuquerque, NM 87102
(505) 842–9918

New York
Buffalo Niagara Convention Center
www.buffaloconvention.com
Convention Center Plaza
Buffalo, NY 14202
(716) 855–5555

Jacob K. Javits Convention Center
www.javitscenter.com
655 West 34th Street
New York, NY 10001
(212) 216–2000

North Carolina
Charlotte Convention Center
www.charlotteconventionctr.com
100 Paul Buck Blvd.
Charlotte, NC 28217
(704) 339–6000

Metrolina Expo Center
www.metrolinatradeshowexpo.com
7100 Statesville Road
Charlotte, NC 28221
(704) 596–4650

North Dakota
Check the convention centers in Minnesota and South Dakota.

Ohio
Duke Energy Convention Center
www.duke-energycenter.com
525 Elm Street
Cincinnati, OH 45202
(513) 419–7300

Cleveland Convention Center
www.clevcc.com
500 Lakeside Avenue
Cleveland, OH 44114
(216) 928–1600

I X Center
www.ixcenter.com
6200 Riverside Drive
Cleveland, OH 44135
(216) 676–6000

Dayton Convention Center
www.daytonconventioncenter.com
22 E. Fifth St.
Dayton, OH 45402
(937) 333–4700

Seagate Convention Centre
www.toledo-seagate.com
401 Jefferson Avenue
Toledo, OH 43604
(419) 321–5007

Oklahoma

Cox Convention Center
www.coxconventioncenter.com
1 Myriad Gardens
Oklahoma City, OK 73102–9219
(405) 602–8500

Cox Business Center
www.coxcentertulsa.com
100 Civic Center
Tulsa, OK 74103
(918) 894–4350

Oregon

Oregon Convention Center
www.oregoncc.org
777 N Martin Luther King Blvd.
Portland, OR 97232
(503) 235–7575

Pennsylvania

Pennsylvania Convention Center
www.paconvention.com
1101 Arch Street
Philadelphia, PA 19107
(215) 418–4700

Lawrence Convention Center
www.pittsburghcc.com
1000 Ft. Duquesne Blvd.
Pittsburgh, PA 15222
(412) 565–6000

Rhode Island

Rhode Island Convention Center
www.riconvention.com

One Sabin Street
Providence, RI 02903–1814
(401) 458–6000

South Carolina
Charleston Convention Center
www.charlestonconventioncenter.com
5001 Coliseum Drive North
Charleston, SC 29418
(843) 529–5050

Palmetto International Exposition Center
www.palmettoexpo.com
One Exposition Avenue
Greenville, SC 29607
(864) 233–2562

South Dakota
Sioux Falls Convention Center
www.siouxfallscc.com
Sioux Empire Fair Office
4000 W. 12th Street
Sioux Falls, SD 57107
(605) 367–7178

Tennessee
Nashville Convention Center
www.nashvilleconventionctr.com
601 Commerce St.
Nashville, TN 37203
(615) 742–2002

Texas
Austin Convention Center
www.austinconventioncenter.com
500 E. First St.

Austin, TX 78701
(512) 404–4000

Kay Baily Hutchinson Convention Center
www.dallasconventioncenter.com
650 S. Griffin St.
Dallas, TX 75202
(214) 939–2750

George R. Brown Convention Center
www.houstonconventioncenter.com
1001 Avenida de las Americas
Houston, TX 77010
(713) 853–8090

Henry B. Gonzalez Convention Center
www.sahbgcc.com
200 E. Market Streets
San Antonio, TX 78205
(877) 504–8895

Waco Convention Center
www.wacocc.com
100 Washington Ave.
Waco, TX 76702
(254) 750–5810

Utah
Salt Palace Convention Center
www.saltpalace.com
100 SW Temple
Salt Lake City, UT 84101
(801) 534–4777

Dixie Convention Center
www.dixiecenter.com
1835 Convention Center Drive

St. George, UT 84790
(435) 628–7003

Vermont
Check the convention centers in Massachusetts and New York.

Virginia
The Greater Richmond Convention Center
www.richmondcenter.com
403 N. Third St.
Richmond, VA 23219
(804) 783–7300

The Virginia Beach Convention Center
www.vbcvb.com
1000 19th Street
Virginia Beach, VA 23451
(757) 385–2000

Washington
Meydenbauer Center
www.meydenbauer.com
11100 NE Sixth St.
Bellevue, WA 98004
(425) 637–1020

Washington State Convention & Trade Center
www.wscc.com
800 Convention Place
Seattle, WA 98101–2350
(206) 694–5000

Spokane Center
www.spokanecenter.com
334 W. Spokane Falls Boulevard
Spokane, WA 99201
(509) 353–6500

West Virginia
Charleston Civic Center
www.charlestonciviccenter.com
200 Civic Center Dr.
Charleston, WV 25301
(304) 345–1500

Wisconsin
Wisconsin Center
www.wisconsincenter.org
Wisconsin Center District
400 W. Wisconsin Ave.
Milwaukee, WI 53203
(414) 908–6000

Wyoming
Casper Events Center
www.caspereventscenter.com
One Events Drive
Caspar, WY 82601
(307) 235–8441

CONVENTION CENTER SPOTLIGHT

A number of state convention centers deserve special attention because of their strategic locations and the important conferences they attract. Here are **OJS** recommendations.

California

The Moscone Center, www.moscone.com. Located in the heart of San Francisco, the Moscone Center hosts some of our largest conventions. For example, in 2015 it attracted the National Auto Dealers Association, the Molecular Medicine Convention, and a number of "Green" conferences dealing with environmental and food products.

Florida

The Orange County Convention Center, www.occc.net. Located in Orlando, this convention center is one of busiest in the world, hosting national and international conferences. There are two separate facilities a block apart and each can accommodate tens of thousands of visitors at one time. Some conventions to attend here are the Orlando Home Show, the Florida Educational Technology Conference, and the Golf Industry Show. The Golf Show attracts 500 companies, which means there are 500 potential employers all gathered under one roof. Attendance usually runs over 50,000. Do you like the sporting industry? Attend the Golf Show.

The Tampa Convention Center, www.tampaconventioncenter.com. This is one of the premier conference centers in the Southeast. It accommodates medium-sized conferences that attract hundreds of companies exhibiting their products and services. Its location is on the waterfront in downtown Tampa.

Miami Beach Convention Center, www.miamibeachconvention.com. The Americas' largest jewelry show meets here each year. It is sponsored by the Jewelers International Showcase (JIS) and features three shows annually that attract hundreds of exhibitors and thousands of attendees. The October show has approximately 1,200 exhibit booths, and the April show has 300 booths. The JIS trade shows attract companies and attendees from 50 countries in the Caribbean, Latin America, and North America. If you like gold, silver, diamonds, rubies, and pearls, this is the place to go to find a job in the jewelry industry. Moreover, if you speak Spanish, you never know where the fun will end!

Georgia

The Atlanta Convention Center, www.atlconventioncenter.com. This large conference facility (more than 800,000 square feet) attracts many national and international trade shows each year. For example, the International Society for Technology in Education (ISTE) held its 2014 convention here the last week in June and attracted 15,000 attendees. This conference hosted 500 exhibiting companies that produce educational technology products for K-12 and higher education. More than 4,500 company representatives worked the booths. As instructional materials are transitioning from textbooks to digital products, the education industry will need more workers, like you.

Hawaii

The Hawaii Convention Center, www.meethawaii.com. This one-million-square-foot convention center is just down the street from famed Waikiki beach and is one of the best of its kind in the world. It holds many large and small conferences around the calendar, many of them with exhibitors staffed by key employees, like hiring managers. The Society for Industrial and Organizational Psychology (SIOP) held its 29th annual convention here in 2014.

By the way, the convention center itself is a prospect for your first job. It has a number of full-time sales reps, a complete staff of IT workers, and an active marketing department. Check out the careers listed under *jobs* on their website. Ready for some sun, surf, and a luau on weekends after convention hours? That's working in Hawaii. Does it get any better than that?

Illinois

McCormick Place, www.McCormickplace.com. This facility, located on the shore of Lake Michigan in Chicago, is Illinois's largest convention facility. Go there now on your smart phone, iPad, tablet, or laptop. Click on "full calendar" and then go to the "monthly calendar." This convention center is one of the most popular in the country because of its central location. Some of the shows it hosts annually are the Progressive Insurance Boat Show, The International Home and Housewares Show, and the National Restaurant Show.

Go to the website and click on the show title. It will take you to that particular website. You will find all the information you need including the names and addresses of hundreds of companies that will be exhibiting.

Indiana

The Indianapolis Convention Center, www.icclos.com. This popular conference center hosts many national and regional conferences representing all industries. Its central location and reasonable attendance fees make it a popular location.

One of the most important regional conferences held here is the Indiana Bankers Association. I checked out a recent conference and it listed all of the attending banks, including many national financial institutions, *as well as the names of the attendees from each bank.* Pay dirt!

Iowa

Iowa Events Center, www.iowaeventscenter.com. The Iowa-Nebraska Equipment Dealers Association hosts the Iowa Power Farming trade show here each year. The convention brings together under one roof manufacturers and dealers of farming equipment, all of which are potential job targets. If you are interested in agri-business, where better to find a job than in Iowa, at the Iowa Events Center in Des Moines?

By the way, when I reviewed the Iowa Events Center website, I found an interesting array of job opportunities and a listing of internships for marketing, sales, events management, and food and beverage operations.

New York

The Javits Convention Center, www.javitscenter.com, is one of the best-known convention centers in the world that attracts an impressive array of important conventions. Companies that exhibit here always send their executives and hiring managers, making the Javits one of the best venues for job-hunting veterans.

One of the most interesting and important annual conventions held at the Javits each October is Photo Plus Expo. It attracts approximately 250 companies that exhibit their latest products and services for the photography and imaging industry. Hundreds of hiring managers staff the various exhibit booths. Attending this conference is not only a good job-hunting experience but also an interesting learning experience.

Washington, DC

The Washington Convention Center, www.dcconvention.com. Our nation's capital has one of the most frequently used convention centers for regional and national trade shows and exhibits. Check the website frequently because conventions in Washington draw a large number of both vendors and attendees. Hiring managers and top-level executives of major companies attend DC conventions.

In addition, many large DC hotels, such as Marriott, Holiday Inn, and Hilton, host trade shows, and I suggest checking their websites for conference information. If you cannot find it online, call the hotel and ask to speak with the conference manager.

BEST TRADE SHOWS FOR JOB HUNTING BY INDUSTRY

The following list of annual trade shows by industry could be your ticket to that first civilian job. Click on the show nearest to your location or the show focusing on an area of interest, like photography, housing, food, shelter, travel, or educational technology and publishing. The organizations listed below hold conferences in different locations each year. To get you started, I'm focusing on only seven industries: Education, Insurance, Healthcare, Transportation, and the *Big Three*: Food, Shelter, and Clothing.

EDUCATION

The Education Industry is truly military friendly. Many veterans are working in this industry because they find there a sense of mission and attractive compensation. At all of these exhibits, you will meet hiring managers working for companies like the College Board, Educational Testing Service (ETS), Scholastic, and McGraw-Hill.

American Booksellers Association (ABA), www.bookweb.com. The ABA holds an annual conference and several regional conferences where you can see many companies in the print and digital publishing industry. The BEA, BookExpo America, is the largest publishing convention in the USA. (See BEA below for more information.)

American Association of School Administrators (AASA), www.aasa.org. Hundreds of companies exhibit here to display their products to school superintendents and other high-level school administrators. The companies attending this convention are publishers and producers of instructional materials, school supply companies, bus companies, insurance companies, security companies, and more.

Association of Educational Publishers (AEP), www.aepweb.org. This organization sponsors an annual conference in June each year in Washington, DC. Attendees include high-level educational technology and publishing company executives, all of whom are hiring authorities. In 2013, this organization merged with the Association of American Publishers (AAP), www.publishers.org.

American Library Association (ALA), www.ALA.org. This conference focuses on books and digital products related to public and school libraries and online education. It is a fascinating show with hundreds of exhibitors from the education, publishing, and online learning industries. Once you are on this website, click on "Education and Careers."

Association for Supervision and Curriculum Development (ASCD), www.ASCD.org. Members of ASCD are involved with curriculum matters at K-12 schools. Thousands of these administrators, called curriculum coordinators or assistant superintendents for instruction, attend this show.

American Society for Training and Development (ASTD), www.astd.org. This nonprofit organization focuses on training and professional development for educators and government workers. It holds an annual conference in a major city plus four regional conferences throughout the country. A recent conference met in Dallas and attracted approximately 9,000 attendees from 80 different countries. More than 300 companies exhibited their products and services. The price of entrance to the exhibits? Free! Track the annual and regional conferences, because this is where you will meet many employers in the flesh, each one being the source for a possible civilian job. Think of it. Three hundred potential employers gathered under one roof. Does job hunting get any easier than that?

BookExpo America (BEA), www.bookexpoamerica.com. BookExpo America is the largest trade show in America for the book publishing industry. BEA held its 2015 annual convention at the Javits Center in New York City. More than twelve hundred companies hosted exhibits on the conference center floor, all staffed by full-time employees. Some held editorial positions, some were marketing managers, some came from sales, others from finance, and still others from information technology. Where in the world could you find so many potential employers under one roof?

Who attends BEA? Here is an example of the caliber of attendees at this convention. A New York City-based trade publisher, Skyhorse Publishing Inc., www.skyhorsepublishing.com, the publisher of this book, attends BEA and displays its publications in an exhibit staffed by some of their key employees, such as an editorial director. He is in charge of the entire editorial staff at Skyhorse and is the person you need to see for potential job opportunities, entry-level or above.

Consortium for School Networking (CoSN), www.cosn.org. This organization conducts an annual conference attended by hundreds of executive-level hiring managers from the educational technology industry. The location changes each year. CoSN is based in Washington, DC, and posts job openings on its website. Check it out.

The EdNET Conference, www.ednetinsight.com. The conference meets in a different city each year in September. In 2015, it was in Atlanta; in 2014, it was in Baltimore. If you are interested in the education business, which consists of companies that produce instructional materials and services for K-12 and higher education, attend this conference. When you register by phone or online, ask for a veteran's discount. Check out the website now to learn more.

Florida Educational Technology Conference (FETC), www.fetc.org. This organization hosts an annual convention in Orlando, Florida, in February. Its focus is educational technology. Hundreds of educational technology companies exhibit at this conference. If you like technology and its application in the education process, you cannot afford to miss this one. By the way, bring a few dozen resumes and several hundred calling cards because you will find a hiring manager in almost every exhibit booth.

International Reading Association (IRA), www.reading.org. This organization is for teachers and administrators who teach reading and literacy to K-12 students. When you access this site, click on "Career Center," where you will find ten or more pages of open positions. If you have any experience in education and are interested in literacy education, you have hit the jackpot.

International Society for Technology in Education (ISTE), www. iste.org. This show focuses on products and services related to educational technology and meets each June at a different location. If you are interested in an industry that makes a difference for kids, this one is for you. Do not miss it, because here you will find hundreds of exhibitors under one roof. Each is a potential employer.

International Education Book Fairs

There are several international publishing conventions each year, and if you are in the area, plan to attend. Attending are companies from America and other countries hosting exhibits staffed by workers who will tell you about job opportunities *and* provide the names and contact information for hiring managers. Foreign companies may be looking for workers to represent their interests in America, and you might be the one for such a job. Here are some of the best international trade fairs in the education and communication industries.

Frankfurt Book Fair, www.buchmesse.de/en/company. This convention attracts 7,000 exhibitors from around the world and is the mother of all international book fairs. It meets in Frankfurt, Germany, every October. Can you imagine 7,000 potential employers under one roof?

The London Book Fair, www.londonbookfair.co.uk. This major bookseller event meets in London each spring. It attracts close to 1,000 exhibitors ranging from retail booksellers to educational publishers and communications companies in general.

Bologna Children's Book Fair. This interesting book fair focuses on products related to K-12 education. Hundreds of companies publishing books and digital products exhibit here. Bologna, Italy, is the host city for this annual conference. Check it out if you happen to be in Italy in spring.

Beijing International Book Fair, www.combinedbook.com. If you find yourself in China during the month of August, visit this fascinating conference to meet more than 500 exhibitors from around the world, with an emphasis on Asian companies. This is a long way to go to meet American companies, but you will find many of them exhibiting alongside their foreign counterparts.

INSURANCE

Many insurance companies have been in business continuously for more than a hundred years and are attractive places for long-term employment. The industry hosts many conventions throughout the calendar year in many different cities. Here is an example.

The National Association of Mutual Insurance Companies (NAMIC), www.namic.org. This is one of the largest insurance organizations in the business, and it hosts an annual convention at a different location each year. The 2014 national convention met in September at the Gaylord National Resort and Conference Center in National Harbour, Maryland. More than three hundred companies exhibited, and there were one thousand senior executives from the insurance industry in attendance.

The best place for information about insurance trade shows is the *Insurance Journal*. Visit the website at www.insurancejournal.com.

If you like the idea of long-term employment, make it a point to attend an insurance industry conference. Attending conferences not only opens the door for job opportunities, but also provides an education about that industry and how it works.

HEALTHCARE

Under the broadly defined label of "healthcare," there are numerous subgroups that include pharmaceuticals, professional providers like physicians, radiologists, certified nurse midwives, physical therapists, medical equipment providers, medicinal packaging companies, and so on. There is no one large catchall convention, but there are many small conventions serving segments of the healthcare industry. Many of these conventions are local or regional in scope. Here are some of the larger national conventions sponsored by professional healthcare organizations:

- NPWH Premier Women's Healthcare Conference, www.npwh.org
- Federation of International Medical Equipment Suppliers, www.fimeshow.com
- Radiographical Society of North America, www.rsna.org
- Healthcare Information and Management Systems Society, www.himss.org
- American Society of Clinical Oncology, www.asco.org
- International Society for Pharmaceutical Engineering (ISPE) sponsors the annual Pharma Expo conference, www.pharma-expo.com
- American College of Nurse-Midwives, www.acnm.org
- American Physical Therapy Association, www.apta.org

The largest in this group is Pharma Expo, www.pharmaexpo.com, a convention devoted to packaging of every imaginable kind for medicines and medical equipment. The 2015 convention was held in Denver in conjunction with PACK EXPO, the national convention for the general packaging industry. Approximately 1,800 exhibitors and over 30,000 industry workers attended this convention.

Veterans whose military experience included healthcare of any kind will receive a hearty welcome from the civilian side of this industry. Learn more about the many facets of civilian healthcare and job opportunities by attending local and national conventions.

THE TRANSPORTATION INDUSTRY

The transportation industry conducts hundreds of conventions each year in locations throughout the country, and it would be impossible to list all of them. As you did for the housing industry, google "auto shows" in the largest city close to home, and you will find all the information you need. Here is an example of a major transportation show to get you started:

New York International Auto Show, www.autoshowny.com. This conference is one of the largest auto shows in the country and hosts hundreds of companies, which exhibit at the Javits Center. Attend this conference and you will find potential job opportunities in the automobile industry. Guaranteed.

THE FOOD INDUSTRY

This huge industry includes everything imaginable, including fast foods, beverages, restaurants, online grocery shopping, and hospitality. There are many local, regional, and national conventions catering to the food industry. Check out those listed below.

Natural Products Expo East, www.expoeast.com. East Expo is an annual conference dedicated to showcasing natural and organic foods and beverages. The convention moves to a new east coast city each year. In September 2015, the exhibit was held at the Baltimore Convention Center and attracted *1,400 exhibiting companies*, each a potential employer. Where else could you find that many employers under one roof?

Natural Products Expo West, www.foodexpowest.com. This is the western states' counterpart to Expo East. It is usually held at the Anaheim Convention Center in Anaheim, California. Last year, more than 1,000 natural and organic food and beverage companies exhibited at this convention.

Specialty Food Association, www.specialtyfood.com. Greek olive oil, gourmet cookies, and Madagascar bourbon. At the Association's conventions you will find such products . . . and more. Here companies producing specialty products of every description exhibit their tempting wares. This nonprofit trade organization was founded in 1952 to promote commerce among companies in the specialty food industry. The Association conducts conventions in cities throughout the country which attract tens of thousands of attendees and hundreds of exhibitors. Veterans with military experience in any phase of the food chain will find job hunting a snap at this conference.

The International Restaurant and Food Service Show, www.internationalrestaurantny.com. Meet 500 exhibiting companies and 16,000 workers in this interesting venue at the Javits Center in New York. The convention is the best in this market niche.

National Restaurant Association, www.restaurant.org. How can you beat a convention with 2,000 exhibitors (all potential employers) and 45,000 attendees? If your interest is the restaurant niche, plan to attend this conference, which meets at McCormick Place in Chicago each year. For general information about this part of the food industry, contact the National Restaurant Association, www.restaurant.org.

THE CLOTHING INDUSTRY

This industry includes a number of specialties, like children's clothing, sportswear, women's fashion, textile manufacturing, footwear, and exercise gear, just to name a few. As a result, there are no national conventions catering to the clothing industry as a whole. The best way to find trade shows in a specialty of the clothing industry is to conduct an online search for your area of interest.

THE SHELTER INDUSTRY

There are many home shows throughout the US that attract thousands of companies exhibiting their products. Each one is a potential employer. Where do you find them? At conference centers throughout the country. For example, do you live in or near the Chicago area? There are several home shows in different area locations hosting many

                Operation Job Search

hundreds of exhibitors. Who knows, one of them may provide your first civilian job. Go here: www.chicagohomeshow.net.

There are so many home shows that it would take many pages to list all of them here. An easy route to find these conferences is to google "home trade shows" in your local area. Sometimes these shows combine home building and improvement companies with garden and horticulture organizations. As an example of what you will find, I will highlight just two.

National Association of Home Builders (NAHB), www.nahb.org. The annual convention is the NAHB International Builders Show. The 2015 conference was in Las Vegas in January. At this show, you will find approximately 1,000 exhibiting companies, all potential employers. If the shelter part of survival intrigues you, attend this show and other home shows that take place in major cities. In addition to providing an opportunity to meet hiring managers or workers who can lead you to them, this show will provide an education about how the shelter industry works in the US. Attend this show or other regional home shows, and your knowledge of the housing industry will increase exponentially. When you visit the website, click on "Careers and Industry Jobs." When I visited the career pages, I found an entry-level job titled computer support specialist, a position requiring a college degree and knowledge of several common applications.

Philadelphia Home Show, www.phillyhomeshow.com. This conference takes place in Philly each February and hosts hundreds of exhibitors. Most are local companies, but some are national, too. While you are there, remember to have one of those famous Philadelphia cheese steak sandwiches.

HOW TO FIND A TRADE SHOW CATERING TO A PARTICULAR INTEREST

There are many resources for finding conventions matching your interests: industry journals, both print and digital, local newspapers, and convention center schedules. In addition, you will find a trade show directory on the website of the following organization:

Events in America, www.eventsinamerica.com/tradeshows. This organization tracks and publicizes the names and locations of industry trade shows across the country.

MOVING FORWARD

Attending trade shows and job fairs is the best method for finding hiring managers who are there searching for candidates to fill open positions. Trade shows convene every month in large metropolitan areas. To learn the who/when/where, search the convention center websites listed above.

CHAPTER TAKEAWAYS

- The best place to meet hiring managers and key executives is at conferences, trade shows, and job fairs.
- Dress in business attire while attending trade shows.
- Never drink alcoholic beverages while job hunting. Never!

THE VETERAN'S LIBRARY

Barry Siskind. *Powerful Exhibit Marketing*. Wiley, 2005.

Chapter 21

Employment Challenges and Solutions for Female Veterans

It comes at you from every direction: right; left; top; and down under. If for some reason you happened to miss the chatter, this is what I am hearing with increasing frequency:

> *"There are large numbers of female veterans transitioning to the civilian workforce."*
> *"The unemployment rate for female veterans, especially those in the post 9/11 group is alarmingly high."*
> *"The unemployment rate for female veterans is twice the rate for male veterans."*
> *"Post-military job searching for female veterans is a no-win contest."*
> *"Why are all of these women who served the country so gallantly unable to find a job?"*
> *"There's nothing out there for female veterans."*
> *"The suicide rate for female veterans is twice that for the female non-veteran population."*

I hear it every day from a range of sources, from First Lady Michelle Obama to the female veteran who submitted 200 resumes and is still without a job. Is all of this just hype, or is there something to it? After all, the national unemployment rate at the end of 2015 was 5.4 percent, which means that America is fully employed when you factor out seasonal and structural unemployment, which we will always have. Why then should there be a problem for female veterans? They had real jobs while serving in the armed forces, and it should be easy for them to make a successful and quick transition to the civilian workplace after discharge. What's the real story?

Moreover, if all of this is true, why are we not hearing more about the *solutions* to correct the problems? Is it just another case of media frenzy to boost ratings?

Here at **OJS**, we always look at the numbers to verify or trash the hype. *Trust but verify* is our mantra. We did just that and found the numbers that show that the problems for women veterans are real. All of our sources indicate that the unemployment rate for female veterans is not only above the national average for the workforce generally, but also *nearly double the unemployment rate for male veterans*. Our sources are media outlets such as the *New York Times*, the *Wall Street Journal*, and *USA Today*; government agencies like the Department of Veterans Affairs (VA), the Bureau of Labor Statistics, and the Census Bureau; and independent sources like the Pew Research Center, Military.com, and CNBC. Never have we found so many sources verifying a problem with supporting statistics like the following:

- As of December 2014, there were 471,894 post-9/11 female veterans and 2,132,000 male veterans.
- Female veterans with a high school degree have the same unemployment rate as non-veterans with a high school degree.
- The unemployment rate for all female veterans is approximately 13.5 percent, almost double the unemployment rate for male veterans and approximately 8 percent above the national unemployment rate.

Clearly, there are challenges facing female veterans as they transition to the civilian workforce, and they need to be addressed not only by the Department of Veterans Affairs and the Department of Defense, but also by the media, non-governmental agencies, and books like **OPERATION JOB SEARCH**.

THE LEADING WORK TRANSITION PROBLEMS FOR FEMALE VETERANS. AND THE SOLUTIONS

There are many reasons for the high female veteran unemployment rate, which is double that of the male veteran population. Some are obvious, but others lurk quietly behind the scenes, wreaking havoc in the lives of transitioning female veterans. Here are the seven leading causes for the high rate of unemployment for female veterans . . . and the **OJS** solutions.

1. **Limited education**. Education is your key to finding more job opportunities that pay living wages. There is a substantial body of research proving that the more education you have, the more money you will make over a lifetime of work.

    OJS Solution. If you volunteered for the military straight out of high school, you must resume your education as soon as possible. The best place to kick-start your education is to enroll at your local community college. If you don't know what subjects to select, head straight for the English curriculum. Honing your written and verbal skills will make you better qualified for any job, in any industry, throughout your career.

    If you completed some college-level courses before the military, continue where you left off through online courses or at a physical campus. Other options include concentrating on something new that interests you, like psychology or business administration, or selecting an entirely new discipline that would qualify you for jobs that are always in demand. The best disciplines for expanding job opportunities are the STEM subjects (Science, Technology, Engineering and Mathematics).

    If the formal classroom is not for you, there are other options, like working in the construction trades where you can expend your creative energy building things of lasting value and beauty such as new homes or commercial buildings. Work in the trades, and for the rest of your life you will look at that house and proudly say, "That's something I had a hand in creating." Working creatively with your hands is a viable alternative to working in the corporate environment where after a year of work you might ask, "What did I really do? Where are visible signs of my creative input and accomplishments?" Work is not always a white-collar activity.

Penny Pritzker, US Secretary of Commerce in the Obama Administration, brings attention to the problems resulting from lack of education, particularly lack of education relating to technology skills. In a recent interview with Katie Couric, she said, *"One of the things that is really important for us to be doing is making sure that we're training people for the jobs that exist today. Since I've been in this job, I've probably met with 1,500 employers. All of them tell that they have challenges finding the skilled labor they need. These are not the manufacturing jobs of 25 years ago. These are technical jobs . . . and they often require some kind of computer literacy."*

Secretary Pritzker went on to say that some companies like CVS and Campbell's Soup have created thousands of apprenticeship programs to help solve the "skills gap" problem that exists today. Veterans, before you continue reading, take a minute to explore career opportunities at these two great companies by going to their websites: www.cvs.com and www.campbellsoupcompany.com.

Read Chapter 6 for more information and advice on continuing your education.

2. **Lack of confidence**. After sitting at home and firing off hundreds of resumes to places like "Box 123" or "Employment Manager" with no response, your confidence erodes to the point where you begin to feel sorry for yourself. You begin to believe that nobody recognizes the significant skill sets you learned in the military. Dejected, you might even begin to think that you are being overlooked because you are a woman and this is just another manifestation of discrimination. Soon hostility sets in and you believe that you are the victim of a

system that is stacked against you. Your descent into victim-hood has a paralytic effect and you begin to ask, "Why should I even try when the odds are stacked against me?" Finally, you become morose and stop your job search believing that it is just an unfair system and you can do nothing about it.

Military.com featured a recent article titled "Study Finds Female Vets Less Confident in Job Hunt." The study found that, compared to male veterans, female veterans feel that the skills obtained during their service in the military were less developed and less relevant to civilian careers.

OJS Solution. The reason why you may not have a job six to twelve months after beginning your search could be that you are going about it the wrong way. This is understandable, because your experience with the civilian world of work is limited. The remedy is to follow the rubrics in **OJS** and to seek counseling from one of the many free sources available to veterans.

Lack of confidence is frequently related to poor communication skills, which are paramount for job searching. For example, if you walk into an interview and relate your experience in military jargon, you will get a blank stare from the interviewer. When she asks you to translate your MOS into civilian terms, you just don't know how to do it. The result? A polite rejection. The solution is to improve your written and verbal communication skills, which you can do by taking courses online or at a local community college.

From my experience as an executive recruiter, I can assure you that the doors of employment are, with rare exceptions, open to women as well as men. At the beginning of every assignment, my clients always tell me to bring them female candidates, as many as possible. I have done just that, and many of my female candidates have been hired for interesting jobs that pay wages comparable to or above those of male candidates. In my twenty years in the staffing business, approximately two-thirds of my placements have been women.

Recently, I interviewed a Marine Captain about her experience making the transition to the civilian workforce and asked what advice she would give to female veterans. Her emphatic response was: *Be proud of your accomplishments.*

3. **Lack of information about the civilian workplace**. You have been in the Armed Forces for the past six years or more working in a unique culture. That environment bears little resemblance to the civilian workplace.

   OJS Solution. Learn how this new world works by reviewing Part II, "Making a Job Search Plan for the Civilian Workplace." There you will learn about the characteristics of the civilian workplace and the numbers and terms that govern it. Also, attend trade shows held at major convention centers, which are located in every state.

4. **Family responsibilities**. Caring for the family is a responsibility that usually falls to women for a variety of reasons. Closely related to this issue is the divorce rate for both active duty and female veterans. There does seem to be agreement that the divorce rate for active duty females and veteran females is higher than it is for males. It is unclear why this happens, but the result is that divorced females are expected to fulfill their own work responsibilities, *and* act as primary caregiver for the children, *and* assume responsibility for the household generally. The added family responsibility places them under considerable stress. Interestingly, the VA reports that approximately 24 percent of all female veterans are divorced (compared to 13 percent for non-veteran females). Moreover, female veterans under thirty-five are more likely to be divorced and have children compared to their non-veteran counterparts. What follows is that divorced female veterans are saddled not only with making the transition to the civilian workplace, but also the responsibility of taking care of the children. Whether by mutual agreement between the divorcing spouses or by court order, custody of dependent children is usually given to the women.

Caring for dependent children places female veterans at a distinct disadvantage when competing for jobs with candidates who do not have childcare responsibilities. For example, many jobs at the managerial level are salaried. You are paid a certain amount of money regardless of the number of hours spent on the job. In addition, overnight travel away from home could be required. How can a single mom work ten to twelve hours a day, travel overnight several times a month or more, and take care of the children, too? As a result, female veterans are disqualified and forced to take jobs that pay less and have meager benefits.

Adding to this challenge is the undisputed fact that employers seek workers with the least number of personal constraints, the least amount of baggage so to speak. Not fair? Well, the employer has a responsibility to the company and to other workers to hire candidates who can be the most productive in order to increase profitability. The so-called bottom line for a company is to maintain profitability to remain in business.

OJS Solution. Explore positions only with military friendly companies, the names of which you can find on Military.com, www.military.com. Human resources managers in these companies make every effort to help female veterans overcome hurdles specific to their situation. In their world, one size does not fit all. They are more likely to permit flex hours to accommodate family responsibilities, like taking the children to school and picking them up after classes. In addition, military friendly companies may provide childcare on company premises for pre-school children or pay for outside childcare.

Another solution, an **OJS** fave, is to seek a position that does not have a 9–5 requirement. Local area sales positions come to mind, like selling insurance, real estate, or automobiles. These positions can be tailored to meet your specific needs, will provide an above average income, and can be a long-term career. For example, I have purchased my last four cars, Toyota Avalons, from Patty, a sales rep with a Toyota dealer in suburban Philadelphia. Patty has been on the job with the same dealership for fifteen continuous years and is the mother of a school-age daughter. She holds a respectable job that pays well and offers flexible hours to take care of her daughter.

Other sales jobs, like selling real estate, do require state certification but you can obtain it easily within a matter of months. Go online or check with a local realtor to learn the specific certification requirements.

How much can you expect to make selling? How does $75,000–150,000 per year sound? What about benefits? Most sales jobs carry a slate of basic benefits, such as life and medical insurance, vacation time, and sick days.

Most sales positions do not require certification or a college degree. They require excellent communication skills, a sense of mission, punctuality, business courtesy, and ethical behavior. To me, that sounds like the skills and values female veterans learned in the military.

5. **Lack of focus**. I have discovered in the course of my work as an executive recruiter that job candidates who want just *any job* regardless of type, industry, or company have difficulty finding gainful employment. The reason might not be obvious. When a candidate goes through the interview process, the hiring manager will always discover a candidate's motive for applying. If the reason is to find a job, any job regardless of what it is, that candidate will go to the bottom of the list. Employers like workers who focus on a particular kind of work and display their passion for the job and the company.

   OJS Solution. Learn who you are and what interests you. Everyone has undiscovered interests. However, your interests may not be identifiable, especially when you have other items on your transition agenda. How do you accomplish this? **OJS** has two suggestions.

First, review the material in Chapters 1, 12, and 13. Second, purchase and read the *Occupational Outlook Handbook*. This thousand-page reference book, which is updated and published annually, lists virtually every job in every industry in America. It provides the job description, requirements, salary ranges, and need for each job going forward. Review this book, note all of the jobs that interest you, and go from there. Armed with this information about yourself, you can focus on a specific job in a specific industry. Your focus and passion will be evident to any hiring manager or human resources director.

6. **Employer ignorance of the female military experience**. The overwhelming majority of human resources directors and hiring managers have had no experience with the military. They have little idea of the training veterans received while in the service. They do not know that your leadership skills and discipline were superbly honed and that these attributes are transferable to the civilian workplace. In short, they know nothing about jobs in the military.

   OJS Solution. Write your resume using civilian language and articulate your military work experience in civilian terms during your phone or personal interview. In effect, you become the teacher and need to be prepared. One reliable method to use is to prepare a career profile instead of just a resume and present this to the hiring manager. There are six parts to the career profile: a cover letter, a resume, a transcript of education credits, business and/or technology certifications, letters of reference, and articles or blogs that you have written attesting to your communication skills. For more information, read Chapter 24, "Writing a Resume and Career Profile."

7. **The Need for Job Benefits**. Most workers need basic benefits that usually come with full-time jobs. However, many female veterans, for a variety of reasons, take part-time jobs carrying no benefits.

   OJS Solution. Until just recently, there were few viable solutions for this predicament. Now that has changed. Some large companies, and a number of smaller companies, have agreed to provide benefits for part-time workers.

Look for large and small military friendly companies that provide benefits for part timers. For example, here are five large companies and one small company that have decided to do so. They are:

- **The Container Store**, www.containerstore.com.
- **REI** (the recreation, sporting goods, and apparel company), www.rei.jobs.
- **Starbucks**, www.starbucks.com.
- **United Parcel Service (UPS)**, www.ups.com. Be sure to review "Women's Leadership Development" and "Veterans Outreach."
- **Whole Foods**, www.wholefoods.com.
- **MMS Education**, www.mmseducation.com. MMS is located in the Philadelphia area and provides editorial, sales, and marketing services for companies in the for-profit and not-for-profit education industry.

TOP 10 COMPANIES FOR WOMEN

Each year *Fortune* magazine, www.fortune.com, evaluates thousands of companies for their attitudes and practices toward their employees and publishes the data in one of their spring issues. The March 2015 issue listed the following companies as the best employers for women:

Fortune's Top 10 Best Companies for Women

1. Meridian Health, www.meridianhs.org.
2. Children's Healthcare of Atlanta, www.choa.net.
3. Perkins Coie, www.perkinscoie.com.
4. Alston & Bird, www.alston.com.
5. Novo Nordisk, www.novonordisk-us.com.
6. Baptist Health South Florida, www.baptisthealth.com.
7. Atlantic Health System, www.atlantichealth.org.

8. Scripps Health, www.scripps.org.
9. Nordstrom, www.nordstrom.com.
10. Wellstar Health System, www.wellstar.com.

Most of these companies are national in scope, even though their name includes a specific location. Other star performers in *Fortune*'s best place to work list include: Whole Foods, Cisco, Wegmans, Four Seasons Hotels, Cleveland Clinic, and Goldman Sachs.

MOVING FORWARD

Job searching comes with multiple challenges for female veterans, but they can be overcome. Use your intelligence, energy, and passion for the task and access every source of advice, guidance, and support. Success will follow.

CHAPTER TAKEAWAYS

- The whole world is there to help with your job search. Reach out and we will find you.
- Continually update your formal education and your job skills.
- Entry-level jobs frequently lead to promotions.
- Do not be trapped by victimhood.
- For every challenge, there is a solution.
- Work includes both hands-on and white-collar jobs.
- Be proud of your accomplishments.
- Become somebody!

THE VETERAN'S LIBRARY

Tanya Biank. *Undaunted: The Real Story of America's Servicewomen in Today's Military*. Penguin Group, 2013.

Travis Bradbury and Jean Greaves. *Emotional Intelligence 2.0*. TalentSmart, 2009.

Chapter 22

Employment Challenges and Solutions for Spouses of Military Veterans

For our purposes, military spouses are women or men whose husbands or wives are active duty military personnel or veterans. Frequently, we assume that the military spouse is a woman, but that notion is becoming "yesterday" as the number of women in the military increases. Women make up approximately 14 percent of today's military, and there are currently 472,000 female veterans. Going forward we will see an increasing number of male spouses. However, the overwhelming majority of military spouses *today* are women, which is the reason why much of our discourse in this chapter targets female military spouses of veterans.

EMPLOYMENT CHALLENGES AND SOLUTIONS

The number one challenge for spouses of both veterans and active duty personnel is unemployment, which just happens to be the number one challenge for female veterans as well. The numbers are alarming. The unemployment rate for military spouses is 25 percent, and the wage gap for military spouses compared to civilian workers is also 25 percent.

Here are the major factors playing behind the scenes that account for unemployment problems for military spouses. I also offer the **OJS** solutions. The term "military spouse" includes both spouses of active duty personnel and spouses of veterans. Both groups have similar problems, and the solutions we provide apply to both groups.

1. **Limited education and skill sets**. Lack of formal education is a common problem for military spouses because of frequent moves from one location to another. Stays of short duration in one particular location inhibit spouses from continuing their formal education in traditional bricks-and-mortar schools like community colleges or universities.

   OJS Solution. Military spouses can take accredited online courses to pursue an AA, BA, or MA degree. Geography is no longer a barrier to continuing one's education. Even if you change locations in the USA and abroad, online courses will always be there for you. Often you can take online courses free of charge from a military friendly college, or you can find tuition reimbursement funds from a variety of sources. The first place to look for more information is the VA website, www.va.gov.

   After your spouse is discharged, your location will be more stable, and you will be able to continue your education without the problems caused by continuous relocation. However, the spouse who continued her education or training online will have a head start on civilian job hunting when that time comes. In effect, your education credentials will make you job-ready.

   The same solution applies for obtaining certifications. For example, if your focus is on education jobs that require certification, you can go online for the required courses. The same applies for certifications in various healthcare occupations, education, finance, and a number of technology related jobs.

2. **Frequent relocation**. This is a common problem, one that has serious ramifications for all military spouses of active duty personnel. Employers always seek job candidates who have no barriers to long-term employment, because they spend a

considerable amount of time and money recruiting, training, and mentoring new employees. The last thing a company wants is constant employee turnover.

OJS Solution. Tell a potential employer that you have transferable skills that you bring to the job, which saves the employer money by eliminating the usual training period and learning curve. Employers know that most civilian workers require ramp-up time, say six months or more before they become productive. Your transferable skill sets could be a big selling point in your favor. Make the case by explaining that you are different because of your family military background, which requires spouses to be productive immediately.

If you have not acquired any specific transferable skills or if you have no job preference, consider working in sales. Selling is a job overlooked by many job seekers. That is unfortunate because a good sales rep can make substantial wages while enjoying a work environment away from the company cubicle. Selling works well for those spouses with family responsibilities, like taking care of the children. Moreover, selling skills are transferable to any part of the world. Does it get any better than that for a military spouse? Successful sales reps possess three qualities: excellent verbal communication skills, intelligence, and honesty. Forget about the stereotypes. Sales reps are smart folks who can take their skills anywhere and make a good living.

So what is there to sell? **OJS** suggests selling insurance or automobiles, both of which are constant needs.

3. **Difficulty writing resumes and interviewing**. These are common problems for most job candidates, not only military spouses. Almost everyone has such problems, which is one of the reasons why I wrote **OPERATION JOB SEARCH**.

OJS Solution. The first rule of resumes and interviews is to be honest. Do not exaggerate or fudge the facts of your background. In today's technology-focused world, the first thing a hiring manager does is google your name to learn more about you.

Resumes and interviews require two different skill sets. Resumes require excellent written communication skills, which include using error-free spelling and grammar. For interviews, it is verbal communication skills, which include correct body language and using civilian terminology, not military-speak. For help with resumes refer to Part V, "Resumes. Career Profiles. Cover Letters. Follow-Ups." For help with interviews, refer to Part VI, "Personal Interviews. Phone and Skype Interviews."

There is a misperception that the resume or the interview alone will win the job. That is just not true. Both are parts of the job-hunting *process*, a multi-step endeavor. For more information, refer to Chapter 12, "The Search Plan as an Operation and a Process."

4. **What to wear**. It's a problem cutting across all demographics. However, it seems that proper business attire, especially for interviews, causes more concern for women than for men. This is understandable because women are more fashion and style conscious than men are, and because there are more choices for women than there are for men. A guy can get away with that fail-safe outfit consisting of a blue blazer, grey pants, white shirt, red tie, and black leather shoes. For women it is not that easy.

OJS Solution. When you are going on an interview or attending a job fair or trade show, always wear business attire, which is always *conservative*. A quick way to learn what is correct business attire is to watch TV channels dedicated to business, such as CNBC and the Fox Business Network. Observe what the women are wearing.

Attire is such an important and troublesome topic in the job searching process that I wrote an entire chapter on the subject for this book. For solid advice, go to Chapter 27, "Communication Begins with Your Appearance." Note the section

"Listen to Linda" for suggestions about what is right and what is not.

5. **Childcare responsibilities**. For military families, childcare is a constant source of concern and at times a source of discord between spouses. Well, guess what? Caring for the kids is a constant concern for non-military families, too, ranking right up there at the top of the problem ladder with divorce, money problems, and infidelity. Do not fall into the victimhood trap, the one that says, "I'm a military spouse, and nobody has problems like mine. Nobody understands me and nobody really gives a good goddamn."

The entire burden of childcare usually falls on the military spouse, hitting on one of her greatest challenges, gaining and maintaining gainful employment.

OJS Solution. For the non-military family, solutions revolve around shared responsibility, but for military families, it is not that easy. Usually the active duty person has military responsibilities that go beyond the civilian 9–5 job. Compounding the problem is deployment overseas, which leaves mom with complete childcare responsibilities.

Spouses of recently discharged veterans have similar problems. There is a period of readjustment to civilian life that all transitioning veterans experience, leaving the spouse to manage everything from tending to the children's needs to maintaining the house.

There are solutions, such as finding a job with flex hours that provides time to take the kids to and from school and other activities or working from home. Flex hour jobs are the ideal solution. One such job is full-time teaching or substitute teaching. If you do not hold teacher certification, consider education jobs like teacher's assistant or administrative assistant. Hours for education jobs coincide with the school day and annual school calendar, providing time to care for the children. You will not find such jobs advertised online or in newspapers.

They are usually filled through networking. The way to find them is to put on your business attire and cold call on individual schools and school district offices. Always ask for the principal or superintendent. Is cold calling old school with all the technology initiatives in place? Don't believe it. Candidates find more jobs through cold calling than one would imagine.

Another job with flextime is selling, as we discussed above. Outside sales jobs provide the ultimate in flexibility and pay well. Cold calling is one of the best methods to find sales positions. Dressed in business attire, cold call on local insurance agents or on automobile dealers.

Working from home is more common than one might think. Technology enables companies to hire workers who can work away from the corporate office. For example, some airlines permit their reservationists to work from home. One that comes to mind is Southwest Airlines. Recently I made a reservation on Southwest using their call-in service. No, the reservationist was not in India or the Philippines. She was working from her home in Denver. Another work-from-home job is customer service. Most small and medium-sized companies hire locals to work from home. To find such employers, cold call on companies located in office/industrial parks. There are many in and around all medium and large cities. To find them, google "office and industrial parks" and add your location.

EMPLOYMENT RESOURCES FOR MILITARY SPOUSES

The world is willing and waiting to help military spouses with employment matters. From the VA and VFW to the local military friendly employer down the street, everyone has respect for the military spouse and will lend a hand with employment matters. Here are some of the best resources.

Defense Enrollment Eligibility Reporting System (DEER). In order to take advantage of your military benefits, you must enroll in DEER and get your military identification card. This site will steer you through the process. It includes instructions on how to locate and complete the Department of Defense Form 1172, a requirement for obtaining your ID card.

The Department of Veterans Affairs (VA), www.va.gov. How many times have you heard, "Go to the VA"? It is good advice because this organization provides benefits in abundance for military families. While writing this book, I contacted officials at the VA for information and advice and was treated with respect and given timely advice.

Contact the VA frequently for updates to programs like the Transition Assistance Program (TAP). Changes for the better are always taking place, and it is your responsibility to stay informed. The Veterans Employment Center should be your first contact.

National Military Spouse Network (NMSN), www.nationalmilitaryspousenetwork.com. As soon as you settle into your new surroundings, join this military spouse group for support and advice, particularly about employment matters.

NMSN describes itself as "the pre-eminent networking, mentoring and professional development organization committed to the education, empowerment and advancement of military spouses." An added feature is the *NMSN Magazine*. A recent issue included an article about VA Senior Advisor Rosye Cloud, which you can access on the website. Don't miss it.

In addition to NMSN, there are local military spouse networks, which you can find through your local VFW.

The Spouse Channel at Military.com, www.military.com. This site makes connections for military spouses throughout the country. Be sure to see "Military Spouse Job Search Tips" for practical job-hunting advice. Study the tip titled "Make that Cold Call. Get the Job." It reinforces what **OJS** advocates for all job seekers: leave the house and knock on doors. For more information on cold calling, refer to Chapter

17, "How to Find Employers through Networking, Print Media, Cold Calling, Trade Shows, and Job Fairs."

Ask Ms. Vicki, www.military.com/topics/ms-vicki. There really is a Ms. Vicki! She is a Dallas resident married to an active duty soldier. She has three children. She is a syndicated columnist offering advice and support to military spouses on a broad range of topics, including employment matters. Check her advice columns frequently.

Grantham University, www.granthamu.com. Grantham brings 60 years of service to military families through scholarships, training, and financial assistance. It offers online degree programs in a number of curriculum areas including business, computer science, and healthcare. When you go to this site, click on "Military and Veterans," where you will find a special section devoted to military spouses.

World Education, www.worldeducation.net. World Education offers online accredited certificate programs in a variety of subjects. WE has working relationships with state and private colleges and universities throughout the country. The website provides a special section on resume writing for military spouses.

Military Spouse, www.militaryspouse.com. This interesting and helpful site concentrates on employment matters for military spouses. The site provides information on the benefits you are entitled to receive from various sources, college funding options, degree options, scholarships, and community forums.

Career One Stop, www.careeronestop.org. The US Department of Labor sponsors this site in partnership with the American Job Center Network. This is a general job-hunting site offering a vast amount of information about jobs in various industries throughout the country.

See the special section titled "Military Spouse Resources." Here you will find helpful information and resources through the links provided.

Those about to transition into civilian life will find employment, training, and benefit information and resources at Career One Stop's "Veterans Reemployment" section.

Next Generation Military Spouse, www.nextgenmilspouse.com. This organization is defining the new generation military spouse. The site includes advice, a current events calendar, press releases, and a career/entrepreneur center.

Military.com, www.military.com. This site reaches out to support and help military veterans and their families. Each year it publishes a list of military friendly companies, which provide special benefits and support not only for the military veteran seeking employment, but also for the military spouses seeking employment. Three of our favorite companies on the list are Johnson & Johnson, Home Depot, and Lowe's.

MOVING FORWARD

There is much information on the Internet for military spouses, and it can become a challenge to sort through it. We suggest that you limit your initial job-hunting activities to the resources in this chapter and this book. The most important action item, whether you are the spouse of an active duty person or a veteran, is to continue your education.

At times, employment-related challenges might seem overpowering for a military spouse. Just remember that America is cognizant of your issues and is ready, willing, and able to help. We have not forgotten you.

CHAPTER TAKEAWAYS

- Continue your education to secure lifetime career opportunities.
- Take advantage of every government benefit you can find.
- General job-hunting rubrics apply to all workers, including military spouses.

- Leave the house and cold call on potential employers in your community.
- Contact local resources like the VFW to build your network.

THE MILITARY VETERAN SPOUSE LIBRARY

There are many helpful books to read as you conduct your job search. Go to the National Military Spouse Network (NMSN) website, www.nationalmilitaryspousenetwork.org, and click on "NMSN Bookstore" for book titles and ordering information. If you are a recent college grad, read the book by the author of this book, listed below.

John Henry Weiss. *WELCOME TO THE REAL WORLD, A Complete Guide to Job Hunting for the Recent College Grad*. Skyhorse Publishing Inc., 2014.

Taya Kyle. *American Wife: Love, War, Faith and Renewal*. Harper Collins, 2015. This book was written by the wife of deceased veteran Chris Kyle, to whom this book is dedicated.

PART V

Resumes. Career Profiles. Cover Letters. Follow-Ups

A resume is you . . . in words that people can understand.

— *John Henry Weiss*

Chapter 23

Writing in Civilian Business Language

One of the challenges facing transitioning veterans is learning to communicate using civilian terminology. Hiring managers and human resources directors do not understand veterans when they use military jargon, abbreviations, and acronyms that mean nothing in the civilian workplace. Transitioning veterans have spent four years or more in active duty military service, which is tantamount to living in a subculture with its own code of conduct, rules, regulation, *and language*. It takes time and effort to learn civilian-speak for both verbal and written communication.

WRITTEN COMMUNICATION

Many of the 200,000 veterans discharged annually need to spend time and effort learning to use civilian workplace terminology. When you place your name under something you have written, like a resume, cover letter, or follow-up letter, you get no second chance. Translating military-speak to civilian-speak is not that difficult, and it will come to you with effort and practice. Read the sample resume in Chapter 25 and mentally plug in military terms. As a veteran, you know where they should be. The original version of this resume was written in military-speak and then translated into the document you see in **OJS**.

To understand the translation process, compare the military version of a resume with the civilian version by viewing them side by side. You can do just that by going to Career Perfect, www.careerperfect.com, and clicking on "Sample resumes." Next, click "Management resume" under the heading "Military to civilian conversion." That will bring up the two resumes of Major Bradford O'Reilly, one in military-speak and the other in civilian-speak. You will readily see how the civilian version leaves no room for misunderstanding.

FREQUENTLY USED MILITARY TERMS AND THEIR CIVILIAN TRANSLATION

The list of military terms that need translation is almost endless when you combine all service branches. Where do you start? Military.com, www. military.com, provides a two-part list, "Job Titles" and "General Terms." Here is a list with the military term on the left followed by the civilian translation. Master this list for use in both your resume and interviews.

General Terms
AI= additionally skilled in
combat = hazardous conditions
company = company, department, or section
medal = award
military personnel office = human resources
mission = task/function/objective
military occupation specialty/classification = career specialty
squad/platoon = team or section
reconnaissance = data collection and analysis
regulations = policy or guidelines
service members = employees
subordinates = employees
TAD/TDY = business trip

Job Titles
Commander = Director or Senior Manager
Executive Officer = Deputy Director

Field Grade Officer = Executive or Manager
Company Grade Officer = Operations Manager or Section Manager
Warrant Officer =Technical Specialist or Department Manager
Senior NCO = First-Line Supervisor
Infantry = Security Force
First Sergeant = Personnel Manager
Squad Leader = Team Leader or Team Chief
Supply Sergeant = Supply Manager or Logistics Manager
Operations NCO= Operations Supervisor

This is just the beginning. When you add "rank," the list expands exponentially. For example, an officer may list rank as *Target Acquisition Platoon Leader: 4–319th Airborne Artillery.* That means absolutely nothing to a civilian human resources director, and placing it on a resume would be nothing but a distraction. That term would not add to your credentials, but using "Operations Supervisor" would.

RESOURCES FOR LEARNING CIVILIAN-SPEAK

Every veteran asks, "Where do I start? How do I get over this hump?" Here are several suggestions and resources to help you translate military jargon to civilian business language. Some of them provide general job-hunting tips and job postings as well.

* **Practice**. It is an obvious place to begin. After writing your resume or other business communication, read it aloud. Then put it aside, even if it sounds great, and start again. Do this several times and you will see an obvious improvement with each new edition. Next, print out three copies of your latest revision and give a copy to each of these individuals for proof reading: a family member, a colleague or friend, and a person working in a civilian job. Make sure that none of the three is a veteran. Ask them to review the resume not only for correct grammar, composition, and spelling, but also for clear and correct civilian terminology.

- **Online Sites**. Google "military to civilian translation," and you will find numerous translation resources. Be sure to access the following **OJS** faves:

  Military.com, www.military.com. This site provides a wealth of information and advice for veterans seeking help translating their military experience into civilian terms. This is a comprehensive site, and it can be a challenge to find the information you need. Be patient.

  Real Warriors, www.realwarriors.net. On the home page, enter "Translating military experience to civilian employment" in the search box, and you can access the information you need.

  TAOnline, www.taonline.com. This is a very practical site where you will learn how to translate your MOS code to a civilian occupation. It is a practical and helpful guide for transitioning veterans.

  The Military Wallet, www.themilitarywallet.com/military-to-civilian. This site provides a wealth of specific information for transitioning veterans, including civilian terminology.

- **Books**. There are a number of excellent books treating written communication for veterans. You can purchase them from Amazon or Barnes & Noble. Here are two **OJS** recommendations:

  1. *Military to Civilian, Resumes and Letters*, by Krannich and Savino

  2. *Expert Resumes*, by Enelow and Kursmark

- **The Veteran Employment Services Office (VESO)**, www.vaforvets.va.gov/veso. Sometimes veterans overlook, or avoid, services from the VA because, like any huge government agency, it can be difficult to navigate. However, VESO provides a number of services pertaining to all phases of military-to-civilian transition. VESO not only provides support, but also serves as a gateway to federal government jobs in the Department of Agriculture (USDA), the Department of Transportation (DOT), and the US Chamber of Commerce. There are multiple VESO offices in every state, and this site provides links to all of them.

MOVING FORWARD

Transition to civilian employment is not a one-time effort. It is a multi-step process, and one of the steps is translating your military experience into civilian terms. **OJS** assures every veteran that the job you held in the military has a civilian counterpart. Write your resume, cover letter, and follow-ups using correct grammar, spelling, and civilian terminology. No compromises. It will take time and practice. There are no shortcuts in the process.

CHAPTER TAKEAWAYS

- Written communication is unforgiving. You must get it right before submitting anything in writing to a potential employer.
- Your mother, father, military commander, and elementary school teachers were correct when they told you that *practice makes perfect.*
- Take advantage of all the resources available. Everyone is eager to help a veteran.

THE VETERAN'S LIBRARY

Ronald Krannich and Carl Savino. *Military-to-Civilian Resumes and Letters: How to Best Communicate Your Strengths to Employers.* Impact Publications, 2007.

Wendy Enelow and Louise Kursmark. *Expert Resumes for Military to Civilian Transitions.* JIST Works, 2009.

Chapter 24

Writing a Resume and Career Profile

Most job seekers believe that writing a "killer" resume is the most important action item in the job-hunting process. This is an outdated assumption. Submit only a resume to a prospective employer, and you are just another look-alike candidate. Companies receive large quantities of resumes for each job posting from both veterans and non-veterans. Remember, the US has a workforce of 155 million people, which generates a lot of action on the hiring front.

Companies find candidates through job boards and social networks like Monster and LinkedIn, from recruiters, and through referrals. Large companies like Google, Caterpillar, and Microsoft receive more than 75,000 resumes per week in response to their job postings. Other large companies like Southwest Airlines have similar statistics. In a recent year, Southwest Airlines received 193,000 new resumes but hired only 4,300 new employees. Walmart hires 600,000 new employees each year and has a turnover rate of 44 percent, similar to that of other large retail companies. When Google posts a job on its website for a web designer, the company receives tens of thousands of resumes.

Keeping these numbers in mind, assume that you submit a run-of-the-mill resume in response to a Google posting and anxiously wait for a response. A week goes by, and you get nothing in return (or maybe just a perfunctory "We received your resume. Thanks."). Six weeks transpire and nothing. Three months? Nothing. Six months? Nothing. This might be discouraging, but let's consider the odds. If 40,000 candidates submit similar resumes for a Google position, your chances of connecting are slim.

What will make your candidacy different from the other 39,999 candidates? Is there anything you can do? Yes, there is. It is your custom designed package of documents about you and your candidacy that I call the **career profile**.

THE CAREER PROFILE

The career profile replaces the stand-alone resume for veterans and non-veterans alike. It is the written version of who you are, your persona. In an ideal world, employers would interview all qualified candidates personally. There would be no phone screenings and no Skype interviews. It would be a face-to-face meeting where the hiring manager and candidate chat for an hour or two and get to know each other on a personal level. However, that usually does not happen in today's world, even with military friendly companies.

Let's assume that a military friendly company is looking for an assistant marketing manager and has decided to reserve this job for veterans. The hiring manager begins the process by screening the resumes of veteran candidates. Most look alike, but you had submitted a package called the career profile, which included five other documents to support the resume. I assure you that your candidacy will stand out from the rest of the pack.

Time is of essence in the business world, and hiring managers do all they can to shorten the hiring process. For example, they hire temp workers to screen resumes using the "key word" technique. If your resume does not contain a sufficient number of company-defined "key words," the screener rejects your candidacy. In addition, some large companies use digital screening software to evaluate your resume. You have no idea what key words and phrases the company has written into the screening program. That is why **OJS** advocates submitting more than a resume. It takes more time to build the career profile, but this empowering tool will place you a step above your competition.

COMPONENTS OF THE CAREER PROFILE

I designed the career profile to make your candidacy a compelling alternative to candidates who persist in the old way, which is sending only a resume to an unknown entity. How do you use it? When you submit your candidacy, you send a package of documents instead of just your resume. It will communicate the full range of your experience, expertise, education, and military background. Here are the six documents in your career profile.

1. Resume
2. Cover Letter
3. College and/or military transcript
4. Letters of reference or commendation for outstanding performance
5. Business and technology certifications
6. Your articles and blogs that have been published or posted, to highlight your writing skills

Don't you think the career profile will be more impressive to prospective employers than just another look-alike resume? Let's go through the process, step by step, beginning with the first item in the career profile—the resume.

1. YOUR RESUME

The resume has only one purpose: to take you to the next step, the personal interview. Everything else is secondary. In other words, the resume is a marketing and sales tool. You are selling your value to the employer, your background and experience, your academic record, your military work experience, your intelligence, energy, passion, and aspirations. It is not rocket science, and you need not spend $200 dollars to get the job done by a resume writer. Follow the instructions from your VA counselor or other advisor and the directions in **OJS**, and you will write a viable resume.

Do Not Use Acronyms

Writing a resume for entry into the civilian workforce presents several challenges. Construct a resume that makes sense to civilian hiring managers and human resources directors, most of whom have no military experience. Having little or no military experience means they will not be familiar with military jargon and acronyms that you consider to be second nature. For example, the acronyms PFC (Private First Class), PO3 (Petty Officer 3rd Class), and SPECWORCOM will mean nothing to the vast majority of civilian human resources directors and hiring managers. The use of acronyms could confuse the reader and diminish your chances of getting an interview.

When you write your resume, you may use acronyms, but only in parentheses following the actual word or phrase. For example, even what you assume everyone will know, like *USN (Ret)*, could be meaningless to a civilian who never went past the Boy Scouts or Girl Scouts. The better way to state this would be *United States Navy, Retired (USN Ret)*. While many civilians would make a correct guess at the meaning of *USN (Ret)*, there are other acronyms that could be very confusing. Here is an example.

On your resume, you will list the branch of service you were in and what your various assignments were. Let us assume that you were on special classified assignment with the United States Naval Special Warfare Command and you would like to include that on your resume. In military jargon, one would refer to your role in this elite branch of the Navy as NAVSPECWARCOM. Everyone in the military knows the meaning of that acronym, but this is not the case for the human resources directors with Walmart, GE, or Microsoft. They would not have the slightest idea what that means. The proper way to present that on your resume in bullet format would be:

* Special classified assignment with the United States Naval Special Warfare Command (NAVSPECWARCOM)

Be sure to explain complicated and extensive military training and education in detail on your resume. Do that by adding an addendum to your resume, titled "Military Training and Education." Highlight all of your field training and experience, your leadership roles, and all of the classes and academic courses you completed.

Job candidates frequently spend hundreds of hours writing the *perfect* resume based upon advice from peers, military organizations, parents, spouses, college professors, and a variety of online resources. When you say "resume," everyone offers suggestions and advice. While some of this input could have value, most of it is redundant or based on personal experience, which may be outdated. Even college professors get into the act and give advice that has no relevance in the civilian business world. For example, they call the resume *curriculum vitae (CV)*, a term used only by the academic establishment. Do not refer to your resume as a CV. In the business world, it is a *resume*.

My experience as an executive recruiter working in the employment industry every day is the basis for the advice I offer. If you follow my instructions, you will design a first-class resume that reflects what is current and acceptable in the civilian business world. If you want general resume writing advice, review a few resume websites. One that I like best is Career Confidential, www.careerconfidential.com. The CEO, Peggy McKee, is one of the best in the business, and I suggest that you attend one of her many free webinars. Her advice is not specific to veterans, but it follows the current rules for sound resume writing.

What about those professional resume writing services that charge $25 to $200 for designing your resume? If these resume-writing gurus sell their services, they must be good. Right? Save your money. What you find in **OJS** is all you need to write a first-class resume. Spend that money to attend a trade show or conference where you will find hundreds of hiring managers in person. You and I know this is money well spent, because landing a job is a matter of building a personal relationship with hiring managers and other influential company workers, like the director of human resources.

GENERAL GUIDELINES FOR WRITING YOUR RESUME

I have reviewed thousands of resumes from veterans and non-veterans. Few are outstanding. Many are just okay. And some are too cute. Cute resumes contain too many unnecessary stylistic features, like a non-standard typeface, multiple colors, clip art, pictures, borders, and other design features. The basic rule is this: *Keep it simple. Keep it clean.* Remember, this is business communication, not a promotion piece for the Super Bowl and certainly not a menu for a French restaurant.

Recruiters working in the staffing business know how a resume should look, and they can tell you what mistakes to avoid. Executive recruiters say these are the five most common mistakes candidates make on resumes:

Five Common Resume Mistakes

         rrect spelling is your responsibility, not the spell
         responsibility. Later in this chapter, I will tell you
         r Patti from St. Louis to illustrate the importance of
         pelling.

         ar mistakes. Hiring managers expect grammatically
         resumes from everyone: veterans, non-veterans, and
college graduates. Make a mistake, and you are finished. There is no second chance.

3. **Inconsistent formatting and style**. Use only one typeface and type size. The current preferred typeface is 12 pt. Times New Roman.

4. **Missing metrics**. Quantify as much as possible. Generalities say nothing about your expertise or accomplishments.

5. **Gaps in employment history**. You do have a work history, which consists of your military experience and pre-military experience, even though it may consist of only part-time jobs during high school or college years. Make sure your work history is in chronological order.

RESUME FEATURES YOU MUST GET RIGHT

Resume File Name. This is one of the most important parts of your resume, and you must get it right. The file name must be brief and to the point so the reader will understand without hesitation who you are and what the file is all about. It should look like this:

"Jerome Michael Resume. Ford Motors: Marketing Associate Candidate."

Resume Length. The resume for an entry-level candidate and a resume for a candidate with eight years of military experience are going to differ in length. Appearance, style, and format, however, are the same for all candidates. The length of the resume for all entry-level candidates should be no more than two pages. However, for workers with six to eight years of military experience that includes "executive level positions" and possibly publications, the resume could be three, four, or more pages.

Resume Appearance. Your resume is your personal appearance in written form. Think of it as the way you would dress for a live interview: uncluttered and neat. Hiring managers are not interested in your picture, graphs, boxed items, borders, charts, shading, and clip art. If they want to see how you look, they can always go to LinkedIn, Facebook, or Twitter. Caution! Make sure your social media images are current and flattering.

Resume Formatting. Consistency is key from beginning to end. Use bullet points consisting of only one line instead of paragraphs in the body of the resume. Use only one typeface and size. The usual business font, the one that I see most frequently in business communication, is 12 pt. Times New Roman. Use uppercase bold for major headings and lowercase regular type for text. Do not use a script typeface, like Segoe Script, under any circumstances. The typeface is not the tool to differentiate your candidacy from the rest of the pack.

Resume Style. Resume styles change over time. Today's readers view content in small bits and pieces. They lose interest when confronted with long paragraphs. Save that for your first novel. The way we convey information in the civilian world of work is to construct the resume using bullet points instead of paragraphs, with one exception. The first major heading of your resume, **_Objective_** or **_Summary,_** should be in paragraph form, but it should not exceed about ten lines. List every other item in bullet points. See the sample resume in the next chapter.

Sometimes you will see **_Summary_** used instead of **_Objective_**. Use **_Objective_** when you are applying for a specific job. Use **_Summary_** if you are submitting your resume to a human resources director to make this key person aware of your search for an unspecified position with the company.

Resume Metrics. One of the most common mistakes candidates make is listing their bullet point achievements using broad generalities, such as "Treated a large number of patients at the emergency facility at McGuire Air Force Base." The statement means much more to the hiring manager if it reads, "Treated an average of thirty patients per day over a six-month period at McGuire Air Force Base."

THE MAJOR HEADINGS OF YOUR RESUME

Construct your resume using this format: major headings followed by bullet points, or numbers, listing the particulars. Here are the major parts of your resume.

1. Personal Identification
2. Objective or Summary
3. Military Work Experience
4. Civilian Work Experience
5. Awards, Recognition, Community Service
6. Technology Skills
7. Technology and Business Certifications
8. Education

Do not include "References on Request" or "Hobbies and Special Interests." Here is a review of each major heading with an explanatory note. In the following chapter, you will find the resume of a recently discharged veteran who served in Iraq, Kuwait, and Afghanistan. I suggest referring to it as you read the following material.

PERSONAL IDENTIFICATION

The first item on your resume, at the top of the page and centered, is your name, address, phone number, and email address. Use only one phone number, the one that you use most frequently for both inbound and outbound calls. Remember that calls regarding employment matters come at all hours. The 9 a.m. to 5 p.m. window is no longer valid. Your address must include your street number, town, and zip code. Your name should be first, in uppercase bold. Beneath your name is the address, followed by phone number and email address in lowercase regular type.

I have received resumes that were missing an address and only included a name, phone number, Twitter hash tag, and an email address. This is the result of a mistaken idea by tech gurus who believe that in a digital world where you live is not important. Tell that to a human resources director, and you are history. Do not buy into the hype. Use common sense. Always include your address.

OBJECTIVE or SUMMARY

This is nothing more than a marketing piece about the product you are selling: your candidacy. Write this in paragraph format and limit your self-advertisement to ten lines.

Write a custom OBJECTIVE for each job application reflecting the qualifications and requirements in the job description. Specifically, state your work expertise, both military and civilian (if applicable), in terms that reflect the job specifications and using key words from the job description. Remember that the reader, the hiring manager or the human resources director, is thinking, *What can this person do for our team and the company going forward?* If there is only a general statement on a company website under "Careers" that reads "Customer Service Representative," think about what this position requires: excellent verbal and written skills, patience, understanding, and courtesy. Build your OBJECTIVE statement around those premises.

There is no need to state your age, number of years in college, or something like "seeking entry-level position." Rather, state specifically the position for which you are applying (e.g. "I am applying for the Associate Finance Manager position"). If appropriate, quantify your experience, because metrics are important. For example, if you are applying for a position that requires writing skills, state, "My written communication experience includes three years of copy editing for the Air Force magazine, *AIRMAN*." In your cover letter, you can elaborate on that experience.

In this section, you may want to include specific competencies in a list of single words or phrases following the OBJECTIVE paragraph. Here is an example.

Core Competencies

PowerPoint   Spread Sheet   Database   Social Media
Personnel Management   Field Manual Writing   Logistics   Cargo Shipping

MILITARY WORK EXPERIENCE

List your military experience chronologically beginning with your most recent job. List each job under a major heading followed by specifics in bullet point format. See the sample resume in the next chapter for an example.

CIVILIAN WORK EXPERIENCE

Many veterans will be seeking their first civilian job and have no work experience outside of the military. What do you include under this heading? While you were in high school or college, you probably had a number of part-time positions that included the usual suspects like retail work, landscaping, childcare, construction, and possibly an internship with a for-profit or nonprofit company. What should be included? Everything that relates to the position for which you are applying.

List all for-profit companies and nonprofit companies for which you worked during the school year, summer months, or holiday breaks. Make this a chronological listing beginning with your most recent experience. To explain what you did at these companies, state your responsibilities in bullet point format. In the following example, note that each contains a specific responsibility, not a broad generality.

Mike's Pizza

- Delivered pizzas and other food items to residential customers and collected bills using credit and debit cards. January - November, 1997.

Run for the Cure (a nonprofit organization raising money for breast cancer research)

- Participant greeter and organizer. June-September, 1996.

Educational Testing Service (ETS)

- Internship program working as Social Media Writing Assistant. June-September, 1995.

AWARDS, RECOGNITION, COMMUNITY SERVICE

This is a section not often found on resumes, but I encourage its inclusion based on my experience with hiring managers. I have noted that one of the first things that a hiring manager will see when scanning a resume is a major heading listing awards and recognition for outstanding achievements.

What do you include? Go back to your high school years and write a list of any citations you may have received for superlative performance. In pre-military life, it could have been a certificate saying "The Most Promising Politician in the High School Class of 2005." In college, it could have been making the Dean's List or graduating *cum laude*. At one of your part-time jobs, you may have received a bonus from the manager of the local Dairy Queen for selling a high quantity of ice cream over an eight-week period.

Be sure to list all of your military awards, no matter how insignificant they may seem to you. For example, the Army Good Conduct Medal says something positive about your character. The company human resources director or hiring manager will note that.

As for community service, many hiring managers and human resources directors will give you a big plus mark for your give-back to those in need. Many companies, like Starbucks, Microsoft, and Bank of America, are community conscious and encourage their employees to participate in outreach efforts. Here is an example of how to state this on your resume:

Washington High School. "Principal's Superlative Community Services Award," 1988.

Do you see how much this adds to your resume? In very specific terms, it tells the hiring manager who you are and what you have accomplished. Flesh out your persona using every means possible.

TECHNOLOGY SKILLS

In today's world, employers assume that candidates have the technology skills required to be productive workers. However, hiring managers have been burned many times because of this false assumption. In Chapter 16, I recommended that you take an online course from HigherNext, Coursera, or another online organization, as verifiable proof to a hiring manager that you are up to speed. This is the place on your resume to include that achievement, because it is a highly visible verification of your technology skills. Here are some examples:

- *Social Media*: Twitter, Facebook, LinkedIn, Indeed
- *Personal Productivity*: Word, Sage/Act, MS Excel, PowerPoint
- *Programming*: BASIC, Java, HTML
- *Technology Expertise Certification*: Completion of HigherNext Technology Course

No matter what your chosen job or industry is, you will be required to use technology to meet your job requirements. If for some reason your technology skills are lacking, take online technology courses or courses at your local community college to enhance your candidacy.

EDUCATION

This is the last major heading on your resume, and it is very straight-forward. Chronologically list your pre-military and military education. In addition, include other professional development courses or courses of interest.

Do not add anything after EDUCATION (such as references, favorite sports, ethnicity, gender, religion, or age). This is how your EDUCATION section might look:

EDUCATION

- *Washington High School, Dallas, TX. Diploma, 1994*
- *Elon University, Elon, NC. BA. Major: Events Management. Minor: Communications, 1999*
- *Elon University Study Abroad in Art History Program, Florence, Italy, 1998*
- *The International Culinary Center, New York City. Graduate level courses in Pastry Arts and Cake Design, 1999*
- *Active Duty Online Web Design Courses, Strayer University, 2000–2006*
- *HigherNext, Philadelphia, PA. Online Certified Business Laureate Degree, 2007*

RESUME WRITING HELP FROM VETERAN'S ORGANIZATIONS

The list of nonprofit organizations assisting military veterans on resume writing at no charge is almost endless. Check the Internet frequently to learn who they are and what they can do for you. The following list will lead you in the right direction:

USO, www.uso.org. This organization was established in 1941 to assist military personnel on active duty and after discharge. There are USO facilities in twenty-six states plus Washington, DC, and overseas locations. All are dedicated to helping military personnel and their families with a variety of challenges and problems. In addition, the USO posts job openings on its website under "Career Opportunities." The last time I checked, there were thirteen posted jobs at different locations in the United States and abroad. Here is a list of advertised jobs I saw on the USO website recently:

Regional Vice President
Director of Operations
Area Director
Area Operations Manager
Center Director
Center Manager
Duty Manager
Information Specialist
Programs Manager
Programs Coordinator
Administrative Assistant
Mobile Program Manager
Mobile Unit Manager
Mobile Unit Coordinator
Volunteer Coordinator
Tours Manager
Assistant Tours Manager

Review positions and job descriptions on the USO website. There may be something for you.

Help for Wounded Veterans. To help our wounded warriors write a resume and position their candidacy, the USO has launched Operation Enduring Care, a fund-raising campaign to assist wounded veterans. This is an important campaign, as 40,000 men and women have suffered physical injuries in Iraq and Afghanistan, and more than 400,000 suffered emotional wounds such as the post-traumatic stress disorder (PTSD). Unfortunately, the media has not done its fair share publicizing this problem. Publicize this by sending emails and Tweets to your friends, congressional representatives, and the president. The USO website provides a link to all senators and representatives on the USO Leadership team. All you need to do is click on their names to access their websites. Voice your concerns and seek their aid. To contribute to this worthy cause, go to www.uso.org and click on "Donations."

VFW, www.vfw.org. The VFW, one of the oldest veterans' organizations tracing its origins back to 1899, provides advice on writing resumes. It has 1.9 million members who not only receive benefits and support, but also contribute their time on a voluntary basis to accomplish the objectives of the organization.

The VFW hosts an annual convention and participates in numerous patriotic functions throughout the nation. In addition, it is actively involved with many employment organizations to advertise the benefits of hiring vets. One such initiative involves the manufacturing sector of our economy that provides hands-on and managerial jobs to veterans.

G.I.Jobs, www.gijobs.com. This site offers resume advice and tips about how to use your military experience in job hunting. Included is a list of military friendly colleges for those seeking a college degree. For example, click on "Military friendly schools," and then click on "Arizona State University." Here you will find a special section titled "Military Support."

US Department of Defense, www.defense.gov. This is a comprehensive site, so plan to spend quite a bit of time here. There are many jobs available within the Department of Defense, and you will find them on this website.

Wounded Warrior Project (WWP), www.woundedwarriorproject.org. The Wounded Warrior Project works to raise awareness and enlist the public's aid for the needs of severely injured servicemen and women. Importantly, WWP also provides support, like resume reviews, for returning military personnel seeking civilian employment.

Yellow Ribbon Programs, www.yellowribbon.org. Yellow Ribbon Programs counsel veterans and assist them in gaining funding and access to education programs ranging from Associate's degrees to professional degrees. This is a far-ranging federal government program offering multiple options, and the place to begin exploring the program is on the following website: www.yellowribboneducationdecisions.com.

Military.com, www.military.com. Military Advantage, a division of Monster Worldwide, owns this site. Services from this organization are hard to beat. I have reviewed some of their resumes and they are spot on.

2. THE COVER LETTER

The next component of the career profile is the cover letter, the purpose of which is frequently misunderstood. Google the words "cover letter," and you will get thousands of hits relating to every conceivable nuance of the term. However, the most important thing to remember about the cover letter is that it is just one of the items in your career profile. Along with the other documents, it has a primary purpose: to take you to the next step, a first or second personal interview with the hiring manager.

The cover letter states your reason for contacting the hiring manager, and it summarizes the other components in your career profile.

Limit the cover letter to one page. In Chapter 26, **OJS** will tell you how to write the cover letter and provide a sample.

3. YOUR COLLEGE AND MILITARY TRANSCRIPT. THE JOINT SERVICES TRANSCRIPT

Obtaining your college and military transcripts is a task easily completed online. I conducted an online survey of several colleges and universities, and all but one offered transcripts bearing the institution's official seal *free of charge*. Obtain a transcript if you completed any number of college courses. Only one of my survey targets, the University of Arizona, charged a $10 fee for obtaining the transcript online. If you order online, the processing time usually takes about two weeks. Plan ahead.

Why do I think the transcript should be a part of the career profile? In my recruiting business, I have observed a growing trend by human resources directors to verify college attendance, mainly because of several high profile cases where candidates outright lied about their academic credentials. In one instance, the multinational recruiting firm Heidrick and Struggles, a company with impeccable credentials, submitted a candidate for the presidency of a major company, Yahoo. The candidate was hired, and a member of its board of directors began to question the new president's credentials relating to technology expertise. A subsequent investigation revealed that the candidate had intentionally misrepresented his master's degree credential. He stated, in the EDUCATION section of his resume, that he had earned a master's degree in Information Technology in a particular year from a well-known university. The company and the Heidrick recruiter conducted an investigation and learned that the university did not even offer a master's degree in Information Technology in that year. Yahoo fired the president. Heidrick was embarrassed, apologized, and returned its recruiting fee.

Military Transcripts

If you completed courses while serving in any branch of service, you can obtain a transcript using the Joint Services Transcripts (JST) system. JST describes the service as "a description of military schooling and work history in civilian language." It is an online service that is easy to use and free of charge. Go to the following link to access the system: https://jst.doded.mil.

Adding an official transcript to your career profile not only adds to your personal credibility, but also helps highlight your academic achievements related to the position in question. For example, if your overall GPA was 3.0, but you had a 3.9 GPA in your major, Business Administration, highlight that in your cover letter and interview. This could be a deal maker if you are applying for a position in finance and the hiring manager notes your sterling performance in business courses. The manager might not care if you had a 2.5 in your required social science courses but will be impressed with a 3.9 in your major.

4. LETTERS OF REFERENCE OR COMMENDATION FOR OUTSTANDING PERFORMANCE

This part of your career profile adds to your credibility. When a job candidate submits a reference letter, I always read it and sometimes follow up with a phone call or email to the individual who wrote it if I have any questions or if I need additional information. This document builds credibility, something that you need when transitioning to the civilian workplace.

Who should provide this letter for you? It is a valid question because you may not have a former boss within reach to vouch for you and your good qualities. My suggestion is to begin with your last military commander or a professor in your major subject who thought highly of your work and commended you for excellent academic performance. Next in line would be your college advisor, if you did indeed have one.

Other references could be the people to whom you reported in one of your part-time jobs or in your community outreach ventures. If you played on any college sports teams, you could ask your coach for a letter of recommendation attesting to your strong team-building skills. Request your reference to comment on your strongest suit, your verbal and written communication skills, for example, and to highlight a project that you initiated and completed satisfactorily.

How many letters of reference do you include in the career profile? One or two at this stage of your job search. An employer who has made you an offer might request additional references. You can solicit more from similar sources at that time. I advise that you have more references lined up to meet that probability.

5. BUSINESS AND TECHNOLOGY CERTIFICATIONS

One of the most impressive documents in the career profile is a written business or technology certification from an online provider like HigherNext (www.HigherNext.com). This is particularly important for Arts, Humanities, and Education majors. You will be competing with Business and STEM (Science, Technology, Engineering, Mathematics) majors, and you need these certifications to enhance your credibility. Usually these online certifications are inexpensive. I suggest that you get busy with this now. Review Chapter 16 for more about online certifications.

6. ARTICLES OR BLOGS YOU'VE PUBLISHED OR POSTED

This is the final item in your career profile. Written communication is one of the key check marks on every candidate's profile, and there is no better way to show these skills to a hiring manager than to include something that you have created and have had published either online or in print media. I cannot emphasize enough the importance of correct written communication in the business world.

If you have any published blogs or articles, be sure to include them in your career profile. Of course, be sure that what you submit is perfect in every respect. Written communication is very exacting. Unlike verbal communication, where you can make mid-stream corrections, a written document is out there for everyone to see. Your article or blog does not have to be the "Great American Novel" quality. It can be plain vanilla, interesting, or entertaining, but it will show the hiring manager that you are a literate person.

SPELL CHECKERS

I am including this section on spell checkers because I have seen many spelling errors on all types of written documents. Candidates often assume that the spell checker corrects everything. Nothing could be further from the truth. Here is a real-life example.

Poor Patti from St. Louis

Patti was a worker with considerable written communication skills. She worked in product development for a company producing testing and assessment products for the K-12 education market. She had risen from an entry-level position to supervising manager and was ready for the next step ahead, a director-level position.

I was conducting a search for a director of professional services for a Boston-based testing and assessment company, and Patti was perfect for the job. The base salary was $135,000 plus a bonus of $65,000, making the total annual compensation $200,000. In addition, the job carried an attractive benefits package. Patti revised her resume several times until she felt it was right for the position, and I agreed. I told her to do a minor tweak on one section of her resume, run it through the spelling and grammar checker, proofread the document, and then submit it to the human resources director and the hiring manager. The response from the company was devastating for Patti. The human resources director and the hiring manager told me that because of a spelling error they were rejecting her candidacy.

All of us have come to trust the spelling and grammar checker without question because it saves time. After all, this is a product from Apple or Microsoft, so you should be able to trust its worthiness implicitly. Wrong! Not all spell checkers are created equal. For example, I have found that the 2010 Word spell checker is close to a disaster. It misreads text, makes erroneous grammatical corrections, and even misses simple misspellings. Recently I was proofreading one of my own documents that contained the proper noun "Bill." In my haste, I had spelled it "Blill," but twice the spell checker did not make the correction. The latest Apple or Microsoft spell checkers are better, but still do not assume they are perfect. Always proofread to make sure you have an error-free set of documents.

MOVING FORWARD

The digital profile, for inclusion in social media such as LinkedIn, is similar in many respects to the resume. Its main characteristics are brevity and clarity. Make sure that your digital profile and resume are coordinated because human resources director and hiring managers will always conduct a Google search to find out who you really are. They are looking for verification that what is on the resume is the real you.

When you write the digital profile, have your resume nearby to make sure they both say the same thing. The digital profile should be a condensed version of your profile. Make sure you get this right. There is a sample digital profile in Chapter 25.

CHAPTER TAKEAWAYS

- Written documents must be perfect. You do not get a second chance.
- Don't trust the spell checker and grammar checker. Before submitting any written document, read it aloud and then have an impartial third person do the same.
- Submitting a stand-alone resume for a job is risky. You need to submit your multi-document career profile to make your candidacy stand out from the rest of the pack.
- A resume is you, in writing that everyone can understand.

THE VETERAN'S LIBRARY

Joyce Kennedy. *Resumes for Dummies*. Wiley, 2011.

Chapter 25

A Sample Resume and Digital Profile

I have combined the sample resume and digital profile into one chapter because each must be a mirror image of the other for consistency. Employers evaluating your candidacy will find every bit of information about you by conducting a Google search using your name. Everyone's life seems to be an open book these days.

After reading your resume, a human resources director and a hiring manager will review the social media to learn more about you. They will look at Twitter, Facebook, LinkedIn, and Indeed. The list goes on and will increase as time passes.

CONSISTENCY. PORTRAYING THE REAL YOU

If your Facebook picture shows you drinking Buds on the beach, and your Twitter picture is you in uniform, and your LinkedIn picture shows you in business attire, the hiring manager might well ask, "Will the real veteran candidate please stand up?" Your profile must be consistent throughout if you want to advance through the hiring process.

I have noted that some online sources are saying that you no longer need a traditional resume. Nothing could be further from the truth, and I advise that you totally disregard such advice. It makes no sense whatsoever. The traditional resume, as part of your career profile, is still the document-in-chief, and you must get it right.

Let's review the major parts of a resume again before looking at a sample. Write your resume following the sample, and you will have a major part of your career profile completed.

THE MAJOR HEADINGS OF YOUR RESUME

Construct your resume using this general format: major headings followed by bullet points listing the particulars. Here are the major parts of your resume. For a full description of each major heading, refer to the previous chapter.

1. Personal Identification
2. Objective or Summary
3. Civilian Work Experience
4. Military Work Experience
5. Awards, Recognition, Community Service
6. Technology Skills
7. Training and Business Certifications
8. Education

You do not need anything more than that. Some candidates include items like references and hobbies, but they are unnecessary and needlessly lengthen your resume.

A SAMPLE RESUME

A U.S. Army Sergeant who served in Iraq, Kuwait, and Afghanistan from 2006–2012 wrote the following resume. This is a well-written document, and I suggest that all veterans use this format.

****

James Silvestri
10527 Komensky Ave.   Chicago, IL, 60934
215–758–0011   JSil@Saturn.com

Summary

Award winning military veteran who served as Transportation Management Coordinator with **Secret Security Clearance.** Six years of active experience in movement control of freight, cargo, supplies, and personnel working for the U.S. Army supporting military operations overseas. Proven ability to process shipment documents accurately, monitor location of supplies during travel, and process Bills of Lading before delivery of cargo. Recognized for strong leadership skills and focus on obtaining results in high-stake, fast-paced environments.

Core Competencies

Bill of Lading Processing	Cargo Load Planning
Cargo Shipping & Receiving	Passenger Manifesting & Reservation
Personnel Management Regulations	Standards Inventory & Requisition
Transportation Management Control	Unit/Overseas Logistics

CIVILIAN WORK EXPERIENCE
SMITHSON PROGRAMS INC. Movement Control Specialist, 2012–2015

- Ensure customer has proper funding codes for billing prior to accepting cargo for transportation.
- Perform day to day air and movement control functions at assigned Aerial Port of Debarkation (APOD)/Aerial Port of Embarkation (APOE), working independently in lieu of specific instructions to accomplish tasks. Enforce the importance of safety continuously.
- Assist military and or contracting personnel with building air worthy cargo for transportation.

- Certify hazardous material using company specifications, and AFMAN 24–204 regulations.

MILITARY WORK EXPERIENCE. UNITED STATES ARMY
Transport Management Coordinator, 2006–2012
US Army Sergeant responsible for scheduling and selecting modes of transportation for personnel and equipment for missions in Iraq, Kuwait, and Afghanistan.

- Requested and coordinated transport capability, monitored movement schedules and programs, and ensured transport capability was appropriate and cost effective.
- Inventoried, marked, and labeled cargo and freight shipments in accordance with regulatory requirements.
- Served as customs officer for shipment releases in overseas theaters, and operated as quality control noncommissioned officer for commercial movement contracts.
- Monitored all freight, cargo, and material shipments to ensure accountability; identified and reported problem areas within traffic management system to prevent additional costs, losses, and damage.

Management Control Coordinator, Afghanistan
Air Passenger Terminal Supervisor, 2010–2012
Assigned to 152nd Movement Control Team stationed at Ft. Carson, CO. Deployed to Afghanistan in support of Operation Enduring Freedom.
Personnel Management
- Supervised and provided technical guidance for staff of eleven conducting Rotary and Fixed Wing Operations.
- Appointed Unit Safety Officer. Conducted monthly counseling meetings on work performance, concerns, and health/welfare of staff.

Passenger & Cargo Transport
- Ensured personnel and cargo were accurately recorded and documented before consolidation of daily Ground and Air Reports. Processed more than 180,000 inbound and outbound personnel over two-year period.
- Tracked and processed 40,000+ short tons of cargo via Global Air Transportation Execution System (GATES).

Management Control Coordinator, Camp Arifjan, Kuwait, 2009–2010

Contracting Officer Representative for both Personal Property Shipping Office (PPSO) and Scheduled Airlines Traffic/Office (SATO). Assigned to Installation Transportation Office at Camp Arifjan, Kuwait.
- Processed more than 146,000 Government Bills of Lading in 12 months.
- Completed 14 audits, including two audits with furniture packers and warehouse vendors.
- Advised Installation Transportation Office in selection process for awarding contract to new vendors.
- Ensured that discrepancies were reported if solutions were not implemented and sustained.

Management Control Coordinator, Iraq, 2006–2009

Movement Specialist in support of Operation Iraqi Freedom.
- Processed and tracked equipment and supplies for 15-month deployment using TCAIMS II and Microsoft Excel.
- Assigned to Kuwait Naval Base to record all cargo and equipment returning to Unit Home Station.

AWARDS RECOGNITION, COMMUNITY SERVICE
- Two Army Achievement Medals | Three Army Commendation Medals | Two Certificate of Achievement Awards
- Two Army Good Conduct Medals | National Defense Service Medal

- Afghanistan Campaign Medal | Army Service Ribbon | Overseas Ribbon | Global War on Terrorism Ribbon
- Awarded the Joint Service Commendation Medal for strong leadership skills and outstanding efforts to move personnel throughout Area of Operation in Afghanistan in support of NATO Forces.
- Two Army Commendation Medals while serving in Kuwait: (1) excellence in reestablishing regulations per PPSO Contract & monitoring PPSO and SATO Contracts; and (2) assisting soldiers returning to place of combat injuries to find closure.

TECHNOLOGY SKILLS

- Microsoft Excel, Word, PowerPoint, and Outlook
- Logistics/Unit Movement Software, including TCAIMS II, BCS3 & TIPS Writer software for RFID Tags to document movement information, contracts, and respond to shipment inquiries, discrepancies, and routine movement transactions.
- GATES, GDSS and SMS Systems to obtain accurate personnel manifest, cargo manifest and arrival/departure times.

TRAINING AND CERTIFICATIONS

- Contract Officer Representative Certification | Basic Combat Service Support System Certification
- Counter Insurgency Training | Company Intelligence Support Team Course
- Additional Duty Safety Officer Course | Combat Life Saver Certification
- Technical Transportation of Hazardous Material (AMMO-62) | Container/CSC Inspection Certification
- Hazard Material Familiarization and Safety in Transportation (AMMO-67)

EDUCATION
Washington High School, Chicago, IL Diploma, 2004
Moraine Valley Community College, Palos Park, IL, Engaged in course work toward a degree in Youth Counseling
****

This sergeant's resume was written in 12 pt. Times New Roman typeface, the standard for all business communications.

Also, note that the Sergeant writes in civilian talk, not military jargon. Acronyms were explained leaving nothing for misinterpretation by the hiring manager or human resources director. SUMMARY was used instead of an OBJECTIVE because this resume was being used for non-specific job-hunting purposes.

WRITING A DIGITAL PROFILE TO USE
WITH SOCIAL MEDIA

The digital profile is used with employment-focused social media like LinkedIn. Think of it as a condensed version of your resume. You may need to make modifications required by the various social media. For example, Twitter allows only 140 characters, which is not sufficient to tell your entire story, so you must be creative. (However, I do not recommend using Twitter as the main tool in your job search.) The medium will define the format of your profile and even limit its length. When constructing your profile, have your written resume at your side and use it as a guide.

LinkedIn is always used by human resources directors and hiring managers. I suggest that you complete your LinkedIn profile first and then move on to other social media that may interest you. In my experience, LinkedIn has proved to be the go-to place for online job hunting, networking, and establishing a digital presence. However, it is important to remember that LinkedIn is only a tool for taking you to the most important next step in the job hunting, the personal interview.

THE DIGITAL PROFILE

To expand the productivity of my executive recruiting business, I use LinkedIn extensively and find it valuable for locating hiring managers, job candidates, and job openings. The LinkedIn profile for my recruiting company, Weiss & Associates, Executive Recruiting, is intentionally brief. According to LinkedIn, my profile is one of the most frequently visited sites. You do not need to write more than is necessary to get the job done. Brevity works. There is more on LinkedIn in Chapter 15.

I know that many of you are already on LinkedIn, but for the uninitiated, let me review the major parts of this popular medium. You might find it helpful to open LinkedIn as you read this material. The first place to visit is the Help Center, which you can access by clicking on the "Help Center" menu. You will find many suggestions for getting started and a list of useful free webinars and videos.

THE COMPONENTS OF A LINKEDIN PROFILE

Your picture. This is where some job-hunters still insist on making fools of themselves by posting an image that is out of sync with the civilian world of work. I will not go into a litany of "do nots." Just look at a few dozen images of LinkedIn members, and you will get the picture. I suggest using a civilian dress photo. You are out of military service and want viewers to see you in civilian mode.

Your picture should be business professional, which means no rings in your nose, beads on your tongue or eyelashes, no tattoos, no orange or purple hair, no t-shirts, and no sunglasses. If you insist the world of work has become informal, go ahead and post a ridiculous image. If this is your view of the world of work, expect calls only from circus hiring managers looking for people to work in a tent called "Freak Show" (I am not opposed to circus employment. One of the best is Ringling Brothers, Barnum and Bailey Circus, www.Ringling.com).

Summary. This should be a condensed version or your resume summary or objective.

Background. Included under this heading are the summary, experience, skills, expertise, and education sections. Complete each section by condensing the major headings on your resume. Notice that solid blocks of type are not in keeping with the overall format of LinkedIn profiles. They look tedious and are time-consuming to read. Use bullet points as you did on your resume.

Additional Information. This section includes "interests" and "advice for contacting." Under interests, several bullet points will be sufficient. Under advice for contacting, be very specific and list your primary choice. Be sure to include your email address. If you wish, include Twitter, Facebook, and your cell number. Also, preface your contact information with a sentence to direct the reader's attention, such as "Seeking full-time employment in finance with a large or medium-sized company."

A SAMPLE DIGITAL PROFILE

Digital profile formats vary with the medium. I have used the LinkedIn format for the following sample.

****

Summary

Multiple award winning military veteran who served as Transportation Management Coordinator with Secret Security Clearance. Six years of active experience in all phases of cargo and personnel transportation in the US Recognized for strong leadership skills and obtaining results in high-stake, fast-paced environments. Ready and eager to begin work with a proven, profitable company to make a positive impact on the bottom line.

Experience
SMITHSON PROGRAMS INC. Movement Control Specialist, 2012–2015

United States Army, 2006–2012

- Transportation Management Coordinator, Iraq, Kuwait, Afghanistan.
- Management Control Coordinator, Afghanistan Air Passenger Terminal Supervisor.

Personnel Management

- Supervised and provided technical guidance for staff of eleven conducting Rotary and Fixed Wing Operations.
- Appointed Unit Safety Officer. Conducted monthly counseling meetings on work performance, concerns, and health/welfare of staff.

Passenger & Cargo Transport

- Ensured personnel and cargo were accurately recorded and documented before consolidation of daily Ground and Air Reports. Processed more than 180,000 inbound and outbound personnel over two-year period.
- Tracked and processed 40,000+ short tons of cargo via Global Air Transportation Execution System (GATES).

Management Control Coordinator/Contracting Officer Representative, Camp Arifjan, Kuwait

- Processed more than 146,000 Government Bills of Lading in 12 months.
- Completed 14 audits, including two audits with furniture packers and warehouse vendors.
- Advised Installation Transportation Office in selection process for awarding contract to new vendor for PPSO.
- Ensured that discrepancies were reported if solutions were not implemented and sustained.
- Management Control Coordinator/Movement Specialist, Operation Iraqi Freedom
- Processed and tracked equipment and supplies for 15-month deployment using TCAIMS II and Microsoft Excel.
- Assigned to Kuwait Naval Base to record all cargo and equipment returning to Unit Home Station.

Technology Skills and Expertise
- Proficiency in PowerPoint, Word, Excel, Outlook
- Working knowledge of social media, including LinkedIn, Twitter, Facebook
- Logistics Software: TCAIMS II, BCS3, TIPS writer software for RFID tags
- Personnel and cargo software: GATES, GDSS, SMS

Education
- Washington High School, Chicago, IL. High School Diploma
- Moraine Valley College, Palos Park, IL. Pursuing major in Youth Counseling.

Advice for Contacting: Jsil@saturn.com.

****

MOVING FORWARD

The resume and digital profile are only tools in the search process. They alone will not get you the job. The purpose of the resume and digital profile is to move your candidacy up a notch to the personal interview, which I will cover in Part VI.

CHAPTER TAKEAWAYS

- A resume may be more than two pages long.
- The digital profile and the resume must be a mirror image of each other.
- Quantify your job experience.
- Avoid the use of meaningless words such as "awesome."
- Always write the resume and digital profile in civilian language.
- Avoid using acronyms, but if necessary, spell out their meaning.

Chapter 26

Writing a Cover Letter and Follow-Up Letter

Write cover letters and follow-up letters with the same care you exercised writing your resume and digital profile. Address both to a living person with a title and company affiliation, not to Box 123, or Position 456, or Staffing Manager. A cover letter reflects your written communication skills, and frequently it is the first document the reader will open in your career profile. A follow-up letter goes to the heart of business etiquette and is another step in the job-hunting process.

The number of Internet hits for "cover letters and follow-up letters" is surprising. Much of what you read is redundant, useless, or incorrect. Follow the rubrics in this chapter, and you will create meaningful cover letters and follow-up letters.

PURPOSE OF THE COVER LETTER

The cover letter serves as a summary and table of contents for your career profile, which you will submit to a human resources director or hiring manager. In addition, the cover letter tells the reader that you have taken time to research the company and that you find it worthy of your candidacy.

COVER LETTER FORMATTING

The cover letter is a business document. Write it on digital letterhead, or print letterhead if you are submitting it by regular mail. Use 12 pt.

Times New Roman typeface. Follow all of the rules for business communication, including an inside address and a date. Sending anything less will diminish your candidacy.

Submit the cover letter on your email communication page, or as an email attachment, or as a print document accompanying a submission by regular mail. There is disagreement on which method to use, but I suggest that you submit it as an email attachment.

THE FIVE COMPONENTS OF THE COVER LETTER

All cover letters should include these five items:

1. The name of a person who referred you to the company or your source of information about the open position, like a job posting on the company website.
2. The purpose of the communication, usually a response to a job posting.
3. A one-line listing of the items attached or enclosed with the cover letter.
4. A compliment to the company.
5. A postscript (PS.) suggesting what you would like to happen next, a true action item. Do not disregard the impact of the postscript. Always include one in your cover letter.

A SAMPLE COVER LETTER

The following sample cover letter contains the five required components, which is all you need to get the job done. Also, note the business formatting, the postscript, and the length—one page.

****

James Silvestri
10527 Komensky Ave;
Chicago, IL 60934

213–476–9909   Jsil@Saturn.com

July 12, 2016
Mr. Howard Jones
Human Resources Director
Nike Inc.
25 Santa Maria Blvd.
Spokane, WA 45667

Dear Mr. Jones:

Nike's Associate Marketing Manager, Linda Mattingham, referred me to you in reference to a position in her department. I am submitting my candidacy for the position posted on your website titled Assistant Digital Marketing Manager. In support of my candidacy, I am submitting my career profile, which consists of the following documents:

Resume, which highlights my military and civilian work experience, education, technology skills, and awards for performance. Note my community outreach initiatives.

Official college and military transcripts, as verification of my BA in English from Ohio State University, and my military transcript verifying courses completed.

Letter of reference, from Dr. Eugene Harris, my college senior class advisor.

Technology certification, awarded by HigherNext Inc., which serves as verification that my technology skills are current and ready to be utilized to accomplish job objectives with Nike.

Article I authored, "The Green Revolution is Changing Our Lives." The *Columbus Times* newspaper published it on May 3, 2014, and it attests to my written communication skills.

My research has confirmed that Nike is *the* leader in the production and distribution of sports apparel for women and men, and that you have a record of profitability for the past twelve quarters. What I like best, however, is that your company has paid a quarterly dividend for the past fifteen years. This is my kind of company, and I would like to move my candidacy to the next step in your hiring process.

Sincerely,
Paul
Paul Silvestri

PS. I suggest that we meet for an interview on Tuesday, July 22, at 9 a.m. at your office. Alternatively, we could meet at a time more convenient for you, or we could continue the conversation by Skype or phone. My contact information is on the resume. Thanks!
****

That is all you need in a cover letter. Do not spend hours or days raking the Internet for more information on cover letters. Spend that time seeking personal contacts at conferences and trade shows.

FOLLOW-UP LETTERS

I never cease to be amazed that candidates forget about an essential part of business etiquette: the follow-up letter or email. When you speak with a hiring manager or human resources director, correct business etiquette requires a follow-up letter, which is a written acknowledgement of your conversation and a thank you. Send this document by email or on a typed note sent by regular mail.

When I receive a follow-up note from a job candidate after an interview, I note that on the candidate's database profile. Hiring managers and human resources directors do the same.

COMPONENTS OF A FOLLOW-UP LETTER

The follow-up letter is brief, a half page or full page at most, and has three main components:

1. A thank you for what transpired, e.g. a phone interview.
2. A brief recap of the conversation.
3. A suggested plan for going to the next step in the process, best stated in a PS.

MOVING FORWARD

Always follow the rules of civilian business, and you will rise to the top of the pack. The cover letter and follow-up letter are tools, sales tools if you will, to move your candidacy to the next level. Even in this world of increasing informality, the rules of common courtesy and discourse still apply.

CHAPTER TAKEAWAYS

- The cover letter and follow-up letter are documents that will enhance your candidacy.
- Always write the cover letter and follow-up letter in business format.
- Write follow-up letters promptly.
- Business etiquette is the rule when constructing a cover letter or follow-up letter.

THE VETERAN'S LIBRARY

Joyce Kennedy. ***Cover Letters for Dummies***. Wiley, 2009.

PART VI

Personal Interviews. Phone and Skype Interviews

Our lives begin to end the day we become silent about things that matter.
— *Dr. Martin Luther King, Jr.*

Chapter 27

Communication Begins with Your Appearance

While there are no hard and fast *written* rules for interview attire, there is tradition to observe. Companies do not tell you beforehand what to wear for an interview. They assume that you know what is appropriate.

YOUR ATTIRE MAKES A LASTING FIRST IMPRESSION

When hiring managers interview candidates, the first thing they notice is appearance. Dress like a sophomore, and the human resources director will think of you, subconsciously, as a candidate not yet ready for the big time. Dress in your military uniform, and the hiring manager will think that you have not yet made the transition. Dress in business attire, and the hiring manager will think of you as a serious candidate, one who is ready to work in the civilian world. Company personnel charged with the responsibility of hiring the right candidates are looking down the road, too. If you are dressed properly, the hiring manager could see you, subconsciously, as a potential manager, director, or vice president.

ATTIRE FOR INTERVIEWING AND FOR WORKING. THERE IS A DIFFERENCE

What you see on TV and in movies like "The Internship" can be misleading. Frequently the workplace portrayed on television and in movies has workers in jeans, t-shirts, and sneakers. While this may be true at some companies, it is not the way workers dress at most companies.

The way you dress for an interview and the way you dress at work *after you are hired* are two different things. You make your first impression when you walk through the door for an interview, and it is a lasting one. Interview attire is business dress; it is conservative. If you hate formal business attire, suffer through it during an interview. When you are hired, you can dress as the culture dictates, usually casual, unless you are a manager, director, or high-level executive.

Chances are that you will find a relaxed dress code at your new workplace. Dress a cut above the crowd, however, and you will make a lasting impression on your managers and executives. When hiring managers and human resources directors are looking for internal candidates to promote, dress subconsciously comes into play. Do you want to appear as a solid member of the "followers" or as a potential "leader"? The way you dress creates a lasting impression on people in the company.

Do Not Dress for Ping-Pong

Most work environments are, by nature, relatively conservative places. They exist to encourage maximum productivity, which results in a profitable operation. Profitable companies make money to pay your salary, and benefits package, and other expenses. Most companies believe that a conservative work environment contributes to productivity.

There is a good reason why the office at most companies is not a free-for-all environment filled with ping-pong tables, frisbees flying through the air, workout rooms, and free pizza and soft drink kiosks liberally sprinkled throughout the building. This may be true for some tech companies, but for most of corporate America, this is not the everyday environment.

ADVICE FROM HUMAN RESOURCES DIRECTORS

When you arrive for an interview at an employer's office, business attire is expected, even if the employer is a tech company noted for its "relaxed" culture. Joyce Boston, Human Resources Manager for Measured Progress, an education company in Dover, New Hampshire, says, "Candidates appearing for an interview dressed in formal business attire stand out from the rest of the crowd. Candidates in business attire, both men and women, get my attention. That means a suit, tie, and leather shoes for men and comparable business attire for women."

In addition, Joyce recommends that you do not bring your smartphone to an interview, even if the ringer is on vibrate or silenced. Turn off the smartphone before you leave the car, *no exceptions*. There is nothing so important that it cannot wait until you complete the interview.

DRESS RIGHT FOR A SUCCESSFUL INTERVIEW. HELPFUL RESOURCES

Selecting the right attire for an interview is a serious concern for all candidates. I have selected a number of helpful resources based on my research and real time spent in the work environment with business people of every rank.

TV Programs

Watch business programs on CNBC and Fox Business News where you will see men and women from the business world. Note how program hosts and guests dress. All represent the business world and hold positions of authority and responsibility. These people will be interviewing you.

Internet Sites

The Internet is loaded with useful information about dressing for interviews. Much of it is redundant because there is only so much you can say beyond "go conservative." Remember to distinguish between proper attire for a personal interview and attire for workers already hired. There is a world of difference. I particularly like the following sites for their helpful advice:

About.com, www.jobsearch.about.com. I like this site because it goes into detail about appropriate dress for an interview for both men and women. While the importance for both men and women is equal, the topic presents a more serious challenge for women because there are more options available in clothing styles. This site sums up suggested attire for women in a few sentences: "Solid color, conservative suit with coordinated blouse, moderate shoes, tan or light pantyhose, limited jewelry, neat professional hairstyle, manicured nails, light makeup, little or no perfume, portfolio or briefcase."

The Limited, www.thelimited.com/Womens-Business. This site provides much good advice and pictures for women exclusively. Review it frequently to see what is in style and what is not.

THE BEST STORES FOR PURCHASING BUSINESS ATTIRE

There are many stores across the country where you can buy appropriate business attire. Here is a list of national stores, which you can find in most large and mid-sized cities.

Ann Taylor, www.anntaylor.com. This iconic retailer of women's clothing offers a wide selection of business and casual clothing. Visit the website and click on "suits." You will see pictures of knockout styles that will make the human resources director remember your name! Ann Taylor holds sales periodically, so check the website frequently. Check out the Careers page as well for job opportunities.

Nordstrom, www.nordstrom.com. Nordstrom sells quality clothing for both men and women. Prices are high but look for sales and you will walk away with stylish clothing at everyday prices. Check their website for the dates of "half-yearly" (semiannual) sales. In addition, Nordstrom has outlet stores in some locations where you can find quality clothing at very attractive prices. Also, Nordstrom has a website devoted exclusively to careers: www.careers.nordstrom.com. This company has a reputation for treating employees fairly and for providing good training.

Joseph Bank, www.josephbank.com. This website gives tips for smart dressing, and you can view a wide variety of both casual and formal business attire. This nationwide chain caters primarily to men.

Brooks Brothers, www.brooksbrothers.com. Brooks produces high-quality clothing for both men and women. The company has retail stores located in shopping malls throughout the country. However, Brooks has outlet stores, too, that sell traditional clothing at very attractive prices. For example, the traditional men's blue blazer, or sport coat, that retails for $500 in its regular stores, sells for $200 at the outlet stores. Shirts go for less than $50 and ties for under $30. You will not go wrong buying at Brooks Brothers outlet stores.

Macy's, www.macys.com. This national chain offers business attire for both men and women at very attractive everyday prices. Macy's carries a number of famous designer labels for both men and women, and the sales reps are very knowledgeable. They will help you construct an entire outfit. If you like the idea of working for a celebrated department store with great clothing products, check out the jobs website at www.macysjobs.com. I saw hundreds of jobs spanning merchandising, sales, marketing, information technology, finance and many others. I presume that employees receive discounts on Macy's products. Check it out!

Paul Fredrick, www.Paulfredrick.com. This Pennsylvania-based clothier specializes in dress shirts for men. The company offers very attractive introductory prices for first-time customers (shirts, $19.95; silk ties, $19.95). Their products are high quality, their service is impeccable, and their prices cannot be beat. Do not mess with shirts and ties from retailers like Target. Go straight to Paul Fredrick to save time and money.

The Limited, www.limited.com. Women, check out the pictures and descriptions of their collection of jackets, blazers, and suits. The

Limited produces conservative business apparel at reasonable everyday prices, but look for sales to save a bundle.

Talbots, www.talbots.com. This nationwide chain offers both casual and business attire for women. Their classic business suits are available as separates or as coordinated outfits. Prices are on the expensive side, so be sure to check out the many Talbots outlet stores. While you are checking out business apparel, go to the career page and see what is available.

Bloomingdales, www.bloomingdales.com. This reputable store carries designer clothing, shoes, handbags, and jewelry and caters primarily to women. On the website, view their suits, separates, and attractive business attire. Prices are high, so wait for sales, which are frequent.

Lord & Taylor, www.lordandtaylor.com. You cannot go wrong with Lord & Taylor. It carries an impressive list of classic business clothing in a number of designer labels. Look online for the locations of outlet stores and frequently check for online discount coupons. The store offers clothing for both men and women. Lord & Taylor has a separate website for job hunters, www.lordandtaylor.com/careers.

FAIL-SAFE DRESS FOR MEN

Men have an easier job selecting proper interview attire than do women. There are two choices that will take men through any interview, and they are available at a modest cost.

The Blue Blazer Outfit

This casual outfit has been around for decades, and it is something that you can wear for a personal interview or while attending a trade show. It consists of the following: a blue blazer, dark gray or tan wool pants, a white or blue shirt (either button-down or traditional spread collar), a conservative tie, black leather loafers or plain cap shoes, and black socks. This ensemble will cost about $400. By the way, patterned shirts can be worn instead of solid white or blue. However, do not go beyond small checks or subtle stripes.

The Suit

The dark blue, dark brown, or gray suit, solid or in pinstripe, will make an indelible first impression. Select a blue or white shirt with a spread collar and a conservative complementary tie. The tie is sometimes difficult because there are so many choices, but a good sales person is always ready and willing to make helpful suggestions. Wear plain cap black leather shoes and black socks and you will not go wrong. The cost of dressing in this ensemble will run between $400–500. However, it will last for at least three years, providing you do not put on any weight.

FAIL-SAFE DRESS FOR FEMALE VETERANS. LISTEN TO LINDA

The first and last rule is to select conservative outfits. Linda Winter, Founder and CEO of the Winter Group, a Denver-based marketing and advertising company catering to the communications and education industries, is noted for selecting the right attire for the right occasion. We asked Linda to provide guidance for female veterans who are agonizing over what to wear for that all-important interview. Here is what she says.

Listen to Linda

Your style should fit the organization you're talking to. For creative companies (publishing, advertising, design, technology, etc.), it's great to dress with a bit of individual "flair." Consider a scarf, a piece of "statement" jewelry, or a jacket with some memorable design elements. For conservative companies (banking, finance, real estate, healthcare, etc.), a skirt or pant suit that's tasteful always works. Add a scarf, understated earrings or bracelet, and a crisp blouse or sweater, and you should be dressed appropriately.

Talbots, Ann Taylor, Banana Republic, Nordstrom, Macy's, and Dillard's all offer great options that you can put together in a variety of outfits. And don't forget Zara, H&M, and other "fast fashion" retailers. These stores often offer great "on trend" pieces at great prices. Personal shoppers at the larger department stores can also be very helpful in showing you how to make the latest trends your own. A white or oxford blue blouse with grey or navy slacks/skirt are great launching pads. From there you can accessorize with scarves, jewelry, shoes, and bags to showcase your own sense of style.

If you're wearing a dress, add a complementary jacket or cardigan. And yes, be sure your bag either holds your files nicely or invest in your own version of an "IT" bag or tote to hold your resume, work samples, notebook, and other business essentials. Cookie cutter? No! The goal is to look "meeting ready" and to show you understand the culture and style of the company you're visiting . . . and at the same time put your own unique personality and style into the mix!

PERSONAL GROOMING

Dress and proper grooming go together. You can dress like a celebrity, but if your hair looks like you just woke up after an all-nighter at the local pub, you are history. Rules for proper grooming apply equally to men and women. Remember them as you prepare for an interview or attending a trade show or job fair.

Hair

Wear your hair in a natural style. It can be reasonably long or short but never looking like you just came out of the shower or just arrived home from a ten-day hiking trip. Your natural hair color is your best color. Orange hair and business do not mix, unless you are in the entertainment business where anything goes.

For men, hair care applies not only to your head but also to your face. A well-groomed beard is fine, but there is nothing better to turn off a hiring manager than a face covered in stubble. *Please* men, shave before an interview and do not cut your chin. If you sport a beard, make sure it is attractively trimmed.

Nails

All of us know the importance of good nail grooming. For some reason, men tend to overlook this part of grooming and show up for interviews with dirt under their nails. It must be a throwback to Neanderthal times. Your hands are always in view so groom your nails carefully.

Women, avoid the use of bright nail polish. Clear nail polish is attractive and business-smart as well.

Cosmetics

Excessive use of fragrances can be offensive to other people. Go very easy on the aftershave and perfume. The hiring manager at your interview may have an allergic reaction to strong smelling fragrances. Women, use common sense with facial cosmetics. Use lip-gloss, eyeliners, foundation, and powder conservatively. Remember that an interview is a business deal and not a weekend party.

Tattoos

There are strict regulations about tattoos in each military branch, the latest being Army Regulation 670–1, which became effective on March 31, 2014. Civilian employers may not have anything in writing about the display of tattoos, but most do not approve of *visible* tattoos. If you have acquired a tattoo after discharge, cover it with appropriate clothing before an interview or a casual meeting with hiring managers at trade shows or job fairs. If you believe that tattoos of any kind and displayed anywhere on the body are okay in the civilian workplace, we suggest that you apply for jobs in the entertainment industry. Once again, Ringling Brothers Circus comes to mind.

DRESS FOR NON-CORPORATE JOBS

I have given much attention to appropriate dress for corporate job interviews, but how does someone dress for a job in a more casual environment, like a garden center or a construction site? Once more, common sense rules. If you are interviewing for an apprentice electrician position with a job supervisor in a construction trailer, then you need not wear a suit. For this kind of job interview, wear a pair of casual cotton khakis, a shirt or top with a collar, conservative sneakers or loafers, and matching socks. Personal grooming is the same for any type of job interview.

MOVING FORWARD

In our appearance- and celebrity-conscious culture, it is easy to become preoccupied with how we look. It is important in the business world because first impressions are lasting impressions. Use the rules and guidelines in this chapter, and you will be fine. Do not obsess over dressing for an interview. Use common sense, and if you want real-life examples, observe how people dress on the TV business shows.

CHAPTER TAKEAWAYS

- Always go to an interview in nothing less than fail-safe, conservative clothing.
- Purchase interview-appropriate clothing, and it will be an investment for multi-purpose use.
- When purchasing interview attire, always inquire about job opportunities. Ask a salesperson for the names and contact information of hiring managers and human resources directors and follow up while you are in the store.
- There is a difference between dress for interviews and dress while on the job.
- Employers consider personal grooming important when evaluating a candidate.

Chapter 28

Speaking in Civilian Business Language

Communicating in civilian language is a distinct challenge for all veterans in transition. In the military, you spoke in the vernacular of that sub-culture using acronyms, technical terms, and abbreviations that everyone understood. Previously, we learned that written communication is an exacting science where second chances do not exist. When you place your name on a written document, you literally own all that you said.

Verbal communication is more forgiving because the listener can ask for clarification and you can respond immediately. For example, if you happen to use the term "military personnel officer" and the listener asks for clarification, you can immediately respond, "that means human resources director in the military." Then the conversation can proceed with little more than a hiccup.

However, even verbal communication is confusing when a veteran continually uses unusual acronyms like *NAVSPECWARCOM*. Veterans know that it means "Naval Special Warfare Command," but the listener could not even hazard a guess at what that acronym means. Using military acronyms in situations critical, like an interview, usually results in a failed operation. So, how do you make the transition? How do you relearn civilian speak?

PRACTICE! PRACTICE! PRACTICE!
You know the drill: practice makes perfect. Before going to an interview, sit down with a friend and play question and answer using the

interview questions in the next chapter. Most likely, the hiring manager will ask, "What did you do in the Navy?" Practice your answers using civilian-speak, totally devoid of military acronyms. Do not assume that the human resources director or hiring manager will know even rudimentary military terms like "commander." Instead, use the civilian equivalent of that term, which is "director" or "senior manager."

LISTEN AND LEARN AT CONFERENCES AND JOB FAIRS

The best way to attune your ears to civilian-speak is to hear it spoken in real-life situations. **OJS** recommends attending conferences and job fairs and viewing TV business channels.

In addition, get rid of the "Yes, sir" and "No, ma'am" drill. In the civilian world, particularly at an informal setting such as a convention center floor, you address people by their first names, which you will find on their nametags. This is not a violation of protocol; it is the ordinary language of business. Once again, practice. "Hello, Mary. My name is Bob Smith and I'm interested in your products. Could you tell me what your company produces and where your products are sold . . . and whether your company has any job openings for a veteran like me?"

After doing this fifty times or more, you will come away with a BA in civilian-speak. Guaranteed.

LISTEN TO BUSINESS-SPEAK ON TV PROGRAMS

Another source for learning civilian business-speak is TV. Here are some of my business TV faves:

CNBC. Here you will see and hear both informal and formal business-speak from CEOs, presidents, business reporters, analysts, and program personalities like Jim Cramer, whose 6 p.m. (EST) show is among the best for learning how civilian business works. Also, skip the networks and tune into CNBC when you awake. The ever-popular "Squawk Box" program at 7 a.m. (EST) will have you thinking in business-speak in no time. Co-host Betsy Quick is one of the best. CNBC has it all: stock recommendations, interviews with business experts, job reports, employment statistics, government initiatives, job locations, and much more.

Fox Business Network. This TV channel will give you an opportunity to hear real-world business-speak while learning how the world of business works. Tune in Monday-Friday, 6 a.m. to 9 p.m.

Bloomberg. This channel is similar to CNBC. Tune in 6 a.m. to midnight, and you will come away with a different point of view on how business works while learning civilian-speak.

MOVING FORWARD

Learning civilian business-speak from real world examples is a vital step in the job-hunting process. If you *say it right* during a phone, Skype, or personal interview, you will rise above the rest of the pack. In the next chapter, **OJS** provides civilian-speak examples and takes you into the heart of the interview process. Stick around!

CHAPTER TAKEAWAYS

- Learning how to communicate in civilian terms is a necessary step in the job-hunting process.
- Practice is a required step in learning how to communicate in civilian terms.
- Attending trade shows at convention centers is the best method to learn civilian-speak.
- Business TV programs provide good examples of business language spoken by the pros.

Chapter 29

The Interview. Purpose and Procedures

Before we get into the heart of the interview process, let's reconstruct the landscape. You are going to the interview because you need a job in order to become self-sufficient and find purpose in your life. You need to provide your own food, shelter, and clothing by working. Ideally, the work you find will have purpose and give you satisfaction and fulfillment in addition to the paycheck.

On the other side of the aisle, the company needs to make money to exist. The company does this by hiring workers like you to make products or provide services, which the company sells to other companies or to individuals. In the process, the company makes money, which it uses to pay expenses, including wages, to its workers. The objective of this game called *business* is to make more money than you spend.

Business is similar to the military; each has its own lexicon. It was confusing at first, but after you learned military-speak, you could play the game and effectively contribute to the mission. The business world is much the same. The more that you learn about business terminology and processes, the easier it will be to have an intelligent and meaningful conversation with human resources directors and hiring managers, the very people you will speak with during the interview.

The bottom line is this: the interview is a part of the process that enables both you and the company to make money. When that happens, everyone wins. The company makes money to pay your salary and benefits, expenses, taxes, and contribute to charitable causes. You win because you make money to become self-sufficient, take care of your family, give back money and time to the community, and find purpose in coming to work every day. Everyone is happy when the bottom line is written in black ink, not red.

WHO'S HOLDING THE ACES?

Even though the interviewer appears to hold all of the cards, it really is not so. While you are there because you need a job, the hiring manager is speaking with you because the company needs workers. The hiring manager needs someone like you to fill an important position. The hiring manager is under pressure, too, to find the right candidate as soon as possible.

While the hiring manager is evaluating the person across the desk, smart candidates are sizing up the hiring manager as well. It is important that the hiring manager is someone you respect, someone who shows intelligence, courtesy, and honesty. If you find that the interviewer lacks these qualities, erase that company from your list. You may need a job, but you do not want it at the expense of working on a ship of fools.

LISTEN AND LEARN

The person sitting across the desk from you is forward-looking. Because the interviewer has a good idea of what you have done in the past from your resume and other sources, he or she is really thinking about what you can do for the company going forward. The questions about what you have done and what you would like to do have one purpose: to determine how successfully you could perform. Forget about all the pleasantries. Listen and comprehend, because it is what you say after you say hello that really counts.

Many people do not really listen because they have other things on their mind. Listening to what the interviewer says and how it is said will tell you how to respond. You cannot listen and comprehend if you are anxious to respond either from nervousness or overconfidence. In his well-known book, *The 7 Habits of Highly Effective People*, Stephen Covey argues, "Most people do not listen with the intent to understand: they listen with the intent to reply. They are either speaking or preparing to speak."

A good example of Covey's theory is the TV interview. Interviewers are more concerned with presenting their own agendas than listening to the responses to the questions they asked. Before the response is even completed, the interviewer interrupts with her own statement. The same might happen in your interview, and if it does, you must deal with it to maintain the integrity of the interview and to make your point. If the interviewer interrupts before you have the last word out of your mouth, you need an appropriate response to keep the interview on an even keel, even though your gut reaction might be, "Shut up. Let me finish my answer to your question." Here is what you might say when this happens: "To complete my response to your first question, here is what I was going to say . . ."

That should keep the interview on the right track and make for a fruitful exchange of ideas and courteous discourse. The interview is a conversation that takes place when two people listen, comprehend, and then respond.

THE TWO GOLDEN RULES OF INTERVIEWS

The two golden rules of interviewing are these:

1. Be courteous.
2. Be honest.

These two rules build the foundation for all personal relationships. Once again, it is basic sociology. This holds true no matter how young, how old, or how senior the interviewer is. The person sitting across the desk from you may be the same age as your parents or even grandparents. This person is probably at the manager, director, or vice president level, and it takes time to reach that point in the corporate hierarchy.

You might detect a note of condescension from more senior workers, but that's just the way it is. Suck it up and deal with it. In addition, the interviewers may know absolutely nothing about your military training. They may not realize that you are job-ready, but once more, keep your cool and deal with it. Gently educate them about your military job.

On the other side of the age situation, the interviewer may be ten years your junior and display arrogance that is nothing short of irritating. Suck it up, because you cannot do anything about it.

Regardless of the situation, the only way to deal with these variables is to be prepared to answer the questions in a mature manner and on your own terms. When you prepare for the interview, resolve that you are going to look at the hiring manager as a potential friend, not an authority figure like your high school principal, or an old-timer like your grandfather, or like the stereotypical drill sergeant.

You are there for an interview because the company needs qualified workers to make the bottom line black. You are indispensable to company success. *You* are holding a full deck of cards loaded with aces!

HOW THE INTERVIEWER JUDGES YOU

Two important things on an employer's checklist appear so self-evident that candidates overlook them. However, if you fall short on either, your chances of moving ahead in the process are diminished.

1. **Dress**. Your appearance is the first thing a hiring manager notices. If you walk into an interview dressed as if you are going to dinner at Chipotle, you are history. Case closed. In fact, this is such an important item that I have devoted an entire chapter to the subject. See Chapter 27.
2. **Appropriate Speech**. After dress, the most important checklist item is verbal communication, which consists of three components: vocabulary, content, and delivery. Vocabulary and content are all-important and will tell the interviewer if you are in ready mode or if you are stuck in military-speak and

street-talk. At all costs, avoid common clichés like "awesome," "cool," "dude." Instead of saying, "your company is awesome," you could say something like this: "I want to work with FedEx because I'm impressed with your record of generating revenue. For example, in the last quarter your revenue was up 10 percent over a comparable quarter a year ago. This tells me that FedEx has a viable business model. I would like a chance to work for such a company and contribute my time and talents to help the company continue to grow."

I don't think you will have any trouble deciding that your business-speak answer is more meaningful than using "awesome." So what's the takeaway? The civilian world of work is *business*, and appropriate speech is expected. Hiring authorities assume that you have the business savvy to use business-speak, and if you do not, they will place you in the "not-yet-ready-for-prime-time" box. Also, couching your answers in quantitative terms will tell the interviewer that you understand business.

BODY LANGUAGE

The interview, like giving a speech or delivering a sermon, has two parts: delivery and content. The delivery part of your conversation includes body language, which reflects your level of confidence and maturity. Millions of words have been written on this subject, but it still comes down to a few basics. Sit straight, make eye contact, relax, smile, and display your personality. If you are not accustomed to using your hands to make a point, do not make an awkward attempt to do this in an interview. You are having a conversation about how you can help the company going forward, not auditioning for a part in a movie.

To learn more on this general topic, conduct a Google search on "body language."

Here is a real situation that I encountered recently while conducting a search for a vice president. This story indicates that delivery, particularly the body language part of it, is just as important as content.

Fred from California

Fred had a personal two-hour interview with the CEO of a major company located in Los Angeles. The position, Vice President for International Sales and Marketing, required the candidate to live in the home office area, and Fred met that requirement. He did not need to relocate. This was a huge problem out of the way. On paper, he met every job requirement and more. So far, so good. However, something untoward happened during the interview process. The CEO rejected his candidacy citing these two reasons: 1. Fred's answers seemed shallow. In other words, the CEO did not buy the content. 2. Fred appeared insecure, lacking confidence and appearing distanced. His body language told the CEO that there was a disconnect. His eyes were wandering during the interview, his posture was strained, his arms were folded much of the time, and his legs were crossed. Fred's body language told the CEO that he was not buying into the conversation.

I counseled Fred on the basics of body language and persuaded the CEO to have a second interview with Fred. The CEO obliged and the results of that second interview were startling. The interview proceeded as a conversation, during which the CEO and Fred learned they had much in common on a personal level. Both were star performers on their college swim teams, for instance. After another round of interviews with company executives, Fred was hired.

PREPARING A WRITTEN INTERVIEW AGENDA

I am always impressed when a job candidate comes to an interview with a written agenda that includes questions about both the position and the company. I'm impressed when the candidate hands me an agenda and requests a brief discussion of each topic if time permits. A written agenda sends a powerful message that you have carefully prepared for the interview and that you are pursuing this particular opportunity, not just *any* job with *any* company. Here is a sample agenda that you can print on your letterhead and hand to the interviewer before you begin the interview.

Sample Interview Agenda

****

Subject: Agenda for Interview with Amazon
Position: Assistant Inside Sales Manager
Candidate: Lisa Hopkins
Human Resources Director: Robert Kowalski
Date: June 7, 2018

I would appreciate the opportunity to discuss the following questions during my interview with Mr. Kowalski:

1. Why is this position open?
2. If someone else had this job, why did that person leave the company?
3. Why are you considering me for this position?
4. Would superior performance in this position lead to a promotion?
5. What are the three major expectations for the Assistant Inside Sales Manager?
6. To whom does this job report and what is that person's management style?
7. What is the background of the person to whom this position reports?
8. What is the company's revenue goal for this fiscal year? How much of an increase is that over the previous year's revenue?
9. What has made Amazon a leader in online retailing?
10. Does the company participate in community outreach programs?
11. Does the company have an employment program for returning military personnel?
12. Why should I join Amazon?

I thank you for discussing these issues during our interview.

Sincerely,
Lisa
Lisa Hopkins
****

Answers to these questions are a tool for evaluating the position and company. You need this information to decide if you want to continue the process or decline. Answers to questions 10 and 11 will tell you much about the company culture.

Using the written interview agenda will also distinguish you from the rest of the pack. Do not hesitate to use this technique for every interview.

THE PURPOSE OF THE INTERVIEW

The interview is one of the key steps in the job-hunting process. It has benefits for the employer and the job candidate. Like anything else in both the military and business, it has a certain set of unwritten rules. Millions of words have been written about interviews. Is the interview process so complicated that we need so many words to define its purpose and processes? Do we really need to read Internet articles like "Ten tips for killer interviews," "Ace the interview in three easy steps," and "Interviews for dummies"? What is it about the interview that compels us to dissect it into very small parts? Please, veterans, do not stay awake trying to figure out the interview "mystery." **OJS** will provide all you need to know about the process and how to do it right.

For starters, the interview has two sides: your side and the company side. On your side, the purpose of the interview is to determine if this is the right place for you based upon your analysis of the company, the interviewer, and the company environment. On the company side, the purpose is to determine your level of maturity, your communication skills, your match with the company culture and the job specs, and to assess how you might add to the company's bottom line. During the course of the interview, the hiring manager is always thinking, "What can this candidate do for the company going forward?"

THE INTERVIEW PROCESS

The interview process has three parts, each with its own set of procedures:

1. The *beginning* of the interview. This is the introductory phase, which sets the tone for the interview.
2. The *body* of the interview, which is what takes place after the greetings are completed.
3. The *ending* of the interview, which is a critically important action item.

Let's explore each part in detail.

HOW THE INTERVIEW BEGINS. SHOW TIME!

After you exchange hellos and informal chitchat ("This is just a beautiful day. I'm happy spring has finally come after such a harsh winter."), it is show time.

Trying to anticipate what the interviewer will ask can be a never-ending game. To level the playing field and keep this a true give-and-take rather than an interrogation, plan to incorporate some or all of these five topics into the interview.

1. You are here because you have learned there is a specific employment opportunity.
2. You have researched the company and would like to work there for several reasons. State what they are. Some reasons could be your interest in their product, company profitability, glowing reports from company workers, or the steady increase in the price of the company stock.

3. You would like an opportunity to increase the profitability of the company by using your military leadership skills, intelligence, energy, and passion.

4. Highlight your successes and awards for achievement. Verbalize the key points on your resume under the major heading "Awards and Achievements."

5. State your career goals, and do not be shy. If you really would like to be the company president someday, say so. Tell your interviewer how and why you believe you could work your way up to that position.

All of this advice may be interesting and helpful, but how does it translate into answers to questions the interviewer might ask? One never knows where an interview will go, and it is really up to the candidate to set the direction and tone of the interview. Your written agenda will help accomplish this. Naturally, the interviewer has a certain number of questions, but you do not know these in advance. However, the interviewer will ask one question in almost every situation: "Would you tell me about yourself?" It appears to be a trivial question, but that's just the way it is, and you have to prepare for it. If you are caught off guard, you might end up reciting your family history or rendering a chronological account of your life from birth to the present. What the hiring manager really wants to hear is what you might do for the company if you are hired, not that you like a latte better than a cappuccino.

How do you answer that question? It could go several ways, but here is a script that you might use. It gives direction to the interview and sets the tone for a dialogue instead of a Q&A session.

Script Answer for
"Would You Tell Me About Yourself?"

I'm the kind of person who takes responsibility for my own life, and that includes finding a position that will give me income to provide for my own needs to become self-sufficient and accomplish some of my career goals. I'm here because I believe that your company can provide that opportunity. My research indicates that your last quarter generated revenue that exceeded expectations and that your past three years were profitable. I want to be part of a company with that kind of track record, because it means that you are doing something right. I would like to build on that success by applying my intelligence, energy, passion, and military training to make this company even better and more profitable. Also, my career vision includes a director-level position, and hopefully I will find that here.

Read this aloud several times until you make it your own. Modify it to include some hard numbers and specifics from your resume.

After you respond, take control of the direction of the interview by asking the interviewer what he or she thought of your resume and whether there are any questions. You need to make sure that the interviewer read and evaluated your resume or career profile. Remember that this is *your* interview and you have every right to ask questions as well.

THE BODY OF THE INTERVIEW.
FREQUENTLY ASKED QUESTIONS

Candidates, understandably, are curious about what the interviewer will ask. The kinds of questions asked in an interview follow a somewhat standard format. Here are questions the interviewer may ask regardless of the company or position.

1. Can you tell me something about yourself?
2. How did you find out about us?
3. Why do you want to work here?
4. What are your major qualifications for this position?

5. Are there any areas where you think you need to improve?

6. What is your career goal?

7. Can you tell me about a work problem you encountered and how you resolved it?

8. What are your compensation requirements?

9. When could you begin work with us if we agree this is the right job for you?

10. Have you participated in community outreach programs?

11. What do you do with your spare time?

12. What is your main academic interest?

13. What books have you read recently?

14. Give me an example of how you use social media like YouTube, Twitter, Facebook, and LinkedIn?

15. What do you want to know about the company and the job?

16. Can you tell me about your military experience?

17. How do you think your military experience will help you in this job?

18. On your resume, you list several positions you held while you were in the Army. Could you translate those job responsibilities into civilian terms?

19. How does your military experience make your candidacy better than that of a non-veteran?

20. Why did you join the military?

You don't know how many of these questions the interviewer will ask, but be prepared to answer all of them. Conduct a rehearsal before the interview by having a trusted friend ask you these questions and then deliver your responses. Practice until you feel comfortable with your answers. Remember to answer in civilian business-speak and to quantify as much as possible.

Note questions 16–20, which deal with your military experience. Human resources directors and hiring managers surely will be curious about this part of your background if they have not served themselves. And, most of them have not. Your replies to their military-oriented questions will be a good opportunity for you to educate the interviewer. Play the role of a teacher, because it will build the relationship and friendship, and that is how you are hired.

This is a good place to begin evaluating the hiring manager by asking questions, such as "Could you tell me about your job experience, such as how long you have been here, what your responsibilities are, and what you did before taking this job? Also, I'm curious about where you went to college and what your major was. And, by the way, do you have any military experience and if so, could you tell me about it? Who knows, maybe we served in the same Company."

This kind of dialogue permits the hiring manager a chance to brag a little and tell you some success stories. Your expressed interest helps build the relationship and provides valuable information to evaluate this person. In addition, it makes the interview conversational rather than interrogative.

Interviewing the Interviewer

Remember, this is *your* interview. You are entitled to ask as many questions as necessary to learn about the company and its people. Do not be intimidated by the interviewer's status or title. You are now part of the civilian world of work, and you are communicating civilian to civilian. The person sitting across from you is not your Commander. What questions should you ask?

Five Questions Job Candidates Should Ask

Most likely, you will create your own list of questions, but here are the five Jeff Haden suggests in his April 2013 piece for the *Inc.* online magazine:

1. *What really drives success for the company?* Every profitable company has rubrics that account for its success. Learn what these are and you will know much about the company and what it expects from its workers. If you hear something like "Everyone here works like crazy, even coming in on Saturdays and

Sundays," consider it a yellow flag. You should not have to spend seven days a week meeting job expectations, and you should not be expected to be on call 24/7, unless you are a medical professional or a law enforcement officer.

2. *What do employees do in their spare time?* This might be a difficult question for the interviewer to answer, especially in a large company. However, the answer will tell you much about the kind of people the company hires and whether these are your kind of people. Do they spend off-work hours at a sports bar? Do they volunteer their off-work hours for company-sponsored outreach programs? Do some of them take graduate level courses to improve their work skills?

3. *How do you plan to deal with . . . ?* The blank part of this question could be any number of items that you discovered while doing your research on the company and the industry. The question could be "How do you plan to deal with lower margins for your technology products?" The answers to these questions will tell you if the company recognizes its problems and what plans it has to deal with them going forward.

4. *What do you expect me to accomplish in the first 60 to 90 days?* This question lets the interviewer know that you are no slouch. You want the company hiring manager to know that you are ready, willing, and able to be productive immediately.

5. *What are the common attributes of your top performers?* The answer to this question will tell you much about the corporate culture, the company expectations, and what workers are willing to do in order to be successful there.

ENDING THE INTERVIEW

There is a definite way to end the interview. Salespeople ask for the order after making their product presentation. They don't just say "Thank you for your time" and leave. The same holds true for the interview. Close by saying "thank you," and if you are interested in the job and the company, ask, "What are the next steps in the process? I really would like to work here based upon your answers to my questions and my research about the company. When can I start?"

If the interviewer gives a nebulous answer to your closing statements, counter with an action item, like "Thanks for your time. I'll follow up with you by phone or email to check on the status of my employment here. May I please have your business card? And by the way, what is your hiring deadline?"

If you are not interested in the job, say, "Thank you for your time. I really do not think this is a good fit. I'm sure that you will find a candidate better suited for this positon."

When you return to your operations center (your home office), remember to send a follow-up thank you note even if you are no longer interested in the job. Always maintain the relationship regardless of the results of the interview.

THE INTERVIEW HAS THREE POSSIBLE OUTCOMES

It does not take twenty books and a thousand Internet hits to learn that interviews can have only three possible results:

1. The interviewer requests that you return for another interview, a serious indication that you are in the running. You passed the first round and you are now one of several finalists for a particular job.
2. Your candidacy is eliminated because you and the interviewer learned that your candidacy did not match the job specs or the company culture.
3. You decided this is not the place for you based on what you heard and what you observed of the work environment, provided the interview took place at the company offices.

PANEL INTERVIEWS

Occasionally a panel rather than one person will conduct the interview for the company. The panel interview may sound intimidating but it can work to your advantage.

Panels usually consist of the hiring manager, the company human resources director, and a worker from the department where the job is located. For example, if you are interviewing for an assistant editor position with a publishing company, the worker may be an associate editor in the editorial department.

The purpose of the panel interview is to save time, not to intimidate the candidate. When you walk in the door you don't know if the interview will be with one person or with a panel so be prepared mentally for both. Usually a panel interview means that the company is seriously interested in your candidacy. It's a positive sign for you. Be reassured and confident that the interview is going to work to your advantage. After the interview begins, determine the person who appears to be most friendly and supportive and make an effort to build a relationship with him or her.

Interviewing with a panel is advantageous for a number of reasons. In the one-on-one interview, if you do not connect with the person across from you, there is nobody else you can turn to for help. In a panel interview, you have options for building strong relationships with more than one person.

CHAPTER TAKEAWAYS

- Build a friendly relationship with the interviewer. Friends hire friends.
- The interview is another step in the job search process.
- Body language is communication.
- Control the interview process by preparing and presenting a written agenda.
- You hold the aces because the company cannot exist without qualified candidates.
- Always use civilian language during an interview.
- Practice your answer to the question "Would you tell me something about yourself?"

THE VETERAN'S LIBRARY

Marc Cosentino. *Case in Point: Complete Case Interview Preparation*. Burgee Press, 2013. (This is a very popular and useful book on case interviewing from an expert in the field.)

Elizabeth Kuhnke. *Body Language for Dummies*. Wiley, 2012.

Stephen Covey. *The 7 Habits of Highly Effective People: Powerful Lessons in Personal Change*. Simon & Schuster, 2013.

Max E. Eggert. *Body Language for Business*. Skyhorse Publishing Inc., 2012.

Chapter 30

Interviews at Offices, Trade Shows, and Restaurants

The corporate office is the usual location for an interview. However, depending upon the industry and the job itself, the location could be a convention center, a restaurant, a small business storefront, a garden center, a construction trailer, Starbucks, or an airport. Wherever the interview takes place, there is a set of common rules to follow for a successful interview: be courteous, be honest, be friendly.

INTERVIEWS AT A CORPORATE OFFICE

Most first interviews take place at the employer's office, a place that is familiar to the interviewer but foreign to you. There is nothing you can do about this except to look at it objectively. The hiring manager needs a place to sit, work, and conduct interviews, but in all probability, he or she would like to be somewhere else, maybe on a golf course or tennis court. Who knows? The corporate office is here to stay, so we might as well get used to it. When you find yourself in the corporate office, envision it as the anteroom at your local Starbucks, which probably is where you and the interviewer would rather be.

To ease the tension, arrive for your office interview fifteen minutes early so you can settle down and feel comfortable. Also, the extra time will give you the opportunity to observe the environment.

INTERVIEWS AT CONVENTION CENTERS

Many interviews take place on the floor of a convention center or even in an exhibit booth. It is an informal atmosphere, and there is a tendency to let down one's guard and fall into sloppy habits like "cool talk" or inappropriate dress. Do not be distracted by the informal environment of the convention center. Even though many of the company representatives and customers are dressed informally, this is still a place where workers transact business and interview job candidates. Always come prepared for business. Wear business attire and bring a dozen resumes, a hundred business cards, and a dozen generic interview agendas.

CONNECTING WITH HIRING MANAGERS AT CONVENTION CENTERS

Hiring managers always attend conferences and trade shows to conduct business and interview candidates, sometimes in the exhibit booth or in a conference center restaurant or coffee shop. The setting is much less formal than an office, and the conversation is more relaxed. Frequently, you will meet hiring managers in their company exhibit booths where they may be talking with customers. When you enter an exhibit booth, ask for the sales manager if you are looking for a sales position, the marketing manager if you are looking for a marketing position, and so on. After introducing yourself and presenting your calling card, state the purpose of your visit and ask for a brief interview. If the hiring manager is obviously involved with customers, ask when you should return for a chat. If the hiring manager you want to see is not at the conference, ask one of the workers in the booth for the hiring manager's name and contact information. Follow up when you return to your operations center.

A convention center interview could be brief, because hiring managers are always watching the clock. They are there to meet with customers, sometimes by appointment, and to attend breakout sessions to learn about competitors' products and industry trends.

BUSINESS ETIQUETTE AT TRADE SHOWS

As a rule of business etiquette, be respectful of the hiring manager's time. In fact, you might want to begin the conversation by saying, "I know this is a busy show and that your time is limited. I'll limit our time to fifteen minutes, and we can follow up at another time if necessary."

Check your iPad or smartphone, and at the end of fifteen minutes, conclude the interview by saying, "I see that our time has passed. Maybe we can continue at another time if you wish. Thanks for taking time for this interview. I hope this is a productive show for you and your company. I'll check back with you after the show."

Do not be surprised if the hiring manager asks to continue the interview. If that happens, continue the conversation and present the hiring manager with a modified version of your interview agenda treated in the previous chapter. For use at a convention center, prepare a generic agenda by deleting the name of a particular company.

After the interview, always get the hiring manager's business card, and when you are back at your OC, send a follow-up message by email or regular mail saying thank you and suggesting the next step.

INTERVIEWS AT RESTAURANTS

Occasionally a hiring manager or human resources director will conduct an interview in a restaurant. The reason is not hunger. The hiring manager wants to learn your level of maturity by observing your behavior in the community at large, in the real world.

Interviews at restaurants can be tricky and sometimes fraught with danger. The hiring manager is placing you in this environment to determine how you handle yourself in a real-life setting. The informal ambiance can be deceiving to say the least. The person across the table from you will be observing the way you interact with restaurant workers, your ability to stay focused despite the numerous distractions encountered at restaurants, your skill ordering from the menu, and your table manners. Here is an example of what can happen during a restaurant interview.

Mark the Marine

I was interviewing a candidate over breakfast for a sales manager position at the Marriott Hotel restaurant, located at Liberty International Airport in Newark, New Jersey. It was a crowded morning, and tables were close together. At the table next to us sat a young couple with a screaming baby who was distracting me to the point where I was ready to ask the host to change our location. However, candidate Mark kept the conversation going as if there were no distractions. He did not even look at the unhappy baby. This caught my attention, and I gained a great deal of respect for Mark because of his discipline and understanding. We proceeded through the interview for ninety minutes, and Mark won not only my respect but also my recommendation for the job. When I asked Mark how he kept his cool, he replied, "In the Marines, you learn discipline and how to stay focused in difficult situations." Semper fi!

Table Manners

Do not snicker at this section on table manners, even though it might remind you of childhood, when your parents were always telling you what to do and not to do. Why are table manners important? Because you represent the company when you are dining with customers, which some workers will do frequently.

Restaurant Interview Etiquette

The rules of restaurant etiquette are important, and violating them will make your candidacy a thing of the past. Here is the **OJS** history-maker checklist.

1. Lick your fingers at an interview, and you are history.
2. Dribble a drink or soup down the front of your shirt or top, and you are history.

3. Rest your arms on the table as you would at a bar, and you are history.

4. Slurp your coffee, soup, or iced tea so that it causes heads to turn your way, and you are history.

5. Spear your meat and veggies with your fork as though you are a Neanderthal, and you are history.

6. Chew with your mouth open, and you are history.

7. Order an excessive number of alcoholic drinks, and you are history.

8. Text or take a call on your smartphone, and you are history.

9. Whine to the waitperson, and you are history.

10. Be demanding and disrespectful to restaurant personnel, and you are history.

Get the picture on table manners? Consider this real-life example.

Bob the Licker

I was interviewing Bob for a vice president sales position over lunch in New York City, and from the beginning I saw a red flag. It was Bob's demanding manner with the server who was busy and trying to do a good job. Strike one! Next, I could not help but notice that Bob chewed with his mouth open making nasty noises that were distracting. Strike two! Toward the end of our lunch, Bob gave three fingers on each hand a great big lick. Strike three! You're out, Bob! I rejected his candidacy for the position, because Bob would have been an embarrassment to the company.

As veterans, you have seen the show while taking meals in the mess. You witnessed the good, bad, and ugly, and cringed when those eating next to you talked with their mouths full. The military provided etiquette training for both officers and enlisted personnel, and if you violated the rules, you heard about it. However, there are other factors to consider in addition to proper table manners at restaurant interviews. Here's a true story from California.

Mrs. Pancakes

Recently, I visited with the human resources vice president for a company in California. During the course of our conversation, I discovered that both of us believed in restaurant interviews, because you can observe so much in a relatively brief amount of time in a real-life setting. As an example, she related that she disqualified a candidate recently because of a menu selection. I asked her to explain. It happened that she was having lunch with a candidate for a marketing position at approximately 2 p.m. The lunch menu included sandwiches, salads, light entrees, and a selection of deserts, typical lunch fare. The candidate ordered pancakes with a side of bacon. The vice president perceived this as odd. A person ordering pancakes at two in the afternoon was not her idea of an ideal candidate, and she rejected the person's candidacy.

This human resources director had it in her mind that breakfast food should be eaten at breakfast, lunch food should be eaten at lunch, and dinner food should be eaten at dinner. This true-life story may border on the absurd, but it illustrates an important point about interviews at restaurants: they are tricky and you don't know what the person sitting across from you is thinking.

As a general rule, do not order the priciest thing on the menu as a matter of courtesy and never order alcoholic beverages, even if the hiring manager does. My advice is to play it straight and be conservative. When it's breakfast time, do not order a filet with a baked potato and creamed spinach for $39.95. And when it's lunchtime, do not order breakfast food like pancakes and bacon. The person sitting across from you could be Mrs. Pancakes! Careful!

WHAT CORPORATE EXECUTIVES EXPECT DURING INTERVIEWS

What do corporate executives advise candidates to do when they come for an interview? I have interviewed many corporate executives across the country and have heard the same sentiments repeatedly. Two such executives offer advice to veterans about interviewing. Follow their advice to the letter.

Advice from Corporate Executives

Susan Meell, CEO of MMS Education headquartered in Newtown, Pennsylvania, offers these four important suggestions for candidates interviewing personally with hiring managers and human resources directors:

- Research the company. You must know something about the company to establish your credibility as a viable candidate. You must show interest in the company.
- Be on time for the interview.
- Dress appropriately. That means business attire, not jeans, a casual top, and sneakers.
- Be ready to articulate and discuss how your military and civilian experiences and accomplishments have prepared you for the position at hand. Remember, the company wants to know how you will benefit the company going forward.

Eric Gootkind, Director of Employment and Employee Relations with Measured Progress, Inc., Dover, New Hampshire, states there are four all-important requirements for candidates engaged in personal interviews:

- Maintain eye contact with the interviewer.
- Wear proper business attire.
- Be prepared to give examples of your accomplishments.
- Follow up with the interviewer promptly.

Thank you, Susan and Eric. This is good advice for all veterans interviewing for civilian positions.

MOVING FORWARD

Rarely will a first interview result in a job offer. It is an opportunity for you and the interviewer to determine if there is enough in common for the next step, a second interview.

This does not conclude our discussion of *the interview*. In today's hurry-up world, phone and Skype interviews are common. Stick around, because we'll discuss this important part of the job search process in the next chapter.

CHAPTER TAKEAWAYS

- When interviewing, be courteous, be honest, be friendly.
- Wear conservative business attire for interviews regardless of location.
- After an interview, send a follow-up message of thanks and suggest the next step.
- Turn off your smartphone before you begin the interview, no exceptions.
- Conclude the interview with a thank you and ask for the job.
- Always use civilian business-speak during interviews.
- Restaurant interviews permit the hiring manager to observe your manners and maturity.
- Never order alcoholic beverages at restaurant interviews. NEVER!
- Do not order pancakes for lunch!

THE VETERAN'S LIBRARY

Shari Harley. *How to Say Anything to Anyone: A Guide to Building Business Relationships that Really Work*. Greenleaf Book Group, 2012.

Chapter 31

Phone and Skype Interviews

The phone interview is a standard part of the job-hunting process because of the large number of candidates applying for posted jobs and because of the distance between the candidate and the interviewer. When human resources directors have many applicants for one position, they make the first cut using the candidate's resume and information from other sources, like social media. After the list is narrowed to a handful of candidates, the next step is to evaluate them with a phone or Skype interview. The process is sometimes called a "phone screening." Company execs claim the phone or Skype interview process is cost-effective.

These interviews are usually interrogations rather than conversations. The interviewer has a list of questions on her/his desk and wants to run through them as quickly as possible. It is akin to a robotic procedure. The candidate is rarely given time to ask questions or offer more than a perfunctory answer to questions posed by the interviewer.

Try to avoid the phone screening by volunteering to come in for a personal interview, even if this means driving three hours each way to the company location. Face-to-face communication is what you need to move forward in the search process, and the phone interview gets in the way.

THE PURPOSE OF THE PHONE INTERVIEW

The only purpose of the phone interview for the veteran job candidate is to move the candidacy to the next step, the personal interview with the hiring manager. Nobody is ever hired after just a phone interview.

For the interviewer, the purpose is to screen out unqualified candidates and select finalists for personal interviews. It does not seem fair, because the hiring manager or human resources director is holding the cards, but that's the way it is. You cannot change some things so you must learn to live with them and do your best. The phone interview is one of them. However, there are some guidelines to make the phone interview work in your favor.

PHONE INTERVIEW PREPARATION CHECKLIST

Talking on the phone comes naturally to some people, but most of us have a less than winning phone personality. However, with adequate preparation, you can become a star salesperson for your own candidacy. Prepare for the phone interview just as you would for a personal interview using this checklist.

- Find a private location for the phone interview, preferably your operations center (home office) where there will be absolute quiet.
- Eliminate traffic noise, barking dogs, crying babies, and music playing in the background. If there are two phones in your location, turn off the one not being used. The last thing you want is your alternate phone ringing during an interview.
- Avoid holding the phone interview in a casual setting, like a beach, restaurant, car, bar, or train.
- Take the call at a table or desk where you can spread out documents for reference. You cannot do this while driving your car.
- Have your resume, the job description, company information, and a written interview agenda listing your questions in front of you during the call. Also, have a tablet or notebook and a pen for taking notes. Handwrite notes instead of entering them on your desktop or laptop computer or smartphone. Keyboard noise is distracting to the person on the other end of the line with today's sensitive audio technology.

- Stay focused. On a separate sheet of paper, write the name of the company, the name of the person with whom you will be speaking (also include that person's title), the date, the time, and the location of the interviewer.
- If the interviewer is located in another time zone, make the adjustment. If you are in New York and the interviewer is in Denver, there will be a two-hour time difference, so plan accordingly. If you miscalculate the time difference and the caller gets your voicemail instead of your voice, you will be history.
- Take the call dressed in business attire, because the way you dress sets the stage for your behavior. If you are dressed in a yoga outfit, your conversation could easily become too casual. If you take the call with your bare feet resting on top of your desk, you could slip into casual mode and begin using words like "awesome."
- Prepare to answer the question "Would you tell me something about yourself?" Refer to Chapter 29 for guidance. Remember, the interviewer is not interested in learning if you are a carnivore or a vegan, or where you were born, or whether your favorite drink is a grande-size-skimmed milk-decaf-cappuccino with a dollop of whipped cream.
- Select the three most important questions from your written agenda. Usually phone interviews are time sensitive, so you want to make sure you have covered what is important *to you*. If the interviewer permits you to continue, go beyond the first three questions. Phone interviews, like personal interviews, should be a two-way conversation.
- Have your laptop or desktop computer running with the company website on the screen.
- Smile during the phone interview. A smile on your face will relax you and make the tone more conversational. Think of the phone smile as virtual body language.
- If you are using a smartphone for the interview, conduct a test run to check the connection. If possible, use a landline, because the audio quality is usually better and the connection is more reliable.

NAVIGATING THE PHONE INTERVIEW

Etiquette is everyone's concern. Should you address the interviewer by first or last name? Is it Mrs., Ms., Mr., Dr., or Mary? It is important to get it right. Here are some guidelines that follow the "listen first" rule.

How to Address the Interviewer

If the interviewer introduces herself as "Mrs. Agricola, Human Resources Director," then you address her as Mrs. Agricola throughout the interview. If she introduces herself as Barbara Agricola, call her Barbara.

If the interviewer introduces himself as "Dr. William Ford," call him "Dr. Ford" throughout the interview. If the interviewer introduces himself as John Cupcake, call him "John," not "Jack." A common error is to assume it is permissible to call a person by a shortened version of his or her name. I have found that the most frequently abused first names are Robert and Barbara. Why does everyone switch to Bob and Barb?

Use Civilian Language

In the military, you were taught to say "Yes, Ma'am" and "No, Sir" when responding to someone in authority. Civilian culture is not so formal. The "sir" and "ma'am" drill has no place in the civilian workforce. Using military lingo in a civilian phone interview will diminish your candidacy.

The same rule applies to job experience. State what you did in the military using civilian workplace terms. If you are having difficulty translating your military experience to civilian language, review previous chapters in **OJS**. Quantify as much as possible. Speak in a conversational tone, as if the person is sitting next to you. Your voice is a critical factor in a phone interview.

After You Say "Hello"

The first thing to ask after you say hello and make introductory chitchat is "How much time do we have?" Knowing this will tell you how much time to spend answering questions and how much time you have for asking questions that are on your interview agenda. Write the end-time on a piece of paper and refer to it throughout the conversation. After learning the amount of time you have, tell the interviewer that you have several questions and ask when it would be appropriate to do so. It could be the last thing on the agenda, or the first. Now that the protocol and time period are settled, proceed through the interview using the guidelines for the personal interview in Chapters 28, 29, and 30.

Closing the Interview

The close is the same for the phone interview and the personal interview. Learn the interviewer's phone number and email address, say thank you for the interview, and ask for the job. The script for closing the phone and personal interview is the same. "Thank you for your time and consideration. What are the next steps in the process? I really would like to work here based on your answers to my questions and my research about your company. When can I start?"

After the interview, follow up by mailing or emailing a thank you note. Review Chapter 26 for follow-up guidance.

SKYPE INTERVIEWS

You may be asked to submit to a Skype interview, which is becoming more frequent. The rules for a Skype interview are a combination of the rules for the personal interview and phone interview. Before committing to a Skype interview, make sure that Skype works in your location. There is nothing worse than a bad Skype connection.

Attire and Location

Think of the Skype interview as a personal interview where proper business attire is a requirement. There are no exceptions. If you take the Skype interview while on vacation and dressed in casual attire, you could be history. Dress in business attire, always. Review Chapter 27 for guidelines.

Your location is critical for a successful Skype interview. Ideally, position yourself sitting at the desk in your operations center with front lighting. For more information on Skype, check out the website at www.skype.com.

Internet Resources for Successful Phone and Skype Interviews

For additional information and guidelines, google "phone and Skype interviews." As always, it is media overkill. There are hundreds of resources available, but after doing all the research, **OJS** recommends *Forbes* business magazine, www.forbes.com. When you reach the website, write "Skype interviews" in the search box. Click, and you will find two excellent articles:

"7 Tips to Nail a Skype Interview" and "Tips for Skype Interview Success." Both articles provide excellent advice.

PRACTICE AND REHEARSAL FOR PHONE AND SKYPE INTERVIEWS

Practice for the phone and Skype interview with the same intensity as you would for the personal interview. Review all of the **OJS** material in Part VI and rehearse your call with a friend using the phone or Skype. Answer all of the twenty questions in Chapter 29 under the major heading "Frequently Asked Interview Questions." Practice until you feel comfortable with the content and tone of your answers.

MOVING FORWARD

The phone or Skype interview can be a challenging hurdle in the job search process, but it will yield positive results if you follow the rules in **OJS.** Preparation is the key. Pay special attention to the "dress-up" rule, because it will guide your behavior during the interview.

In Part VII, **OJS** provides rubrics for evaluating a job description, a company, and its executives. Not all are created equal. Stay with us.

CHAPTER TAKEAWAYS

- Wear business attire for a phone or Skype interview.
- Exercise business etiquette and protocol during a phone or Skype interview.
- Use civilian-speak from beginning to end.
- Practice! Practice! Practice! Rehearse! Rehearse! Rehearse!
- Adjust for time zones.

THE VETERAN'S LIBRARY

Peggy McKee. *How to Ace Your Phone Interview*. www.CareerConfidential.com.

PART VII

Evaluating a Job Description and a Company. Negotiating a Job Offer

If ethics are poor at the top, that behavior is copied down through the organization.

—*Robert Noyce, inventor of the silicon chip*

Chapter 32

Evaluating and Responding to a Job Description

Job descriptions are simply a concise rendering of the job title, job responsibilities, and qualifications. Sometimes they include a description of the company. They rarely include compensation and benefits, or names and titles of the hiring manager. Veterans should make a thorough evaluation of all job descriptions before responding to them. Do not respond to a job description that is lacking in details and information necessary for understanding what is at stake.

THE EVALUATION PROCESS

A job search is a process. Evaluating, interpreting, and responding to a job description are integral parts of that process. You learned process skills in the military, and now it is time to put that experience to work in your transition to civilian employment.

Patrick Kelly, the portfolio manager for the very successful Alger Spectra Capital Appreciation mutual fund, said in a recent issue of *Barron's*, "Having the best process maximizes opportunities and minimizes mistakes." While he was referring to evaluating a company for investment purposes, the same applies to any endeavor. Another believer in process is Bill Walsh, former coach of the San Francisco 49ers football team. Coach Walsh believes that if you follow a winning process to the extreme, the score will take care of itself. I like what Walsh said because of his enviable NFL success. He won three Super Bowls!

INTERPRETING THE JOB DESCRIPTION

A candidate's gut reaction after reading what appears to be an interesting job description is to respond with a resume and other requested information without a second thought. This is unfortunate, because job descriptions exist for a number of reasons, and what you read is subject to misinterpretation. To begin, where do these job descriptions originate?

WHO WRITES THE JOB DESCRIPTION?

One of three people writes a job description: the hiring manager, the human resources director, or a recruiter working collaboratively with both. Hiring managers write the most reliable job descriptions. They are realistic and portray the position and requirements honestly. It is in their best interests to fill an open position as soon as possible.

Human resources directors write credible job descriptions, too, but many times they lack details about the job known only to the hiring manager, the person to whom the position reports.

Recruiters sometimes write job descriptions at the request of the hiring manager or human resources director. Usually they are credible documents because the recruiter knows what will motivate qualified candidates to respond.

ARE JOB DESCRIPTIONS REALISTIC?

The job description is written with the *ideal* candidate in mind, and rarely, if ever, does that person exist. In all of my years recruiting for positions from entry-level to CEO, I have never found a job candidate who met every one of the requirements and qualifications on the job description. Employers *always* make compromises, and experienced candidates know this. When you read a job description that states "four to six years' experience required," do not disregard it if you have only two years of experience.

WHY JOB DESCRIPTIONS EXIST

Company personnel write job descriptions to attract candidates for a job opening within a company for one particular position or for multiple positions with identical requirements but in different locations. For example, a single job description might cover three sales representatives who will work in different parts of the country.

Also, sometimes job descriptions exist because the company needs to avoid the appearance of discrimination, or to meet OEO requirements, even though the company hiring manager may have already selected a candidate. (The Office of Economic Opportunity, OEO, is a federal government agency that oversees fair employment hiring practices. All companies doing business with the federal government must sign an OEO document agreeing to meet rigid recruiting and hiring practices.)

BEATING THE INTERNAL CANDIDATE

When a position opens up for any reason, the first place a company looks for a replacement is within its internal workforce. After a reasonable amount of time during which the company gathers resumes from both internal and external applicants, the pre-selected internal candidate gets the job. All of the candidates who applied for this position unknowingly submitted their candidacy in vain. Unfortunately, there is nothing you can do about it.

During the interview, one of the first questions to ask is "How many internal candidates are you considering? If you already have your selection and are interviewing me for other purposes, I'd rather not waste your time and mine by proceeding through the interview." If nothing else, it will let the interviewer know that you have the experience and maturity to play the game.

WHERE ARE JOB DESCRIPTIONS POSTED?

A job description is posted in various places, not just on a company website. The job description could appear on various job boards, like

Monster, on social media sites, like LinkedIn, and on websites of recruiters. It could easily find its way to a dozen or more places, which is one reason why companies receive so many resumes in response to a posting. When you see the same job posted in multiple locations, it is a sign that the employer may be looking for many resumes to satisfy OEO or other requirements.

Always respond to the job description posted on the employer's website. If the selected candidate is hired directly by the employer rather than an outside source, the company saves money, because it does not have to pay a fee to a job board or contingency recruiter.

WHAT JOB DESCRIPTIONS REALLY SAY

The typical job description will state the title of the position and where it is located. It will list the job responsibilities either in bullet point format or in a text paragraph. Usually these are broadly stated items. The job requirements and/or qualifications specify the educational background, years of experience, and fields of expertise. The requirements are usually overstated, and nobody on Earth or Mars will ever possess all of them. Do not be frightened away by the experience "required" on a job description.

There are always exceptions and compromises companies will make for certain positions. However, some jobs require strict adherence to the specs in the job description because of legally required certifications and licenses, which I will discuss later in this chapter.

A good job description will also include the posting date, an important bit of information because it tells you how long the company has been looking for the "right" candidate. An active job search that began six months ago is a warning that something is not quite right.

The final item on most job descriptions is a request to send your resume to a particular place, or there may be an "Apply" button. A click here will take you into a list of procedural requirements for submitting your application and a request for much personal information.

Warning!

If the job description or online application requests your age, driver's license number, or social security number, do not apply. This is your personal and confidential information. Share it with the employer only if you get the job, because such personal information is required for tax and identification purposes.

JOB DESCRIPTIONS WITH STRICT REQUIREMENTS

Job descriptions for positions requiring certification and licensure have more strict requirements. Examples are jobs for medical personnel that by law require licensure and certification. The requirements stated on job descriptions written for physicians, certified nurse midwives, nurses, radiologists, physical therapists, and other medical personnel leave no room for compromise, and this is understandable. The performance of medical procedures, and the prescription of medications are truly life and death matters. The employer relies on certifications and licenses to verify that the candidate can perform the job.

Educators face strict requirements as well. All states require certification for classroom teachers, and most states require an advanced degree for school principals and superintendents. Most colleges and universities require a PhD for teaching and administrative positions. You cannot negotiate compromises on requirements of this kind.

Other job categories carry legal requirements as well. For example, lawyers must be licensed to practice in a certain state and must show proof of passing the bar examination.

WHAT JOB DESCRIPTIONS DO NOT SAY:
THE BIG RED FLAGS

Frequently, postings on job boards, or even on LinkedIn, are tricky to say the least. I have identified the big red flags of job descriptions. Note them well.

Red Flag #1. The job description does not disclose the name of the company or its location. The company could be a back alley operation or a prominent company on Wall Street or in Silicon Valley. You just don't know. The reason for this non-disclosure is known only to the entity writing and posting the job description, and you do not have time to play games. Do not send a resume or click the "Apply" button if there is no company name. Make this one of your cardinal rules of job hunting.

What if the job sounds interesting and matches your search criteria? When this happens, respond by asking for the name of the company, the hiring manager, and the job location.

Red Flag #2. The job description does not state the name of the company contacts or their titles. It might ask you to "Send your resume to Position # 256." Sending your resume or answering online application questions in response to a job number is equivalent to sending your candidacy to the third moon of the planet Jupiter. There is no reason why the company should have all of your personal information while hiding the identity of the human resources director or the hiring manager. Once more, this is a game you do not want to play.

If there is no name and title on the job description, but you really like the position, call the company customer service department and ask for the name and contact information for the human resources director and hiring manager. Then you can submit your candidacy to a living person by email or ground services like UPS or FedEx.

If an unnamed recruiter posts the job description, respond by email asking for the name of the person to whom you should send your credentials. If the recruiter responds by saying they are the exclusive recruiting agent for the company, ask if they are conducting the search on contingency or retainer. If it is on retainer, the recruiting firm can be trusted, because it is the only agent working with the company. In this case, the recruiter is really an extension of the company human resources department. If the recruiter has the search on contingency, it usually means that the company has given the search to multiple recruiters. Work only with recruiters who are conducting the search on retainer.

When I write a job description using the name of my company, Weiss & Associates, Executive Recruiting, I always disclose my name and contact information and state that I am working this search on retainer. All reputable recruiters will do the same.

Red Flag #3. Some job descriptions are nothing more than a general statement about a particular kind of job. Recently, I saw one of these on the LinkedIn site. It was called "Recent College Grads." The job title was "Virtual Executive Assistant to the CEO." It had several bullet points about responsibilities and qualifications but did not include the name of the company, the hiring manager, or location of the company.

In addition, it had a deceptive major heading, "Professional Chemistry," under which were three bullet points: "upbeat demeanor," "adaptable attitude," and "composure under pressure." This could have been a bogus job description. It gave you nothing but asked for much personal information after you hit the "Apply" button.

Handing out your personal information to an unknown entity is a recipe for potential disaster. Never submit your resume or application for what appears to be a bogus job description, even if it comes from a reputable source.

ELEMENTS OF A CREDIBLE JOB DESCRIPTION

Job descriptions come in all sizes and shapes and are written by any number of sources. They are not all created equal. Some are bare bones; others are encyclopedic. There is a natural tendency for all candidates to respond to every job description that seems to match, even tangentially, their vision for employment. However, you can spend useless hours responding to job descriptions that have no merit and will not yield even a thank you from the employer. Learning which job to disregard and which to address is just another part of the search process. Here is a list of elements that credible job descriptions should have, as well as a brief example of each:

1. **The name, location, and description of the company**. Example: "Facebook, a social media company located at 127 Smith Rd., San Jose, California."
2. **The job title and the title of the person to whom it reports**. Example: "IT assistant reporting to the IT department head, Mary Smith."
3. **The job location**. Example: "The job location is the corporate regional sales office in Seattle, Washington."
4. **A list of responsibilities and expectations**. Example: "Selling product line to hospitals; meeting sales goals; reporting customer concerns to marketing; daily expense accounting."
5. **Background qualifications for the position**. Example: "5 years in residential HVAC installation and repair and HVAC certification."
6. **Desired level of education**. Example: "BS in biology."
7. **Required certification or licenses, if any**. Example: "State of New Jersey issued Certified Nurse Midwife certification and license."
8. **A general description of the compensation and benefits package**. Example: "Salary, bonus based on performance, life and medical insurance, IRA, paid annual vacation, paid holidays, paid sick days, long-term disability insurance."

Do not expect every detail of the job to be on the job description. As you read it, make notes for discussing the particulars with the hiring manager during the interview.

HOW TO RESPOND TO A JOB DESCRIPTION WITH A CAREER PROFILE PACKAGE

If you decide to pursue a position you found through any source, and it does not contain any red flags, what do you do next? Conventional wisdom says that you should submit your resume to a person with a name, a title, and company affiliation. However, is that all one should do? Send *just* a resume?

Consider this. Hundreds or maybe thousands of other candidates probably saw the same job description that you saw on a company website. What happens next? Hundreds or thousands of candidates will, like sheep, send *only* their resumes. Why? Because that is what the job descriptions requested. To distinguish yourself from the rest of the crowd, you must submit a career profile, which **OJS** covered in Chapter 24.

SAMPLE JOB DESCRIPTIONS

Talking about good and not-so-good-job descriptions is academic. There is nothing like a real-life example to distinguish one from the other. Here are two job descriptions to illustrate what I mean by a good job description versus a poor one.

A CREDIBLE JOB DESCRIPTION

****

Position: Inside Sales Representative
Solberg Manufacturing, Inc.- Itasca, IL (Greater Chicago Area)

Job Description:
We are looking for a hustler at the start of his/her career to join our Inside Sales Department. The position is fast-paced and involves intensive customer contact, order management, and intra/interdepartmental coordination.

Our Inside Sales Representatives are responsible for fulfilling customer needs to ensure customer retention and satisfaction while supporting the outside sales effort. Our team members with well-developed organization skills and the ability to communicate effectively are top performers and eligible for opportunities for advancement. All excelling employees at Solberg are encouraged to set challenging personal and professional goals.

This is a great opportunity for those who have recently moved into a sales role or those looking to begin a career in sales and marketing.

We will train the right candidates on all aspects of our business. Solberg invests in their employees and coaches those willing to be coachable. As we continue to grow and expand our operations, advancement opportunities are available for the high achievers seeking continued professional challenges.

Desired Skills and Experience:
We welcome recent and upcoming college graduates.

Previous sales and customer service experience is a plus. (Preferably in an industrial B2B setting) Any of the following experience is welcomed: project coordination, purchasing, use of design, and drafting CAD programs.

Requirements:

A team player. You work well with others, love high fives, and jump at opportunities to support your colleagues.

Driven. You have superior follow through, integrity, and always meet deadlines. You don't get overwhelmed easily. A tough goal to reach? No problem!

Creative. You're innovative, curious, and constantly looking for ways to improve upon things.

Communication wiz. You have exceptional writing skills, natural grace under pressure, are well-spoken on the phone and eloquent in emails.

Fun. You're a charismatic people person who can talk to anyone; you're flexible, fearless, and excited to help build something awesome and share it with the world.

Smart. You get mechanics (maybe tooled around with cars in your day), are an expert at Office Suite, and hold a bachelor's degree in business or something technical.

Bottom line? You're ready to hustle. You love people, are naturally motivated, and get a thrill from accomplishment. You must *be excited* *to dig in and help a business reach the next level of success . . . are you ready?*

Company Description:
Solberg is an exciting growth-focused organization with twelve facilities located throughout North America, South America, Europe, Asia, and Australia. Through our corporate headquarters just outside of Chicago, IL, Solberg provides filtration and separation solutions to customers ranging from original equipment manufacturers to resellers to end-users in highly diverse industrial markets. Our commitment to partner with customers creates a fun, energetic, focused and fast-paced team environment that facilitates personal and professional growth. We have an excellent training and development program to ensure our employees are given the tools and knowledge to succeed. Please visit www.solbergmfg.com to learn more about our company and culture.

Additional Information:
Posted: June 14, 2013
Type: Full-time
Experience: Entry level
Functions: Business Development, Sales, Customer Service
Industries: Machinery
Job ID: 6073491
****

This job description was posted on the Solberg Manufacturing Company website. It is well written and supplies all the information you need to make a decision about submitting your candidacy. There is one exception. It does not give the names of the sales manager or the human resources director. However, it does give the company website, so you can find the names of those individuals. If that does not work, call the customer service department to obtain that critical information. Once you have the name of the person and contact information, you can safely submit your career profile to a named individual at Solberg to begin building a personal relationship.

Many job descriptions found on Internet job boards or other places are not reliable documents. Poor job descriptions lurk everywhere, and you should never respond to them. Here's one that I found online recently.

A POOR JOB DESCRIPTION

****

Sales Representatives Needed!
New technology company has many job opportunities for sales reps nationwide. Sell game changing software apps that can only be described as "awesome." Good starting salary and exciting bonus and commissions for those who can cut it. You must be a self-starter and work with little or no supervision.

We want entry-level candidates with a college degree who have an intuitive sense of selling and who can hit the ground running with little or no training.

Join us and be part of a team that will make us a Fortune 500 Company in the next three years. If this exciting opportunity is right for you please respond by sending your resume to our job counselors at, www.salesjobsforcollegegrads.com. Reference Job # 297.

****

You can easily see the difference between the credible and poor job descriptions. It would be a waste of time to respond to the latter posting, which does not even give the name of the company, much less the name of a person with a title. Never respond to job descriptions similar to this one.

MOVING FORWARD

Let's assume you have submitted your candidacy for the Solberg Manufacturing position to the sales manager whose name you learned by calling customer service. You aced the phone screen and the personal interview. Three days later the sales manager says, "You're hired," and presents you with a written job offer. What's next? Do you sign on the bottom line? What do you *really* know about the company? How do you learn about the company, its culture, and the executive staff? In the next chapter, **OJS** will tell you how to evaluate a company. Stay with us.

CHAPTER TAKEAWAYS

- Never respond to a job description that does not provide the name of the company.
- Never respond to a job number or a generic title like "employment manager."
- Respond to a credible job description by submitting your career profile, not just a resume, to a named person with a title and company affiliation.
- Job descriptions are not literal documents. Companies always make compromises.

Chapter 33

How to Evaluate a Company, Its Culture, and Executive Staff

Learning the names of potential employers in a particular industry is a relatively simple matter with the technology we have at our disposal. However, learning about a company's finances, culture, reputation, and practices is quite another story. It requires research to see what is behind the name. This cautionary note applies to all employers: for profit, nonprofit, government, and even military friendly companies.

Company evaluations usually focus solely on finances, and while finances are critically important, there are other criteria to determine if a particular company is a good place to work. Company evaluation is another part of the job search *process*, not the sole determining factor in deciding whether to cast your lot with a particular employer.

As you proceed through the job search process, you will learn that potential employers can be divided into several categories, like Fortune 500 companies, mid-sized companies, small capitalization companies, and startups. How do you evaluate companies in each category? This process could consume many hours and even days of research, but I have created a checklist for evaluation purposes based on our experience in the retained search business. It is a good starting place for most veterans who are in the thick of making the transition to civilian employment.

While the **OJS** checklist applies to evaluating all companies, there are special criteria that apply to each. For example, startups are frequently exciting places to work because of the enthusiasm and sense of mission of the executive staff and founders. Type "How to evaluate a job at a startup" into Google to find the many websites with information on how to evaluate a startup company. Do the same for companies that fall into other categories.

COMPANY EVALUATION IS A PROCESS

Many times companies are judged solely by word of mouth, a dangerous practice because unsubstantiated information can be misleading. Take, for example, a situation where a worker I will call "Anthony" was fired from XYZ Corporation. After word circulates through his circle of friends, you might believe that Anthony was unjustly fired and think that XYZ Corp. is a nasty place to work. The truth, however, could be that Anthony was fired because he was not able to fulfill his job responsibilities after repeated warnings to improve his performance. You need more than hearsay to evaluate a company. What's needed is a company profile based on verifiable information. To help you through the process, I have created the following checklist to use as a guide for evaluating any company, large or small.

COMPANY EVALUATION CHECKLIST

1. Company Finances

A history of profitability is one of the most important things you need to know about a company. A consistent record of growth and profitability means that a company has a viable business plan that its employees know how to execute. For example, Procter & Gamble has an impressive record of consistent growth and profitability over the past *175 years*. The company employs more than 126,000 workers and generates more than $83 billion in annual revenue. Moreover, P&G has paid its stockholders dividends over many years because of its record of profitability. You can review job openings at www.pg.com.

All financial information is disclosed in a company's printed or digital annual report. You can find the report online or you can call customer service and request a print copy.

Research every company you find interesting by using any number of online resources. For a quick summary, go to the company website, as well as Wikipedia and Hoovers (www.hoovers.com), a Dun and Bradstreet business research and evaluation firm. Also, read books that tell you in everyday language how to evaluate a company's finances. I recommend that you read these two books by Jim Cramer: *Stay Mad for Life: Get Rich, Stay Rich* and *Jim Cramer's Real Money*.

2. Company Mentors

Some companies assign a mentor for every employee regardless of rank, even for their presidents and vice presidents. Companies with a formal mentoring program have found the process to result in increased productivity, worker satisfaction, and long-term employment. As a worker new to a company, you will find mentors to be of inestimable value. They will help you learn not only how to fulfill your job responsibilities, but also how to work within the company culture. Having this information will contribute to your success and job satisfaction. When you research a company of interest, check its website to learn if it has a mentoring program. If you do not see it, send an email to customer service or human resources inquiring about such a program. If you cannot find this information before an interview, make sure it is on your written agenda for the interviewer.

How Many Companies Have Mentoring Programs?

Some sources estimate that 70 percent of the Fortune 500 companies have mentoring programs, but the quality of each program has not been determined. Large companies that have formal mentoring programs are Citigroup, Nationwide Insurance, McGraw-Hill, and Texas Instruments.

3. Company Benefits

Most large and medium-sized companies offer a similar array of benefits: medical and dental insurance, life insurance, long-term disability insurance, paid holidays and sick days, vacation time, and Individual Retirement Accounts (IRA). All of these benefits are important, but what distinguishes one company from another are the following:

Retirement plans like an IRA or a Roth IRA. If the company makes a monthly contribution to your IRA, it's a check mark in the plus column.

Company paid pension plans, which are fast disappearing from the corporate landscape. If the company does have a pension plan in addition to an IRA program, it is a check mark in the plus column.

Tuition reimbursement for college courses, like an executive MBA.

Professional development courses that focus on your job responsibilities.

Flexible hours for workers with family responsibilities, especially female veterans.

Student loan repayment programs are very important if they apply to dependent children.

Programs for returning military personnel, a sign of a military friendly employer.

The benefits program will tell you how much the company values its workers. When you interview for any position, learn the extent of the company benefits. Most companies will honor your request by furnishing you with a brochure detailing specific benefits. Remember, too, that benefits are part of your total compensation program. Reliable sources indicate that benefits cost the company 30 percent of an employee's base salary.

4. Company Litigation Record

The last thing you want to do is to work for a company involved in numerous lawsuits filed by employees, customers, or both. This is a matter of public record, but finding this information could be time consuming. It is appropriate to ask the hiring authority during your first interview about the company's record of litigation. Inquire about the number of lawsuits filed against the company over the past five years and the issues that caused the litigation. Ask if there are any *pending* lawsuits.

Many companies have been sued by their employees for reasons such as harassment by a boss, favoritism, and gender, age, racial, or religious discrimination. However, one must be judicious in determining culpability. The filing of a lawsuit always makes headlines, but the result of the lawsuit, which could be acquittal two years later, often goes unreported.

5. Reputation

Some companies are American icons; others are thought of in dubious terms. One must be careful when making a judgment based on hearsay. Consider the source and conduct your own research using all of the digital sources at your disposal, such as Facebook, Twitter, LinkedIn, and others. Even then, it could be difficult to make an honest assessment of a company to determine if it is worthy of your time and talents.

6. The Boss to Whom You Will Report

Your supervisor is the person who can make the difference between loving your job and hating to report for work each day. In fact, worker dissatisfaction with the boss is the number one reason why workers quit their jobs. Therefore, it is important to learn who your boss will be *before* you start working for the company.

How does one learn about the future boss? In most large and medium-sized companies, the human resources director handles the hiring process and does the upfront work like searching for qualified candidates, conducting phone screens, and conducting personal interviews. If you are one of the finalists, the human resources director will arrange an interview with the hiring manager, the person to whom you will report. That person will be your boss.

In your initial interview with the human resources director or a member of the executive team, learn the name of your potential boss and ask about his/her background and qualifications. Learn how long your future boss has been with the company and how many jobs this person has had over the last ten years. Ask if any lawsuits were ever filed against this person by subordinates. Ask about the boss's management style. After you learn that person's name, conduct a Google search to see what you can find. Also, go to LinkedIn and read the hiring manager's profile.

If you see any yellow or red flags, contact the human resources director and express your concerns. Do not accept any job, no matter how good it appears to be, if you observe something questionable in the boss's background. The last thing you need is a boss who does not meet your standards for leadership and ethical behavior.

7. The CEO or President

There is another boss to consider when evaluating any company—the person running the entire show, the CEO or president. Use the investigative procedures described above to learn about that person.

An example of a good and competent Big Boss is Marc Benioff, CEO of the world's largest cloud computing company, Salesforce. Com, www.salesforce.com. Another is Gary Kelly, CEO of Southwest Airlines, www.Southwest.com, the only American airline with a consistent record of profitability. Another is Meg Whitman, CEO of Hewlett-Packard, www.hp.com, who is making great progress restoring a company that once was a leader in the technology business. All of these CEOs have a verifiable reputation for fair play, concern for company workers, a record of proactive outreach to the community, and a record of donating a portion of company profits to charitable causes. Google their names to learn who they really are and what they have done for their employees, shareholders, and the community at large. Also, watch CNBC and Jim Cramer's *Mad Money* show, which often includes interviews with CEOs and presidents.

8. Corporate Physical Environment

You can learn much about a company from its work environment. While you are visiting a company for a personal interview, observe the physical workspace, the décor, the location, and the behavior of its employees. Also, ask the human resources director or the hiring manager where your future workspace would be. If it is in a cubicle near an elevator that is constantly buzzing, or next to a restroom where the only music you hear is the constant flush of toilets, you may want to consider another company. You do not want to work in a depressing environment.

You may find that the *real* corporate environment is much different from what is depicted in TV ads for tech companies like Google. Most companies do not provide recreational facilities. They have a traditional work environment and a regular work schedule with rules to follow, with little time for recreational pursuits during work hours. If you find general mayhem, consider it a big red flag. Here is an example of a dysfunctional work environment that I found in New York City.

Yo-yos in Manhattan

Recently, I visited a tech company in Soho to discuss a search with the CEO. When I walked through the door, I found empty boxes piled high in a large open space with desks scattered here and there. There were young workers sitting on desks preoccupied with iPads or tablets, and others were walking around the room in circles while talking on cell phones. Most were playing with yo-yos. Yes, most were playing with yo-yos. Immediately, I surmised that something was wrong, drastically wrong.

> *I entered the CEO's office, which had a large window overlooking the yo-yo playground, and he said, "Look at that. These are all smart, young people, but they can't focus. All of them have good tech minds. Many have dropped out from places like Yale, Columbia, NYU, and the like. They are more interested in playing with those damn promotional yo-yos than connecting with customers." My first thought, which went unspoken, was,* Well, you're the CEO. Why not do something about it? *This was truly a chaotic environment and a dysfunctional corporate culture. What I observed reflected a total lack of training and discipline. This company went out of business nine months later.*

This real life example confirms that you *can* judge a book by its cover. Observe carefully what you see happening in the corporate workspace. Yo-yos and good business practices do not mix. Use common sense when evaluating a company

9. Anecdotal Information

One can learn much about a company and a potential boss by conducting a survey among friends, acquaintances, and seasoned workers. Social media, like Twitter, are also excellent sources for gathering information about a company. Some scoff at using anecdotal information, but often this research method yields interesting results.

One of the best methods to learn about a company is to find current employees and ask for their opinions. Use social media, like Twitter, Facebook, and LinkedIn, to locate current employees.

10. Community Outreach

Companies, like individuals, have an obligation to participate in community affairs to make this world better. Corporate outreach programs involve proactive participation in the community. Other programs include monetary grants for any number of programs designed to help those in need, to build medical facilities, or to foster participation in the fine and performing arts. Company donations for scholarships reflect good executive leadership and management.

A recent example comes from Facebook. In 2015, the CEO, Mark Zuckerberg, and his wife Priscilla Chan donated $75 million to the San Francisco General Hospital and Trauma Center. This is the largest gift from an individual to a public hospital in US history. No matter how much money one has, donating $75 million is commendable, and it shows that Mark and his wife care about the welfare of others in the community. For more about giving back to the community, read Chapter 39.

11. Company Etiquette

Observe the behavior of company employees. Did the receptionist treat you with courtesy and respect? Did the person on the other end of the line put you on hold for ten minutes? Did the interview take place at the appointed time, or did you have to wait an hour to see the hiring manager? Did the hiring manager read your resume *before* the interview? Did the interviewer answer all of your questions and concerns? Did the interviewer interrupt your phone interview to take another call?

Everyone has a story about the breakdown in human decency in the workplace. Here are two examples from my experience in the executive search business, the real world of work:

Sergio from Chicago

Sergio, a candidate for a $250,000 job, went for an interview with the president of a communications company. After the perfunctory greetings, the president said he had not had time to read Sergio's resume and asked for fifteen minutes to review it before getting down to business. The president scheduled the meeting a week prior, and Sergio had taken a half day off from his job for the interview. What's wrong with this picture? The president knew about the interview well in advance but was not respectful of Sergio's time, which was just as valuable as his own was. Someone's rank or position does not excuse him or her from showing respect and exercising basic courtesy.

Marcia from San Francisco

Marcia was a regional sales manager with an educational technology company and was recruited by a competitor for an executive vice president for sales position. The CEO had scheduled a 4:00 p.m. interview at the company corporate office. Marcia was on her way to another appointment half-way across the country but rescheduled her flight to make time for the interview. She arrived promptly but had to wait in the reception area for 45 minutes before the CEO called her in. He then proceeded to tell Marcia that he had just skimmed her resume before she came in and issued no apologies. He proceeded to a Q&A session that was not only challenging but also hostile. One hour later, Marcia left the interview and withdrew her candidacy, which is the smart thing to do when a company executive does not show respect and courtesy.

There is more to evaluating a company than looking at the finances. You can tell much about a company by observing the little things that often go unnoticed. If you see yellow flags during the search and hiring process, you will surely find red flags when you begin working there.

EVALUATION QUESTIONS FOR USE DURING INTERVIEWS

When you interview with a company, try to learn as much as possible about its culture and operations. Remember, this is a two-way street. You are entitled to as much information about the company as the company is entitled to learn about you. The interviewer will pepper you with questions and it is your prerogative to do the same. You need to know about the company and people to whom you will give your time, intelligence, energy, and passion. You will spend eight to ten hours a day working there, and you want to make sure that you are not aboard a ship of fools.

Prepare a checklist and present it to the interviewer during the course of your conversation. You can present this checklist along with the interview agenda. The interview agenda addresses the job specifically while the checklist below concentrates on the company.

Sample Company Evaluation Checklist for Use during an Interview

Company: Safeway Foods
Interview: June 1, 2015
Candidate: Marilyn Edinburgh
Interviewer: Marshall Blakemore, Human Resources Director
Subject: Company Information

1. What was company profitability after taxes over the last three years?
2. How long has the CEO been with the company?
3. What is the annual rate of employee turnover?
4. Does the company have any community outreach programs?
5. Is there litigation pending against the company and if so, what are the issues?
6. Does the company have a mentoring program?
7. Could you describe the company culture?
8. Could you please tell me something about your own career with this company?
9. What is included in your benefits program?
10. Is your company military friendly?
11. How many veterans have you hired over the past five years?

This is a long list, and you may not have time to cover every item. Select the top five that interest you the most and discuss them first. Continue if time permits.

SOURCES FOR COMPANY INFORMATION

There are many online and print sources for information about companies and the individuals who work there. Here are seven that I have found most useful:

1. *CNBC Business News*. On TV and online, www.cnbc.com.
2. *FOX Business News*. On TV and online, www.foxbusiness.com.

3. *Forbes*. In print and online, www.forbes.com.
4. *Hoovers*. www.hoovers.com.
5. *LinkedIn*. www.linkedin.com.
6. *Wall Street Journal*. www.wsj.com.
7. *Barron's*. www.barrons.com.

MOVING FORWARD

Using all of the tools in **OJS**, you have made it through the job search process. You have researched the company and found it worthy of your trust and time, and you really want to work there. The company sends you an enticing job offer. Do you just sign on the dotted line and report to work the following Monday? What about all that small print you saw in the job offer? What does it all mean? The salary looked okay, but can you get more? Is anything negotiable? Stick around for the next chapter. We're going to tell you how to evaluate a job offer.

CHAPTER TAKEAWAYS

- Learn about the company, its CEO, and your potential boss before accepting a job.
- Do not work for a company that refuses to disclose information you request.
- When you are on the job, you work for your boss, not the company name.

VETERAN'S LIBRARY

Jim Cramer and Cliff Mason. ***Jim Cramer's Stay Mad for Life: Get Rich, Stay Rich (And Make Your Kids Even Richer)***. Simon & Schuster, 2007.

Jim Cramer. ***Jim Cramer's Real Money***. Simon & Schuster, 2009.

Troy Adair, PhD. ***Corporate Finance Demystified***. McGraw-Hill, 2011.

Chapter 34

Evaluating a Job Offer: Salary, Bonus, Benefits . . . and the Small Print

Your worth on the job market will fluctuate with the economic cycle and other factors. For example, the median salary for MBAs with one to three years' experience is approximately $54,000, according to an article in the *Wall Street Journal*. This is down considerably from median salaries for MBAs in the year 2001. Salaries for those holding bachelor's or master's degrees will vary, too, depending on the state of the economy, geography, the industry, and the position. There is no accurate and consistent way to measure the going rate for entry-level or executive-level jobs. However, by aggregating the data from a number of sources, one can make some educated guesses. Contrary to what the Internet wizards say, compensation packages are negotiable, even for veterans entering the civilian workplace for the first time. However, there are exceptions. For example, government jobs and very large companies have compensation tied to certain grade levels that carry strict requirements.

READING THE JOB OFFER

Assume that you have made it through the interview process and are ready for a trip to the islands for some relaxation. But wait! You have been offered a civilian job paying real money and benefits with a profitable company in an industry you like. You have to postpone your trip to evaluate the offer, which states the terms of employment: start date, salary, bonus potential, position title, responsibilities, benefits, and other things about which you know nothing, like passing a drug screening. Now what do you do?

Let's say the offer you received by email included these items:

Annual Base Salary: $60,000.

Bonus for Meeting Objectives: 5 percent of base salary.

Benefits: shared-cost group medical insurance; term life insurance at two times annual salary; company contributory IRA, eligible after twelve months of continuous employment; two weeks paid vacation; nine paid holidays and family leave days; eight paid sick days.

Start date: August 23.

In addition, there were three pages of small print detailing the company's rights, some of which were confusing. Here are five "standard" items, usually written in legalese, which could be difficult to understand:

The "termination-at-will" clause, which means that the company can fire you at any time for any reason without explanation, and that you agree not to take legal action against the company.

A "non-compete" clause stating that if you are terminated or leave the company voluntarily, you agree not to work for a competing firm located within a 50-mile radius of the company office where you worked for six months.

A drug and alcohol screening test upon which your employment is contingent.

A credit check upon which your employment is contingent.

A criminal and law violation record check for charges such as DWI and other misdemeanors and felonies.

The small print seems never-ending. What is going on here?

EVALUATING THE OFFER

Although you might be pleased, thankful, and even flattered to receive this offer, it raises some concerns and legitimate questions.

- Don't I deserve more than $60,000 per year in base salary? Is that all I'm worth?
- Can I pay all of my personal expenses after deducting federal, state, and city taxes, plus my share of medical insurance?
- And what about this "termination at will" clause? Can they fire me for no reason? I've never heard of that!
- What is this "non-compete" clause? Again, I have never heard of that.
- And how about the 5 percent bonus? It states that I will receive it only if the company exceeds its revenue goal by 20 percent.
- The benefits seem okay, but can I do better?
- And what's all this I hear about the provisions of the Affordable Care Act (Obamacare) kicking in and costing employees a ton of money?

You probably thought the offer was the final step in the process. You just sign on the dotted line without reading the fine print and start work the following Monday. Now you're learning there is more to it than that.

Let's take a closer look at this offer point by point to discover what it means and how much a "package" like the one above is really worth. As we learned in Chapter 10, it's all about the numbers. The job offer is a compensation package, and to determine the total dollar amount, we need to examine each component part. In our hypothetical offer, the bottom line compensation is more than $60,000, because the benefits add another 30 percent to your package, making the total $78,000.

BASE SALARY

Every company offers a base salary in language and style that implies it is final, but that is not the case. In all my years as a retained recruiter, rarely has a company told me that a base salary offer for any job at any level is final and that if the candidate does not like it the deal is off. Most private sector companies are open to negotiating. They usually establish a base salary range for a particular position, say $55,000 to $70,000 for an associate marketing director and $35,000 to $45,000 for an assistant marketing manager.

Salary Tied to a Job Grading Level

Base salary at any level in the corporate hierarchy is highly negotiable. An exception is a government job or one with a large company, like Microsoft, where base salary is linked to a grading level. For example, an associate marketing manager might carry a Level One designation, an assistant marketing director a Level Two, and a marketing manager a Level Three. Usually the very large companies have salary grading systems that make it difficult to negotiate upward. Government jobs, whether city, state, or federal have grade level designations that make it next to impossible to negotiate upward.

Job Location Affects Salary

Another factor affecting the base salary is location. For example, the base salary for an assistant marketing manager in New York City could go as high as $90,000, but in Casper, Wyoming, the base salary for a similar position would be in the $40,000 to $50,000 range. Considering the cost of living in New York City as opposed to that in Casper, the difference in base salary makes sense.

To make sure that any offer you receive is at market value, research what a particular job is paying in *your local area,* not across the US generally. Frequently, certain job rating agencies, including the US Department of Labor, quote average US base salaries, but these numbers are misleading. There are many online resources to help you find local average salaries.

BENEFITS

Workers often forget that benefits add to your compensation number. The entire benefits package must be monetized and added to base salary in order to determine the *true* value of the offer.

Benefits cost employers approximately 30 percent of base salary and are an important part of the package. For example, if your base salary is $60,000 per year, your benefits cost the employer $18,000, making your *true* compensation $78,000.

Traditional company benefits include health insurance, term life insurance, disability insurance, retirement plans such as an IRA, paid vacations, paid sick days, and paid holidays. A retirement program, such as a company-sponsored IRA (Individual Retirement Account) or Roth IRA, will most likely become effective after you work with the company six to twelve months and cannot be negotiated to kick in at an earlier time. IRAs, paid holidays, life insurance, disability insurance, and medical insurance will not be negotiable. However, vacation time is sometimes negotiable, or it can be used as a tradeoff for other benefits.

Your most important benefits are medical insurance and disability insurance, because one never knows when illness or an accident will strike. Medical and disability benefits are as important as base salary. Of course, these benefits have even greater importance if you are married and have children, or plan to do so.

THE AFFORDABLE CARE ACT (OBAMACARE)

The Affordable Care Act (ACA) goes by many names. It is frequently called Obamacare, or the Health Care Act, or just ACA. All mean the same thing. Even though you are a veteran and receive many benefits from a number of federal government programs, you need to be familiar with the terms of Obamacare so you are not caught off guard during an interview with a hiring manager or human resources director. This important piece of legislation is the law of the land, and the Supreme Court has, so far, upheld its many provisions.

Prior to October 1, 2013, when the Affordable Care Act became effective, a company would say, "Here is our medical and hospital plan.

The plan is through Aetna, and your benefits and costs are contained in this booklet." That is no longer the case.

Obamacare includes the Health Insurance Marketplace provision, which permits employees to purchase health insurance individually through several approved insurance companies. The companies could be different from one state to the next. Costs vary, and so do the benefits.

Health benefits are a matter for serious discussion with potential employers, so do not hesitate to ask for explanations about your options. The human resources director will be familiar with the new provisions and will share them with you. The provisions of Obamacare are still evolving, so keep an eye on how its provisions will affect your benefits program and its cost to you.

A prudent thing to do now, however, would be to go online and research this important topic yourself, because new information is becoming available every day through a number of different sources. Review the official website, www.healthcare.gov, and google "Obamacare" and "Affordable Care Act."

VA HEALTHCARE BENEFITS

Do not count on VA health benefit programs exclusively for the long term. The VA is a government agency and as such, it is subject to politics, which can alter the benefits packages at any given time. A number of VA hospitals were caught in major scandals over the past few years that deprived veterans of their benefits, making due diligence mandatory for all veterans. Check the VA website frequently for updates on medical benefits. Also, discuss the issue with the company human resources director. There could be a company medical benefits program that works in conjunction with or in addition to VA medical benefits.

BONUS AND COMMISSION

Like base salary, bonuses can be negotiated. In fact, companies could be more flexible on the bonus than on the base salary. In some companies,

certain workers receive a fixed bonus based on total company performance; in other companies, bonus is based on individual or department performance.

Some workers, like sales representatives, receive a commission
based on revenue goals. For example, an outside full-time sales representative selling into the school market for John Wiley Publishing
Company might receive 5 percent on all sales revenue after reaching
an established revenue quota of $2,000,000. If the sales rep delivers
$2,800,000 ($800,000 over the revenue goal), the commission would
be $40,000. If the sales representative had a base salary of $60,000, the
total income from base salary and bonus would be $100,000, plus the
value of the benefits, usually 30 percent of base. Thus, the total package
would come to $118,000.

To determine the true value of your compensation package, always
include the cost of benefits and the bonus.

There are as many different bonus and commission arrangements
as there are companies. Rarely will you find two bonus and commission programs that are the same. In small- to medium-sized companies,
the bonus and/or commission plans are sometimes negotiable. Large
companies are usually not open to negotiation. The bottom line is this:
always try to negotiate a higher bonus or commission. If the offer says
the bonus or commission plan is 5 percent, ask for 7 percent. There
is nothing to lose by asking. Your potential employer will probably
appreciate that financial reward is an incentive for you.

PROFIT SHARING

Some companies offer profit sharing in addition to, or in lieu of, a
bonus plan. The higher the company profits in any given fiscal year, the
higher the profit sharing for each employee. For example, some companies, like Texas Instruments, have a profit sharing program based on
total company revenue. Many Texas Instruments workers have become
very wealthy working there over an extended period. If you do not see
"profit sharing" in the job offer, always ask if you might be eligible to
participate in the program. Most companies have a profit sharing plan

for their key executives, but *might* offer it as an incentive for mid-level workers as well. Some companies, like Starbucks, offer profit sharing for all employees regardless of rank.

STOCK OPTIONS

Another benefit in publically traded companies is the stock option plan, which permits workers to purchase shares of company stock at a price that is below market price. The number of shares of stock an employee receives is directly proportional to rank and length of time with the company. Presidents get more than vice presidents, who get more than directors, who get more than managers, and so on.

Companies offering attractive stock option plans usually have a workforce that is stable and long lasting. I have noted that workers in companies offering stock purchase plans retain workers for longer periods. For example, Apple provides a discounted stock purchase plan for its workers, which has created many millionaires. I know Apple employees who joined the company in 1980 and are still there, primarily because of the stock purchase plan.

Negotiating stock option plans is easier with a smaller company than it is with an established company like Google or Apple. The risk of continued long-term employment with a startup or small company is greater than that with an established company, so small companies are often more amenable to offering generous stock options to compensate workers for the added risk.

WHAT IS YOUR JOB REALLY WORTH?

Salary fluctuates with the economic cycle, workforce demand for a particular skill, and geography. For example, in a very robust economy where annual GDP growth is near 5 percent, compensation in a high-demand field, like information technology, will be higher than it would be when the country is in a steep recession.

OJS cannot determine what a particular job is worth at any given time because of these variables, but there are many resources, both print and digital, for veterans to use as a guide. On the print side, the most valuable resource is the *Occupational Outlook Handbook*, which I have cited a number of times. Online, review the following sites, remembering that the numbers you find are *estimates*, not firm and final numbers:

Salary, www.Salary.com.

Pay Scale, www.payscale.com.

Bureau of Labor Statistics, www.bls.gov.

Job Star, www.jobstar.org.

Career Builder, www.careerbuilder.com.

Conduct periodic online searches for salary information, because numbers change and new sources of information are always emerging.

COMPANY COMPENSATION PARAMETERS

When you are negotiating base salary, it is important to remember that the company must work within established parameters in order to keep peace in its workforce and maintain profitability.

For example, assume that a company has a staff of twenty customer service representatives working from offices in Scottsdale, Arizona, all making a base salary in the $35,000 to $45,000 range, depending upon length of service, experience, expertise, and education level. In that situation, it would be impossible to negotiate beyond $45,000. There would be a breakdown of trust if a customer service rep with two years of experience and making $40,000 learns that an entry-level veteran is making more. How will you learn the salary range for a particular position? Ask the director of human resources or the hiring authority with whom you are negotiating.

There are parts of the compensation package other than base salary where the company may have more flexibility, like paying tuition for an undergraduate or graduate level degree or increasing the amount of vacation time or agreeing to flexible working hours.

INTERPRETING THE SMALL PRINT CLAUSES

Job offers could contain a number of provisions or clauses that are frequently overlooked because they are written in small print and in legal jargon. They just don't seem that important. However, it is critically important that you read and understand the small print provisions. They could affect your employment status, both short and long term.

Termination-at-Will Clause

Many job offers contain this provision. It means that the company can terminate your employment for no reason. It can happen at closing time any day of the week. Your boss or the human resources manager can call you into the office and say that this is your last day working there. The real reason why you are being fired may be that you did not perform up to expectations, and the most expeditious way to terminate your employment is to use business-speak, euphemisms like "downsizing," "rightsizing," or "reorganizing." Your job is not an entitlement, and you have no statutory right to your job. There is usually nothing you can do about it.

However, there are exceptions, and you can research the issue by googling "termination at will." Also, if you are a member of a union, the contract may include provisions for termination. Learn what is included in any union agreement.

You can refuse to sign a job offer containing this clause, but your candidacy could be rejected because of it. Candidates with minimal or no experience in the civilian workplace have little bargaining power for this job offer provision. I advise you to agree to this clause and sign the offer.

Non-Compete Clause

This clause means that you agree not to take a job that would be in competition with your company or to disclose proprietary company information after separation. Usually this limitation is time sensitive and limited to one year after separation from the company. There is a geographical component to this clause as well. For example, the clause may prohibit you from working for a competitor located within a three-mile radius of your employer.

There is an entire body of law governing the non-compete agreement. Google "non-compete agreement" and add your state for current legislation. A veteran new to the civilian workplace has little negotiating power to remove this clause. I advise you to sign and get on with the job.

Drug and Alcohol Testing Clause

There is a growing trend for companies to require a drug and alcohol screening as a condition of employment. Employers usually outsource these pre-employment tests to companies specializing in this type of activity. The potential employer always pays the bill for these screenings.

Refusing to submit to the pre-employment drug or alcohol screening will jeopardize your chances of employment. If you have nothing to hide, agree to the screening. What about Alaska, Colorado, Oregon, and Washington, where recreational use of marijuana is legal? Most employers in these states still require the pre-employment screening and do not permit or condone use of pot or alcohol while on the job. If you live in Alaska, Colorado, Oregon, or Washington, do not assume that employers permit use of controlled substances.

The Credit Check Clause

The credit check clause may be in the job offer for a number of reasons, the foremost of which is that employers do not want to deal with wage garnishment requirements. In addition, an employer may believe there is something lacking in a candidate's sense of responsibility if they have a history of unresolved debt or bankruptcy. If you have any long-term debt or substantial credit card debt, try to resolve these issues while in the search process. Do not object to the credit check clause. It could cost you a job.

The Starting Date Clause

A job offer will contain a start date clause. For example, assume you received the job offer on December 5 and it contains a start date of December 10. Do not fear the start date clause. All employers consider this a negotiable item, especially with recently discharged veterans who are transitioning to civilian life and have a variety of family matters to address.

The Relocation Clause

If a company offers you a job based in another location, the job offer will contain a relocation clause. The terms vary widely from company to company, but usually they state how much the company will pay to relocate you, your dependents, your spouse or partner, and your household goods. There is much flexibility here, and companies are willing to negotiate the terms of relocation. This is a highly negotiable item, and in the following chapter, I will give you a vivid example to illustrate that anything is negotiable when it comes to relocation. You will not believe what happened to Peggy from Phoenix!

REJECTING A JOB OFFER

There are two ways to reject an offer after negotiations reach an impasse.

1. Tell the hiring manager that the job sucks and that you would be dumb to accept it. For emphasis, close the conversation by reciting the title of a song made famous by folk singer Johnny Cash, "Take This Job and Shove It!"
2. Thank the hiring manager for considering your candidacy and wish him success finding an alternate candidate. Close the conversation by telling him that your rejection is nothing personal; it just does not provide what you need at this time.

If you use method #1, you will derive great satisfaction bragging to your friends that you just told the human resources manager at GE to take the job and shove it. Your friends will laugh and tell you what a gutsy call you made. Bravo! The downside is that you have severed the possibility of ever being considered for a future job opportunity at GE. In addition, the person on the other end of your message could move on to another company, and guess what? You will find no job opportunities at her new company. Method #1 is a dumb move.

Method #2 is the route to select when declining a job offer. It says that you have a sense of business etiquette, maturity, and good judgment, and may help you with a future job opportunity.

STOP! YOU ARE NOT YET READY TO SIGN!

So you thought that dealing with a job offer would be a piece of cake. If the money is right, forget about the small print. The $60k base salary and all those benefits look good. Why not just sign and get on with it? Are you ready to take the path of least resistance and sign on the dotted line without negotiating? Stop right there.

MOVING FORWARD

There are many ways to negotiate a better employment package in a friendly way. Negotiating need not be hostile. You still have a way to go before celebrating, and I will tell you how it works in Chapter 35, "Negotiating the Best Compensation Package." Sit tight until you read this chapter. If you do not, you might leave a lot of money, and better benefits, on the table.

CHAPTER TAKEAWAYS

- Benefits are a vital component of the job offer.
- Drug and alcohol screenings are not negotiable.
- Freedom from personal debt will set you free to discover your niche in the workplace.
- If relocation is part of your first job, or second, or third, remember that relocation expenses are negotiable.

- Read and understand all of the small print provisions in a job offer.

THE VETERAN'S LIBRARY

Suze Orman. *The 9 Steps To Financial Freedom*. Three Rivers Press, 2012.

Chapter 35

Negotiating the Best Compensation Package

Negotiating may sound intimidating for the uninitiated, but the concept is easy and the implementation can be fun and profitable. It means that when someone makes you an offer, you say "thank you" and make a counter offer.

Does that work? You bet. Many of us have had fun negotiating with street vendors in San Francisco, Chicago, New York City, Athens, Mexico City, Istanbul, or Delhi. In most cultures, negotiating is an accepted, and even expected, way of conducting business. The process of negotiating is universal. The seller always starts with a high price and the buyer always counters with a low-ball offer. The final price is usually somewhere in between. For example, a street vendor in Delhi, India, where street bargaining is an *expected sport*, might offer you a Gucci knock-off purse or wallet for $20, knowing full well he will not get that price. You respond offering $8, and the vendor says, "Do not insult me," but counters with $15. You say, "That's a rip-off and the most I will pay is $10." The vendor says he is losing money, but the weather is hot and he wants to go home, so he will give it to you for $10. You close the deal at $10, and both you and the vendor are happy.

YOU DON'T GET WHAT YOU DESERVE. YOU GET WHAT YOU NEGOTIATE

In America, the cost for most products and services we purchase is negotiable, and that includes salaries and benefits found in job offers.

American workers tend to believe that what is stated in a job offer is firm and final and never think to negotiate a better deal. Just the opposite is true. Like the Gucci knock-offs in Delhi, job offers are usually negotiable.

Dr. Chester Karrass, author of four books on negotiating, offers negotiating advice in his book *In Business as in Life, You Don't Get What You Deserve, You Get What You Negotiate.* I suggest that you take time to read this book, as well as two others by the same author, *Give and Take* and *The Negotiating Game.* These are classics, and Dr. Karrass will tell you what can be negotiated, how much can be negotiated, and how it is done.

THE PROCESS OF NEGOTIATING A JOB OFFER

Negotiating a job offer is usually conducted person-to-person, in the employer's office. The process can be intimidating, especially for veterans new to the civilian workplace. Remember that the corporate office is nothing more than a gussied up street vendor cart where everything is negotiable. A carpeted floor, a wood desk, a two-story window overlooking a beautiful park and other trappings are just that, trappings. The corporate office is just a convenient place for the hiring manager and human resources director to conduct business.

Negotiating a Compensation Package is not a Hostile Event

Negotiating need not be hostile. Proceed with a plan, a sense of adventure, a smile, and good intentions, and you will come away with more than what was offered. The process breaks down when one of the two parties becomes greedy. The key to successful negotiating is to make sure that everyone is a winner. Let's consider a real-life story that I encountered when placing a director-level candidate with a large company in the education industry. This true story illustrates that everything in the job offer is negotiable, *even relocation expenses for a goose.*

Peggy from Phoenix

I was conducting a search for a director level position with a company that published testing and assessment products for high school students. Peggy, who lived in Phoenix, had much to offer by way of experience and accomplishment and was willing to relocate. My New York-based client found Peggy to be the ideal candidate and made her an offer that consisted of a generous salary, bonus, and benefits, which included health, life, and disability insurance, an IRA, and a relocation package. Peggy negotiated a higher base salary, extra vacation time, and a number of extras in the relocation package.

The relocation package included reimbursement for moving household items and transporting a spouse and dependent children. After negotiating a higher base salary, she told the human resources director that she needed a more generous relocation package. The company balked, and this is where my recruiting firm stepped in to salvage the deal.

Peggy said she needed the relocation package to include reimbursement for transporting her aging parents to the East Coast so they could be close to her new home, and that she wanted the company to pay relocation costs for her pets. I convinced the company that the additional cost was worth the price because Peggy was a one-of-a-kind candidate. In the end, the company agreed, and this is what Peggy's relocation package included: reimbursement for moving all household goods, transportation to New York City for her aging and infirm parents, two house hunting trips, and transportation for her pets, which included her cat, dog, and a goose.

There is a postscript to this story. My research indicates this was the only time in recorded history that a company paid to relocate a goose for a job. As Dr. Karrass says, everything is negotiable!

NEGOTIATING BEYOND THE PACKAGE

All veterans, even those new to the civilian world of work, can negotiate base salary, bonus, and some benefits *within reason*. Some benefits are highly negotiable, but others are not because employers do have parameters beyond which they cannot negotiate.

Creativity is one of the keys to successful negotiation. Let's assume that you negotiate an initial salary offer of $70,000 up to $80,000. Is that the end of the line? Do not be fooled by the statement "That's the best we can do." Remember, everything is negotiable, even when the transaction is taking place in a corporate office rather than on the street. This deal is not yet done, and here is what you do next.

Going Beyond "That's the Best We Can Do"

Before you begin negotiating a job offer, make a plan, and then work your plan. Prioritize and write down those items of the job offer that you would like to negotiate, like a higher base salary.

First, research the average base salary for a comparable job in your location so you will have numbers to use in negotiating. How do you ask for a higher base salary? Here's a simple script you can use. Practice it before you begin negotiating with your potential employer:

"I like many of the items in your offer, but I must admit, I was thinking of a higher base salary. You offered me $80,000, but I was expecting $85,000. I think that number is in keeping with the norm, and I really need that much to take care of current expenses. If I accept your offer of $80,000, I might have to take a second job or go on food stamps."

Injecting a bit of humor into negotiations lightens the mood and makes it easier for both parties to arrive at a compromise.

On the benefits side, you could select an area of your education that needs upgrading, like digital marketing. Make that an item for negotiation. Your skill sets will need to be upgraded going forward, particularly your technology skills, and that costs money, whether you are taking courses online or at a bricks-and-mortar school. Another benefit item on your list could be tuition for learning a second language, like Spanish. Strengthening your technology skills and learning a foreign language are benefits to the company. After you get that intimidating "That's the best we can do," counter-offer with something like this:

"I'm really flattered that you have made me an offer to work here, and I'd like to share something with you. In order to make my employment more beneficial to your bottom line, I would like to continue my education by taking two courses in digital marketing at Florida Tech. Tuition is $1,800. Also, I would like to take the Berlitz online introductory Spanish course. The cost is $1,200. I would appreciate your including those two education courses in my benefits program. Would you consider that?"

The hiring authority can respond in one of three ways:

1. "Yes, we will pay the entire cost for these courses."
2. "No, we just cannot afford to pay these costs."
3. "We can pay a portion of the tuition cost."

If you do not ask, you get nothing. A simple question, courteously put, can result in significant benefits, like flex time to take the kids to certain events on a given day of the week.

A key to successful negotiating is to persuade your potential employer that your requests ultimately benefit the company. This requires preparation and understanding your potential employer's business. The classic book *How to Win Friends and Influence People* by Dale Carnegie will help you in the preparation process.

YOU CAN'T LOSE BY NEGOTIATING

There is always more to negotiate beyond the "final" package. No matter what happens, you win. If the company says *no* to any or all of your requests, you can rest easy with the satisfaction that you stepped up to the plate and tried your best to negotiate additional salary and benefits. If the company says *yes* to any of your requests, you have hit the jackpot.

MOVING FORWARD

The art of negotiating can be used in the workplace just as it is on the street. After negotiating the best deal and finding yourself in a very attractive civilian job, you will be happy. You will begin work on the appointed day and love being there to begin your civilian career. However, before we let euphoria rule the day, let's think about how to make the best transition to civilian employment both short and long term. How does a veteran ease into a civilian job after several deployments to Iraq and Afghanistan? **OJS** has guidelines to help you take charge of your career in the next chapter. Don't go away.

CHAPTER TAKEAWAYS

- You get what you negotiate.
- Do not settle for the first offer. Base salary, bonuses, and some benefits are always negotiable.
- When negotiating compensation and benefits, do not be greedy. Be reasonable.
- If relocation is required for a job, remember that relocation expenses are negotiable. Do not hesitate to ask for expenses to relocate your pets, even a pet goose.
- Personal debt is debilitating. It sucks money out of your pocket like nothing else, and it plays upon your psyche like a never-ending nightmare. Avoid it by negotiating a higher compensation package to offset your living expenses.

THE VETERAN'S LIBRARY

Chester Karrass. *In Business as in Life, You Don't Get What You Deserve, You Get What You Negotiate*. Stanford St. Press, 1996.

Dale Carnegie and Associates. *How to Win Friends & Influence People*. Simon & Schuster, 2012.

PART VIII

"You're Hired!" Mission Accomplished. What's Next?

Two roads diverged in a yellow wood . . .
I took the one less traveled by,
And that has made all the difference.

—Robert Frost, "The Road Not Taken"

Chapter 36

Easing into Your Civilian Job

Landing a job was a hard-fought victory. Take the time to give yourself a pat on the back and say a prayer of thanksgiving for winning the opportunity to become a self-sufficient human being. When you began your search, maybe six months or a year ago, it seemed like a no-brainer. Send out a few resumes and job offers will follow, or so you thought. After all, America has created a workforce of 155,000,000, so there should be a job on demand for everyone who wants one. Right?

Well, as you witnessed in your job search, a civilian job is not an entitlement for anyone, not even a veteran. But now that you have a job, you can look back and see that job hunting is a process. You followed the systematic rules in this process, from creating a plan to acing the interviews, negotiating a great compensation package, and accepting the offer. Your job hunt is over.

AFTER YOU ACCEPT THE OFFER, WHAT'S NEXT?

Going to work in an environment entirely different from the military requires some adjustments. For veterans like you, however, the art of switching gears is something you have already learned in the military. You probably recall how many times you were transferred from one job to another, often in a different location and on very short notice. Transitions take time and planning.

What can you expect when you report to work? What challenges will you find? Whom can you trust? These are all valid concerns, but if you ease into the learning curve, a productive and satisfying work experience will follow.

ACTION ITEMS FOR NEWBIES

All veterans come to a new job with different experiences and different expectations. Some were leaders and some were followers. Some saw combat; others worked behind the lines. Every veteran had an MOS. Regardless, when you find yourself in a new civilian job, you can take measures to make your new career a success. Here are the **OJS** guidelines to help you move forward.

- Keep your mouth shut and your eyes and ears open for the first six months on the job, or however long it takes to reconnoiter the premises. Learn the landscape. Learn who will be a trusted friend or a ruthless competitor. You will never learn anything if you are constantly talking.
- When the bullets fly, duck. Veterans usually like to take a stand when they hear something controversial. In the civilian workplace, you are going to hear a lot of back-and-forth on issues ranging from politics to religion to sporting events, and even about how to run the company. What do you do when you are new on the job and someone says, "How do you feel about that, Bob?" Your gut reaction might be to vent your opinion in strong language, but where does that leave you once the conversation stops?

   The diplomatic way to handle such issues is to say, "I understand and appreciate your point of view on this issue. However, there is another side to it that some people feel is valid. There are two sides to everything." Is this merely wimping out? No, it is not, because leaders always see both sides of an issue. Taking that position says much about your maturity, intelligence, and judgment, all honed to a fine point during your military service. That said, there will be issues where saying *anything* will move the conversation to a heated debate that you cannot win. When that happens, go into your foxhole until the bullets stop flying.

- If you have a leadership role in the company, be a good leader by following your employer's success formula. Resist the temptation to tear up the script during your first month by implementing new rules and regs and by firing half of your subordinates. Take it slow and success will follow. What may seem to be reality after six weeks on the job could be a smoke screen. It takes time to tell. All people like stability, and gradual change is usually best.

- If you are in a follower role, become the best follower in your group. Support your manager, show loyalty, and become the best worker on the team. Being a good follower is necessary for the company to be successful. Work is not only about the highly touted worker with a leadership role. It is also about workers with followership roles. Leadership. Followership. One cannot exist without the other. It is a symbiotic relationship.

- Leadership does not only mean a management job. Leadership wears many different hats. For example, good leadership means setting a good example for team play. It means adhering to ethical practices. It means taking a proactive role in community outreach initiatives. Leadership means contributing a portion of your income to charitable causes. Leadership means mentoring those who are falling behind the curve. All veterans can be good leaders in many ways regardless of rank or title. Leadership is for everyone, not just those in managerial positions.

- Find a company mentor, a seasoned company worker to help you through the learning curve. You are new to the job, the company, and the culture. A good mentor will help you find your way.

- Each day you report to work, affirm your value to the company and build your character by applying your intelligence, energy, and passion to the mission. It has been said that punctuality is the best barometer for observing a person's sense of responsibility. Practice it.

- Do the best you can in your new job. The best preparation for a promotion is to excel in your present position.

THE JOB SEARCH PROCESS CONTINUES AFTER YOU ARE HIRED

When you are hired, do not believe that your job is forever. When you think you have arrived, you stop growing and do not see the danger signals. Think of your new job as another step in the lifelong career process.

Nothing is forever, and you must continue developing your career. Here are five action items that will help you win the game called *W-O-R-K*. **OJS** calls these initiatives "career insurance."

Career Insurance. A Six-Part Policy

1. Continually update your resume and your career profile by adding notes about your accomplishments and new experiences. Be ready to begin another job search when this job comes to an end, which it can on any given day. Something entirely out of your control could happen. Your company could be sold, resulting in your being laid off, along with hundreds of your colleagues. Alternatively, your company could miss its quarterly number by a wide margin, and your boss could be given orders to slash the department workforce by 30 percent. Guess who goes? The most recently hired workers usually are the first to be cut in situations like this.

2. Continue adding new contacts to your network through LinkedIn and through personal networking. Your personal network is the best avenue to continued meaningful employment.

3. Remain current about what is happening in the economy generally and in the job market specifically. Review financial

programs on CNBC and read financial magazines like *Forbes*. Review job boards and websites.

4. Continue attending conferences and trade shows in your area, even if you have to give up a weekend to do it. This is where you meet people face-to-face and develop personal relationships that result in jobs.

5. Maintain your operations center (home office) to continue research on the job market and to refine your career aspirations. Work continues wherever you happen to be. It does not happen only when you leave home and put in work time in a specific location.

6. Continue your education by working toward the next degree or certification and by taking online courses to learn new technology skills.

MOVING FORWARD

It might seem counterintuitive to begin preparing for a new job days after being hired. You have worked hard to reach this point in your transition, so why worry about the next step? Do not kid yourself. Your new job is not forever. To believe that you will remain in your present job until you retire is a delusion. I have witnessed heart-breaking events, like workers being fired during the holiday period from Thanksgiving through New Year's Day. Always look ahead to the next opportunity with your present employer or with an alternate one. Do not be caught off-guard! In the next chapter, **OJS** will help you prepare for the day when you might be laid off or decide to quit and look for alternate employment opportunities.

CHAPTER TAKEAWAYS

• You cannot afford to rest on the laurels of victory. Your present job will not last forever. It is subject to a sudden ending, so you must be prepared to begin another job search immediately.

- Be both a good leader and a good follower.
- Find a company mentor to help you through the learning curve.
- For the first six months in your new job, keep your mouth shut and your eyes and ears open.
- Your new job is not the end of your search. It is just another step in the lifelong career process.

Chapter 37

Your Job Is Not Forever. Reinventing Yourself Is a Continuing Operation

Why is **OJS** including a chapter on losing your job? This book is about finding a job, not about being fired. Sorry, veterans. Being the *complete* guide to careers and job hunting, **OJS** believes you should temper your successes with a strong dose of reality. You cannot afford to become complacent, because your present job will not last forever. It is subject to a sudden ending, so you must be prepared to begin another job search immediately.

The biggest mistake a veteran can make after starting a new job, whether it's an entry-level position or a presidency, is to assume the job will last throughout the work cycle. That is not the way it works. How long will this job last? It could be six days, six weeks, six months, or six years.

EMPLOYEE TENURE

According to figures released by the Bureau of Labor Statistics, the average length of time on the job in any private sector company (for both men and women, veterans and non-veterans) is approximately 4.5 years. In addition, the number of workers employed for *less than one year* from 2012 to 2014 was an astounding 21 percent of the workforce.

NOBODY IS IMMUNE

Some members of the workforce believe their job is secure and forever because of social status. They might think, "But I'm a veteran. My employer won't let me go" or "I'm a woman, and if they fire me, that's gender discrimination." Dream on! This is not your grandparents' generation. Anyone can get whacked on any given day for any reason. Here's an example.

Brenda from California

Brenda had a job as VP for the education division of a well-known technology company located in California. She had been with the company for twelve continuous years and was managing the education division for six of those years. She made her quota every year and had a compensation package in the $350,000 range. One day between Christmas and New Year's Day, the boss called her in for a chat. He told Mary that the education division was being folded back into corporate and she no longer had a job. Brenda was devastated, because she assumed she had it made long term. She had not seen this coming. She was given a severance package and walked out the door.

WHACKED!

In today's world of work, everyone must prepare for any event that could affect one's employment status. Assume you have been on the payroll for six months when your boss calls you in for a chat. In the past, she has given you high-fives for performance, but now she tells you that your job has been eliminated because your division is not profitable. She has been ordered to reduce her staff by 50 percent. The company gives you two weeks' severance, and you are escorted from the building. Your being a veteran did not seem to make any difference. When an employer decides that you are expendable, you are going regardless of social status or length of time with the company. Not fair? Sorry. That's just the way it works.

You are on the street again looking for a job, but this time the experience is much different. Added to the weight of going through the job search process again is the psychological trauma that comes with being fired or laid off. (In **OJS** we use the terms "fired," "whacked," and "laid off" interchangeably.)

You are now just another human being trying to make it in a seemingly unfair world. Suddenly, you no longer have that all important tag-line "I work with XYZ Publishing Company as regional sales manager" or "I'm president of Big Brother Technology Company." You are now just plain John or Mary. You feel immense pressure to get a job, sometimes any job, to relieve the pain. Losing your job will crush your ego like no other event because in our culture self-esteem and identity are closely tied to a job title and the name of the company employing us.

FIRST AID FOR FIRED WORKERS

Fired workers handle the trauma in different ways. Recently, a newly fired senior account manager in California related that after cleaning out her cubicle she headed straight for her favorite expensive restaurant for a stiff drink to help overcome the initial shock. Then she ordered a sumptuous dinner and paid the outrageous bill in cash.

Joe, a president who was relieved of his duties as head of a major retail company, went to the golf course, alone, and smacked the ball with all he had for the next three hours just to reassure himself that the recreation he liked best was still available to him as a "lay person."

The point is this. After being fired, it usually helps to apply first aid by leaving the premises, both physically and mentally, and engaging in something you like to do, preferably alone. It is important to reaffirm your self-worth and to prove that you can continue your favorite pursuit as Joe or Mary, and not as "Joe, President of Ajax Software" or "Mary, CFO with Finance Unlimited." After applying first aid to survive the initial shock, you are ready to move forward into what could be the most rewarding time of your life. Look at it this way. You have just won an opportunity to look at who you are independent of the support, or crutch, provided by your past employer. This is the beginning of building, or rebuilding, your character, and it will be an exciting trip.

REBUILDING YOUR CHARACTER

Character is the aggregate of traits and features that form and identify the *real* you. Are we going back to Psychology 101 or what? Well, sometimes you have to go back in order to move ahead a step or two. This period of downtime affords an opportunity to see where you have been in the military and the civilian workforce, where you want to go, and who you really are now that you cannot hide behind a corporate title or affiliation.

Looking back, you might find that the real you was disguised by the corporate culture or a preoccupation with being politically correct. In the process you may have forgotten who you are or what you truly think or feel. It's time for a homecoming with the real you. Day to day, the rebuilding process may be tough, but you must put it in perspective. Get rid of the two demons, regret and fear, that will inhibit your growth. As you move forward, here are guidelines to begin the rebuilding process.

Guidelines for Rebuilding Your Character

1. Take stock of all the good things in your life: your spouse, partner, children, friends, family, and personal possessions. Notice the abundance of things your work has provided, such as the best of the basic three: food, shelter, and clothing. Be thankful for what you have and remember that you are among the most fortunate group of workers on planet Earth—a worker in America, a country that employs 155,000,000 people. It does not get better than that. You have also served in the US military

and in the process acquired skills that are valuable in the civilian workplace.

2. Do not rush the process of reconstructing your work life. In fact, you may want to consider a vacation, alone, to clear out the chatter from within and the extraneous chatter from companions. The rebuilding process is not a group affair. It takes place in your own self-contained classroom where you are both the teacher and student. You don't need teachers, coaches, or tutors. You are smart enough to work through this yourself. In the past, you may have permitted others to tell you where to go, what to do, what to think, and even how to feel. Being fired has given you another chance to define yourself on your own terms.

3. Study the numbers related to the economy here in the USA. These numbers are unbiased, and they seldom lie. Tune out the media babble regarding the dire state of the economy and the tragedy of "underemployment," which are myths created to support an agenda. These are good times, and here's why. We have a workforce of approximately 155 million workers generating trillions of dollars in goods and services annually. We now have an unemployment rate of about 5.5 percent, which translates into an employment rate of close to 94.5 percent.

4. The US economy is the best place in the world to find meaningful work. Need more evidence? Look at the immigration numbers, both legal and illegal. Workers from around the world are flocking to the USA in record numbers in order to find employment opportunities that their native countries could not provide.

5. Define your ideal job, what you really want to do with your work life. Compare that with all the jobs you have had in the military and civilian workplace. If there's a disconnect between your ideal work vision and your experience so far, this is a splendid opportunity to begin planning how you want to use your intelligence and your acquired skills to do what you really

want to do. Evaluate your work history. Did you really like working in your last civilian job, or did you take it because you believed any job to bring home the bacon is satisfactory?

6. Through self-examination, determine what it is that you love and do it. Once I saw a resume with a string of twelve sales jobs over ten years, followed by three years in the Peace Corps teaching English in a newly liberated country in Eastern Europe. This fifty-something worker reentered the US workforce after the Peace Corps, this time as a teacher and administrator in a private school. Finally, he found the right niche.

7. Examine your personal life. What do you do after work? In your last job(s), was there any "after work," or were your work life and personal life one and the same? Define and write down what brings you pleasure and satisfaction after working. If you are like most workers, time on the job leaves little time for strictly personal pursuits. Right now, vow that you will never again allow an employer or a job to rule your life and define who you are, what you should do, and when you should do it. It's your life. Take charge!

8. Do you want just another job, or do you want to do something that also gives you a sense of satisfaction? These are jobs that stimulate creativity and provide generous compensation packages. Decide what kind of job will give you the best combination of compensation and satisfaction.

9. Once you have redefined who you are and what you want to do, you are ready to jump back into the world of work, but this time on your own defined terms. At this point, you may be undecided about how to begin your employment search. Whether you have decided to continue in your previous career or to pursue something entirely different, the search process is the same. Activate all of your existing personal networks. Network with individuals with a history of success in the civilian workplace. Read publications covering job opportunities. Watch TV programs devoted to business. Contact executive

recruiters working in the industry that appeals to you. Executive recruiters and search firms have a realistic handle on the job market and will point you in the right direction. Believe what they say, because the workplace is their work. Use the Internet judiciously, because it is the least effective method of job searching. Attend conferences at major convention centers and visit all of the exhibit booths. Every exhibitor is a potential employer. In short, follow the advice in **OJS**.

10. Carefully review your financial status, because you will need money to carry you through the unemployment period. Apply for unemployment compensation as soon as possible after being fired, because you are entitled to collect these safety net benefits. This is nothing to be ashamed of. Also, do not tap into your 401K or IRA, because you will incur severe financial penalties.

11. Make a budget to purchase the basics for yourself and any dependents, and to continue payment of insurance premiums, auto, and home loans. Avoid the temptation to charge all of your purchases to credit cards. Outstanding debt is the last thing you need at this point.

12. Those who are working with outplacement firms should not assume that this is their ticket to a new job. Although these firms provide excellent support services for fired workers, do not assume that you are going to find another job just because you report to "class" three times a week. Outplacement is primarily for networking, support, and education, not for job hunting.

13. Begin networking with your veteran colleagues. You will probably find that some of them are in the same boat. It is always reassuring to learn that others have similar problems. Also, reach out to your local VFW for support.

MOVING FORWARD

After a brief hiatus to redefine your character, what can you expect? Based on our research and anecdotal reports, we can almost guarantee that six months from now you will be gainfully employed in one of four ways:

1. As a worker in a job that you love and that pays more than your previous position.
2. As an employee of a company engaged in meaningful work that brings you great personal satisfaction in addition to a good income.
3. As an entrepreneur who has decided to "do it alone," using your skills, your newly found character, and your intelligence to build a profitable business.
4. As a worker in an entirely different industry, pursuing what you always wanted to do but could never find the courage to try.

Whatever you decide to do with your new perspective on work and your rebuilt character, stay the course, veterans. Success will follow.

CHAPTER TAKEAWAYS

- A job is not forever. Be prepared to move on.
- Nobody is immune from being laid off on any given day. Social status is no defense.
- Losing your job provides an opportunity to rebuild your character.
- Do what you love, and you will never work a day in your life.
- America is the job basket of the world. There is something here just for you. By applying your intelligence, energy, and the rules in **OJS**, you will find another job.
- It isn't the burdens of today that will drive you to distraction. It's the regrets over yesterday and the fear of tomorrow.

Chapter 38

How to Quit Your Job Gracefully

There will come a time when you decide to move on from your present employer. It could be in six months or six years. There are many reasons why workers quit their jobs, and all are valid.

How do you leave your job when you decide to say good-bye? Resigning is another part of the process of employment. There are two methods of bowing out, one is graceful and the other crude.

THE PROCESS OF LEAVING YOUR JOB

Leaving gracefully means departing on friendly terms and observing the rules of business etiquette in the process. Before handing in your resignation, write down the reasons why you are leaving and rehearse how you will break the news to your boss or the human resources director. Your opening resignation statement should go something like this.

The Verbal Resignation Statement

Mrs. Petrocelli, I'm here to submit my resignation. This is not easy for me, because there are many things I like about the company. However, in order to accomplish my career goal, which is becoming a Vice President for Marketing, I need to work as a Marketing Manager first. Ajax Security offered me that position, and I have accepted. Thank you for everything you have done for me while I was employed here. Here is my written resignation, which includes two weeks' notice.

Note the four essential characteristics of this resignation. 1. It was courteous. 2. It explained the reason why you are leaving. 3. It included proper notice. 4. The resignation was delivered verbally and in writing.

The Written Resignation Statement

The written statement is part of the process, but it does not need to be lengthy or state the reason for leaving. The written notice should just state that you are resigning and the date you are leaving the company. Here is a sample.

I am resigning my position as Marketing Associate, effective April 30, 2017. Thank you for giving me the opportunity to work with the company for the past two years.

Always give ample notice. Announcing your resignation on Thursday and leaving on Friday violates business courtesy. Two weeks' notice is standard for most jobs, but some require more. Always consult your job contract or human resources guidelines before giving notice. Some jobs, such as those in the medical profession, carry longer resignation notice, which could be four to six weeks or more. Adhering to the company notice requirement will be a plus mark in your personnel file.

The resignation process applies to all jobs, not just those in the corporate arena. The process is the same whether you are resigning from your job as a carpenter for Toll Brothers Home Building Co., a truck driver for FedEx, or a Biology teacher at King High School in Atlanta.

HOW NOT TO LEAVE YOUR JOB

The other way to leave your job is to vent your anger about the job and/or the company and do something stupid, like walking into the human resources director's office and saying, "I've never really liked it here, and I'm leaving tomorrow. I've found something much better." This method of resigning will tear down any bridges to future employment with that company and with that human resources director.

TEN GOOD REASONS WHY WORKERS QUIT THEIR JOBS

There are trigger points for deciding to leave one's employer, and most are valid. Sometimes workers are criticized by outsiders for leaving what appears to be an ideal position. Don't worry about what others are saying. It's your life, and it is up to you to make the best of it, even if it means leaving a job that pays well and is only a few minutes' drive from home. Here are the reasons cited most frequently by workers who leave their jobs.

1. The boss is the number one reason why workers leave their jobs. She might be a micromanager, a gossip, a bully, untrustworthy, or discriminatory. All are valid reasons for leaving your job. A recent Gallup poll of one million workers confirmed that the boss is the main reason why they quit their jobs.

2. The company has consistently missed its revenue goals. When this happens, it is time to seek alternate employment. If a company is not making money, reorganization will happen, because a company cannot exist without being profitable. Along with the reorganization, there will be mass firings. Guaranteed. Resign and move on before you get laid off.

3. The company is acquired by one of its competitors. What usually follows is a complete reorganization, where the acquiring company places its own workers in strategic jobs. It only makes good business sense to begin searching for an alternate job when the acquisition is announced.

4. Some workers resign because they just do not like their jobs. Taking the job was a mistake, because it was not aligned with one's qualifications and vision. If you do not find your job interesting or challenging and never see daylight ahead, move on.

5. Workers resign because of relationships with their coworkers. The job itself may be fine, but the group you are working with is just not "your kind of people." It could be that they are potheads, heavy drinkers, or just behind you in intelligence and work ethic. Why continue working on a ship of fools? Move on.

6. Company culture is another reason why workers quit their jobs. It is difficult to determine the company culture until you are actually on the job. A difference in values is usually at the heart of it. Your idea of work may include a culture that is community conscious and reaches out in a number of ways, including contributions from company profits to charitable causes. If there is a culture disconnect, move on and do a better job examining a potential employer's culture before signing on next time.

7. There is a disconnect between your lifestyle and working conditions. Assume you are a single mom or single dad with two kids in elementary school and you need flex hours to attend to their needs. The company does not permit flexing under any circumstances, even though they had told you during the interview that they are cognizant of family situations and make allowances. It's time to move on.

8. Workers quit because they no longer find "fulfillment" in the job. **OJS** does not believe that a job should provide satisfaction and fulfillment every working minute. Much of work is routine and even boring, but some workers need the job to provide everything all the time. This expectation is unrealistic, but still it is a reason why workers quit. **OJS** advises you to reexamine the meaning of work before resigning for this reason. If you just cannot find anything more than a paycheck at the end of the week, it's time to move on.

9. The company rarely promotes people from within the company. Instead, the company recruits outside workers for attractive jobs of higher rank. If this is your situation, move on. There are other employers who show loyalty and offer promise for their employees.

10. The company rarely provides increases in compensation. This happens more frequently than one would think. Some workers meet all the requirements, are productive, are good team players, and are loyal, yet they never receive recognition in the

form of a pay increase. A good employer will always reward its productive and faithful employees with something tangible. If this is where you are, turn in your resignation . . . after you have found an alternate employer.

The list of valid reasons why employees leave their jobs could go on forever, but the ten reasons listed above rank high on the list.

MOVING FORWARD

At some time in your career, you will find reason to resign your job and move on, but that is not something easily accomplished. It takes courage to quit! The easy thing to do is to stick it out with your present employer. Stay the course as long as there is a paycheck. While this may be a valid strategy depending on your financial circumstances, it is not a good way to spend your whole working life.

There are two rules that all workers, regardless of rank or compensation, should observe:

1. Have another job before turning in your resignation. It is much easier to find alternate employment while you are still employed.
2. Have enough money in the bank to provide for the basics during your transition to alternate employment.

In the next chapter, **OJS** will discuss an important part of work—giving back and community outreach. Hang with us.

CHAPTER TAKEAWAYS

- Resign from your job respectfully and courteously.
- Find another job before resigning.
- Resigning is a two-part process. First, make a verbal resignation statement to your boss and/or the human resources director. Next, submit a written notice, which includes the date you are leaving, to your boss and/or the human resources director.

Chapter 39

Charitable Giving, Philanthropy, and Community Outreach

Critics say that making money, *really big money,* is unethical. The criticism targets both individuals, like Mark Zuckerberg, CEO of Facebook, and companies, like Salesforce.com, the world's largest cloud computing company. It seems that the noise is getting louder day by day. One would think there is something wrong with making money to become a self-sufficient human being. If you do not make a good buck, who will pay for your children's education, the house mortgage, car payments, insurance premiums, recreation, retirement funds, and donations to charity? Veterans, do not buy into this sentiment. If you learn that someone is making more than you are, find out what their secret is.

MAKING BIG MONEY

Who are some of the wealthiest Americans, and what do they do with their money? A recent issue of *Forbes,* www.forbes.com, profiled the wealthiest 400 people in America. Ninety-five percent of these people made it on their own. They did not acquire their wealth through inheritance. Here are fifteen of America's most wealthy people and their net worth.

Steve Ballmer, owner of the Seattle Seahawks, and former Microsoft executive, $23 billion.

Mark Benioff, CEO, Salesforce.com, $3.3 billion.

Jeff Bezos, CEO, Amazon, $30 billion.

Michael Bloomberg, former mayor of New York City and CEO of Bloomberg LLC, $35 billion.

Warren Buffet, CEO, Berkshire Hathaway, $67 billion.

Larry Ellison, CEO, Oracle, $50 billion.

Bill Gates, founder of Microsoft, $81 billion.

Diane Hendricks, co-founder and chair of ABC Supply (roofing and siding), $3.6 billion.

Charles and David Koch, Koch Industries, $84 billion.

Ralph Lauren, CEO, Ralph Lauren Inc., $8 billion.

Larry Page, Google co-founder, $32 billion.

Alice Walton, $40 billion (through inheritance from Walmart).

Meg Whitman, CEO, Hewlett Packard, $2 billion.

Oprah Winfrey, talk show host, actor, author, producer, philanthropist, $3 billion.

Mark Zuckerberg, founder and CEO of Facebook, $34 billion.

What do these people do with their money? Buy yachts? Live in multi-million-dollar houses? Own airplanes? Drive expensive and prestigious cars? It may be all of the above, but why does it matter? Does that imply they have done something "wrong"?

This elite group of Americans acquired their wealth through hard work and education. With few exceptions, all hold college degrees and work sixteen hours a day or more at their jobs. The time and effort they put into reaching the pinnacle of wealth is remarkable. Remember, they earned this money in our free market economy.

HOW DO THE WEALTHY MAKE BIG MONEY?

Most wealthy Americans did not inherit their wealth; they earned it. While Joe Six-Pack was drinking Buds in a sports bar arguing about who was the American League MVP in 1995, these people were working toward their graduate degrees and working sixteen-hour days. To learn how to make it in America, follow the example of these individuals. Study the list of the 400 wealthy Americans listed in the *Forbes* article to learn how these people accumulated such wealth. Their contributions have provided much for those in need here in America and across the globe. Make a million, make a billion, and contribute in proportion to your success.

CHARITABLE CONTRIBUTIONS OF WEALTHY AMERICANS

Wealthy Americans who make it big give it away big, too. *Forbes* and other sources have investigated the charitable contributions of many wealthy Americans. Here is how some of them spend their money.

Marc Benioff, CEO, Salesforce.com. He has given away more than $30 million and counting. In addition to personal money that he donates to charitable causes, his company, Salesforce.com, donates a portion of corporate revenues to charity each year. So far it has donated hundreds of millions of dollars to worthy causes.

Michael Bloomberg, CEO, Bloomberg LLC. He has donated $1.1 billion to Johns Hopkins University. This is a remarkable story of a true outlier and a model to emulate. Michael Bloomberg was an average student at a Massachusetts high school, but Johns Hopkins University accepted him. There he learned the leadership and financial skills that he used to create businesses that made large sums of money.

His contributions to Johns Hopkins University in Baltimore have funded construction of a Physics building, a school of public health, a children's hospital, a stem-cell research institute, a malaria institute, a library, and many works of art. Mr. Bloomberg plans to give away all of his billions before he dies. This is a noteworthy example of what you can do when you make a lot of money.

Warren Buffet, CEO, Berkshire Hathaway. His $17.5 billion in donations to a variety of causes, mostly to education, is almost hard to believe. Mr. Buffet has no problem sharing his wealth with others. In addition, he has established a foundation operated by his son that addresses the critical needs of agriculture in foreign countries.

Larry Ellison, **CEO, Oracle**. He has given $444 million to the Ellison Medical Foundation for research on aging.

Chuck Feeney, founder of Duty Free Shoppers. Feeney founded Duty Free and other businesses and accumulated billions in the process. Today, however, he is worth a paltry $2 million. What happened to the rest of his money? He donated the billions he made to a variety of charities across the globe.

Bill Gates, founder of Microsoft. He has donated $30 billion, most of it for education and health initiatives in America and Africa.

T. Boone Pickens, Chair, BP Capital Management. This titan of the oil and gas industry has donated $625 million to education, mostly to Oklahoma State University.

Stephen Schwarzman, CEO and co-founder of Blackstone Private Equity. He has made billions but has given much of it away to a variety of charitable causes. He provides several hundred scholarships for New York City children each year. His best-known gift was to the New York City Library. The amount? $100 million.

Oprah Winfrey, actress, talk show host, TV producer, philanthropist. She has given away over $400 million, most of which goes to education and scholarships for female students in America and Africa.

Mark Zuckerberg, CEO and founder of Facebook. Despite being only thirty-one years old, he has already given away hundreds of millions of his own personal money. His most recent charitable donation was to the San Francisco General Hospital and Trauma Center. The amount? $74 million.

HOW ABOUT THOSE RICH ENTERTAINERS AND ATHLETES?

The media takes delight in reporting only the scandalous exploits of workers in the entertainment industry. But look behind the headlines, and you will come away with another point of view. In addition to contributing their money, many wealthy Americans in the entertainment and sports business have donated their time as well. Here are three good examples.

Jon Bon Jovi. He earns millions annually from his entertainment feats, not bad for a song and dance routine. However, he has donated not only millions of dollars, but also hundreds of hours of his own time each year helping those in need. He has helped build twenty-six houses for Habitat for Humanity and health clinics for the poor in New Jersey. In addition, he is the founder of the Jon Bon Jovi Soul Foundation, an organization to combat issues that force individuals and families into economic despair. His charitable contributions have touched thirty-one causes across the United States.

Beyoncé Knowles. She is another entertainer noted for her philanthropy. Beyoncé not only donates large sums of money, but also volunteers her time to support Goodwill programs. She has very quietly donated $7 million to the Knowles-Tenemos Place Apartments in her hometown of Houston, Texas, to help victims of Hurricane Katrina. In addition, she donates a portion of ticket sales for her concerts to a variety of charities. Beyoncé's donations often go unnoticed, at her request. For Beyoncé, life is more than show biz.

LeBron James. Star NBA basketball player LeBron James's 2014 income was $72.3 million according to *Forbes*. His salary as a pro basketball player was $19.3 million, and his endorsement earnings were $53 million. That's a lot of money for any professional athlete! However, his story does not end there. LeBron considers himself a man of the people, so he makes every effort to be a good role model by participating in children's initiatives through the LeBron James Family Foundation. His favorite targets for charity include the following organizations: After School All-Stars; Boys and Girls Clubs of America; and Children's Defense Fund. His contributions include not only his time and millions of dollars in cash, but also technology equipment and Nike clothing.

Corporate leaders are not the only ones who make it big, and give it away big. Professional athletes and entertainers are right in there with them and serve as role models for all of us.

HOW MUCH DO AMERICANS DONATE TO CHARITY?

The bottom line about philanthropy in America is nothing short of astounding. Reports from a number of reliable government and private research sources indicate that Americans gave $360 billion to charitable causes in 2015. If the folks with an agenda against the wealthy would just look at the numbers, they would be shouting from the rooftops that Americans are the most charitable people on planet Earth!

HOW VETERANS CAN GET INTO THE GAME OF GIVING

When you have a steady job, I strongly advocate setting aside a portion of your income, regardless of the amount you make, for charitable giving. The more you make, the more you have to give away. There is *nothing wrong* with making big money. There is *something right* about giving some of it away.

In addition to donating money, consider also donating your time. It could be as basic as helping handicapped veterans make the transition or teaching kids to read. Where you give your charity dollars is your call. Whatever you donate will come back to you in different ways and provide that feeling of fulfillment all of us desire.

I have prepared a list of nonprofit organizations that will spend your donations responsibly. The list of organizations deserving of your support could fill dozens of pages, but I recommend the ones below based on personal experience and research. As you review each website, remember to look at the career postings. Your research about where to donate your money could open the door to a job as well. People you meet in the course of charitable activities are often the movers and shakers in your community. They will become members of your personal network.

WHERE TO DONATE YOUR MONEY AND TIME

The American Red Cross, www.redcross.org. This icon of charitable works has a long and storied history. Donating money and time on a regular schedule to this organization will help those less fortunate overcome obstacles to a quality life. This is a huge organization and its administration requires significant dollars to support its infrastructure. Less than 78 percent of your charitable contributions will get to those in need, but the Red Cross is worthy of your support.

Catholic Charities USA, www.catholiccharitiesusa.org. Ninety-three percent of donations to Catholic Charities go directly to a particular charitable cause. The remaining amount pays for infrastructure costs. This organization is one of the best among charitable organizations. Catholic Charities supports all people in need, not just those of the Catholic faith.

Robert Wood Johnson Foundation, www.rwjf.org. This New Jersey-based charity is the country's largest philanthropic organization devoted exclusively to health-related initiatives. Programs include solving problems of childhood obesity, substance abuse, and age-related problems. Princeton, New Jersey, is home to RWJF, founded in 1972. This organization spends more than $400 million per year on its various initiatives. When you review the website, remember to check out the career page. RWJF is a first-rate employer.

United Way Fund, www.unitedway.org. In 1887, a Denver woman, a priest, a rabbi, and two ministers came together to found the United Way. Its initiatives include improving the quality of general education, health education, and health care for the needy. If you donate $35 per month, you can go to bed knowing that your job is doing more than providing for your own food, shelter, and clothing. It's a good feeling. Give generously.

Your Local Church. You do not have to be a church member to contribute to local church-sponsored charitable programs. It does not make any difference if your local church is Catholic, Protestant, Jewish, or non-sectarian. All churches provide food, shelter, clothing, and career support for those in need. Most of your donations will go to the needy, because infrastructure costs are almost non-existent. Church members contribute their time to make it work.

If your base salary is $55,000, you will never feel pinched if you contribute just $25 per month to your local church. Go online or call your local church to learn where to send your contributions.

The Kosciuszko Foundation, www.thekf.org. The Kosciuszko Foundation is dedicated to promoting educational and cultural exchanges between the United States and Poland and to increasing American understanding of Polish culture and history. It was founded in 1925, on the eve of the 150th anniversary of Thaddeus Kosciuszko's enlistment in the American Revolutionary War, where he was a Brigadier General in the Continental Army reporting directly to General George Washington. The Foundation is a national nonprofit, nonpartisan, and nonsectarian organization.

Contributions primarily support higher education initiatives and provide scholarships (over $100,000 per year) for deserving students with leadership skills who are pursuing graduate-level and professional degrees. You cannot go wrong making contributions to this worthy organization, named for a veteran who served in the American Revolutionary War.

OPERATION JOB SEARCH funds an annual scholarship for candidates applying for graduate level assistance through The Kosciuszko Foundation.

Doctors without Borders, www.doctorswithoutborders.org. Medical professionals staff this organization and render assistance to needy people in more than sixty countries in the developing world. Their services prevent and cure diseases and save the lives of people who do not have access to regular medical care. Give generously to this organization. Their professional staff is dedicated to humanitarian ventures and needs your help.

Susan G. Komen, www.komen.org. This well-known nonprofit organization is the premier foundation dedicated to finding a cure for breast cancer and for providing education and support to women afflicted with this disease. It is active in more than fifty countries and is highly ranked for its effective services. You can donate your time as well as money to Komen. Your donations could not go to a better cause. If you make $70,000 per year, donating $50 per month to Komen is not going to send you to the poor house.

Wounded Warrior Project, www.woundedwarriorproject.org. WWP is a nonprofit organization with one mission: to support our military veterans who suffered physical and mental injuries while serving our country. The organization helps wounded military veterans regain their health so they might participate in an active and productive post-service life. In addition, Wounded Warriors provides career counseling and recruiting services for military veterans seeking their first civilian jobs. In addition to donating some of your income to this program, consider donating some of your free time to make this organization work. You will find much satisfaction assisting your wounded colleagues returning to civilian life.

Goodwill Industries International, www.goodwill.org. Goodwill is a nonprofit worldwide organization that assists needy individuals on a number of different levels. It provides clothing, food, housing, job training, career guidance, and a number of other services. One of Goodwill's most ardent supporters is the talented and prominent entertainer Beyoncé Knowles. There is a Goodwill location in almost every city across the United States.

Other potential targets for your charitable gifts could include local museums, art galleries, hospitals, and universities. Select causes that you believe in and care about most.

COMMUNITY OUTREACH

If you simply cannot afford to donate money to charities, consider volunteering your spare time to community outreach projects instead. Every community, from a large city like Chicago to a small town like Dover, New Hampshire, sponsors outreach programs. To find these opportunities, google "Community Outreach Projects" for your hometown.

MOVING FORWARD

According to the latest Gallup poll, 83 percent of Americans donate part of their income to charitable causes and 65 percent volunteer some of their time to community services, both religious and secular. A complete life is one that includes giving back to those in need. Give back generously to the community. Your charitable donations of time and money will provide much personal satisfaction and help those in need.

CHAPTER TAKEAWAYS

- Be generous with the fruits of your labor.
- Do good works for those in need by contributing your time and expertise.

- Share what you earn with others who are less fortunate than you are.
- Learn from those who have made big money in their successful careers.

THE VETERAN'S LIBRARY

Jim Cramer and Cliff Mason. *Jim Cramer's Stay Mad for Life: Get Rich, Stay Rich (And Make Your Kids Even Richer)*. Simon & Schuster, 2007.

Jim Cramer, *Get Rich Carefully*. Blue Rider Press, 2013.

Suze Orman. *The Money Book for the Young, Fabulous & Broke*. Riverhead Books, 2007.

Standard and Poor's. *Standard & Poor's 500 Guide 2013: America's Most Watched Companies*. McGraw-Hill, 2013.

Robert Kiyosaki. *Rich Dad Poor Dad*. Plata Publishing, 2011.

ACKNOWLEDGMENTS

I owe thanks to many veterans and non-veterans for contributing to **OPERATION JOB SEARCH**. They helped me stay the course by reviewing the manuscript, relating their transition experiences, and by offering advice to veterans seeking civilian employment. They are:

Leslye Arsht, Chair, StandardsWork, Inc., Member of the Board of Trustees of Franklin Pierce College and the Center for Education Reform, and former Senior Advisor to the Ministry of Education in Iraq.

Marilyn Baker Weiss, my wife and Certified Nurse Midwife.

Lisa Bingen, Director of Marketing, Heinemann Publishing Company.

John Boyle, Lieutenant Commander, (USN, RET.), Manager, Yardley Borough, Yardley, PA.

Rosye Cloud, Senior Advisor for Veteran Employment, Department of Veterans Affairs (VA).

Russell Davidson, Commander, VSO VFW Post 6393, and Vietnam Veteran.

Robert Ivery, Sergeant, U.S. Army (RET.), Veteran who served in Iraq and Afghanistan.

Terry Jemison, Public Affairs, Veterans Benefits Administration, Department of Veterans Affairs.

Kiel King, 1st Lieutenant. U.S. Army (RET.), Founder and Owner, *Kings of Fitness*, Physical Therapy, Strength and Conditioning.

Dr. John Meeker, Founder and Owner, Meeker Search and Consulting.

Ed Meell, Veteran, U.S. Army. Founder, MMS Education, former Editorial Director, McGraw-Hill Films.

Susan Meell, CEO, MMS Education.

Randolph Norris, Esq., Partner, Norris and Norris LLC, Former Senior Prosecutor, Mercer County New Jersey, and Vietnam Veteran.

Dr. Stephen Payne, President, Leadership Strategies LLC.

Kevin Treiber, former Army Medic in Operation Desert Storm and Desert Shield, founder and owner, TDY Medical Staffing.

Cabot West, Veteran, U.S. Air Force. Senior Human Resources Manager, Measured Progress Inc.

Linda Winter, President, Winter Group, Education Marketing and Advertising, Denver, CO.

I owe special thanks to Skyhorse editor Olga Greco, who made it all come together. Without her, there would be no **OPERATION JOB SEARCH**.

INDEX